THE MUCH-LAMENTED

# DEATH OF MADAM GENEVA

# THE MUCH-LAMENTED

# DEATH OF
# MADAM GENEVA

❖

## THE EIGHTEENTH-CENTURY GIN CRAZE

# PATRICK DILLON

review

First published in 2002
by REVIEW

First published in paperback in 2003
by REVIEW

An imprint of Headline Book Publishing

10 9 8 7 6 5 4 3 2 1

ISBN 0 7472 3569 4

Typeset in Poliphilus by Palimpsest Book Production Limited,
Polmont, Stirlingshire
Printed and bound in Great Britain by
Mackays of Chatham plc, Chatham, Kent

HEADLINE BOOK PUBLISHING
A division of Hodder Headline
338 Euston Road
London NW1 3BH

www.reviewbooks.co.uk
www.hodderheadline.com

The illustrations on p.xi (title page from the satirical poem, 1736) and
p.xiv (woodcut from *Treasure of Euonymus*, 1559) are both courtesy of the
British Library.

# For Nicola

Patrick Dillon was born in London in 1962. He has lived there all his life and has developed a broad knowledge of the city and its social history. As an architect, he has worked on a number of eighteenth-century projects, including Benjamin Franklin's London house. His previous books, the novels *Truth* and *Lies*, were set in London. *The Much-lamented Death of Madam Geneva* is the result of detailed research into contemporary archives, court records, pamphlets and newspaper reports. Patrick Dillon is married with two children.

# CONTENTS

———•—•———

# ACKNOWLEDGEMENTS

I am particularly grateful to my agent, Andrew Lownie, and commissioning editor, Heather Holden-Brown, for their support, ideas and encouragement throughout the process of writing this book. Matthew Parker has been a sensitive, sharp-eyed and clear-headed editor. For their help in research, I am grateful to the staff of various archives and libraries, particularly the British Library, Public Records Office, London Metropolitan Archive, Guildhall Library, London Library, City of London Records Office and Cambridge University Library. I would also like to thank Penny Fussell, at the Draper's Company, and Christine Jones, at the Diageo Archive Department, for giving me access to material at their disposal. I am grateful to Professor John Chartres of Leeds University for putting me on to Jessica Warner's articles on the Gin Craze.

But most of all, for ideas, suggestions, criticism and patience, this book is indebted, as well as dedicated, to my wife, Nicola Thorold.

# AN
# ELEGY

On the much Lamented

# DEATH

OF THE

## Most Excellent, the Most Truly-Beloved, and Universally-Admired LADY,

# Madam *GINEVA*.

Worthy to be perused by all DISTILLERS,
Whether Simple or Compound.

*Dum Memor ipse Mei, dum* SPIRITUO *hos regit Artus,
Semper Honos, Nomenq; Laudesque manebunt.* VIRG.

*Sapiùs in Nosmet Legem Sancimus iniquam.* HOR.

LONDON:
Printed for *T. Cooper*, at the *Globe* in *Pater-Noster-Row*.
M.DCC.XXXVI.

# AUTHOR'S NOTE

The term 'Gin Craze' was not a contemporary one. Reformers of the early eighteenth century were more likely to talk about 'the pernicious consequences of the common people drinking spirituous liquors.' But 'Gin Craze' has gained some currency in subsequent histories of the period and is too useful a shorthand to abandon.

The balance of early eighteenth-century prices, incomes and tax revenues was very different from our own, making a single multiplier confusing. An income of £20 a year was usually thought to be the subsistence line, but many lived below it. Daniel Defoe reckoned a hard-working poor man without skills would find it difficult to earn more than £10–£15 a year. A large section of London's skilled tradesmen and 'middle classes' lived around the £40–£50 mark. £300 a year was reckoned the minimum for a gentleman. From his income, a poor man would probably spend a shilling a week on lodgings (£2–£3 a year) and five shillings on food. The cheapest dosshouses charged a penny a night. Jonathan Swift, by contrast, paid eight shillings a week (£20 a year) for his two rooms in Bury Street. Government revenues fluctuated around £5m–£6m a year throughout most of the period, rising in the 1750s to an annual figure around £7m–£8m.

Statistics for spirit production are taken from the collection made by the Commissioners for Inland Revenue in 1870. Figures in original Excise Office records and reports to Parliament differ only marginally from these. Gin was measured in the wine gallon of 231 cubic inches.

—•—

# THE ALCHEMISTS

It started as alchemy.

It started with secrets. The Greeks knew how to take the salt out of sea water. Chemists of the Levant brewed mysterious potions in odd-shaped vessels. When Henry II's soldiers raided monasteries in Ireland in the twelfth century, they sometimes came across casks of a heady liquid they didn't recognise. The liquid was hot on the tongue and burned their throats. Just a few gulps could leave them roaring drunk.

When the magic of distilling began to be whispered around Europe in the late Middle Ages, it was 'Books of Secrets'[1] which passed on the formulae. Distilling transformed the nature of matter, and that had always been the alchemist's dream. The distiller put ordinary wine into his still. He lit a fire beneath it. And at the touch of the fire's wand, a mysterious transformation took place. Vapour rose from the broad base of the still to its narrow neck, condensed, then dripped from the spout. What the distiller collected in the vessel he had waiting was clear and odd-smelling, slightly oily. It was nothing like the wine he had started with; nature had been transformed. The distiller had reached out and placed one hand on the philosopher's stone.

The philosopher's stone produced the elixir of life, and that was the name distillers gave to the clear, pungent liquid that dripped from their stills. It became aqua vitae, eau de vie, usquebaugh, the water of life. No one doubted its power. Distilled spirits were the new wonder-drugs in the apothecaries' cabinet. Their medical possibilities seemed limitless. They cured palsy and prevented scurvy, some claimed. They were good for the eyes. They would even protect drinkers from the most terrible scourge of all, the plague. An English doctor who set down his own recipe not long before the terrible outbreak of 1665 boasted that 'this water . . . must be kept as your life, and above all earthly treasure . . . All the Plague time . . . trust to this; for there was never man, woman, or child that failed of their expectation in taking it.'[2]

The ingredients distillers put into their stills were exotic, the recipes complex and fantastical. One, of 1559, was for 'a certain Aqua Vita such as is made at Constantinople in the Emperor's Court.'[3] The most refined of all spirits were 'compound waters' (*aquae compositae*), which were made in two separate processes. First a raw spirit was distilled, usually from wine. Then a complex bouquet of flavourings was added to the spirit, and it was distilled again. This time, the liquid which dripped from the still carried with it a powerful aroma and taste. Its flavourings were herbs from the medieval medicine chest, spices carried halfway across the world in small sealed boxes: 'rue, sage, lavender, marjoram, wormwood, rosemary, red roses, thistle, pimpernel, valerian, juniper berries, bay berries, angelica, citrus bark, coriander, sandalwood, basil, grain of paradise, pepper, ginger, cinnamon, saffron, mace, nutmeg, cubeb, cardamon, galingall.'[4] It was no coincidence that the flavoured spirit called gin would be developed in Holland and England, the two countries that would dominate the spice trade.

Time soon showed that the alchemists had missed the philos-opher's stone again. Spirits didn't grant eternal life; they didn't even cure the plague. But they did have other effects. Even the most earnest doctor couldn't help noticing that. Spirit-drinking 'sharpeneth ye wit,' one wrote. 'It maketh me merry & preserveth youth ... It agreeth marvellously ... with man's nature.'[5] Spirits may not have conquered death, but they did make life more palatable. Compared to distilled spirits, beer and wine were just flavoured water.

Something else was about to become clear as well. You didn't have to be philosopher, alchemist or magician to make these powerful new drugs. You didn't even need a ready source of wine. They could be distilled from anything – even from grain, the staple food of northern Europe. Soon, on a tour to the Baltic, the Dutchman Caspar Coolhaes noticed that, 'in Danzig, Königbergen and similar White Sea towns, just like in our countries at Amsterdam and neighbourhood and also at Rotterdam, Hoorn, Enkhuyzen and other towns, corn-distilleries were founded.'[6] Lucas Bols established his distillery near Amsterdam in 1572. Schiedam was growing as the home of the Dutch distilling industry by the 1630s. The stage was set for Europe to be flooded with a cheap and intoxicating new drug.

That was a more dangerous kind of magic, and many were scared of it. Way back in 1450, a Brandenburg Codex had tried to slam shut the lid of Pandora's box. 'Nobody,' it decreed, 'shall serve aquavit or give it to his guests.' Augsburg legislated in 1570 against grain spirits as 'harmful to the health, and a useless waste of wheat.'[7] In France, where distilling would remain focused on wine, rather than grain, brandy was banned in 1651. In Russia the rapid spread of vodka-drinking led to a panic clamp-down on drinking houses in 1652. Neither measure lasted long. But in 1677, only five years after the ban had been replaced by taxes, the Paris authorities again noted the spread of the *limonadiers*, and warned against 'those sorts of liqueurs of which the excess is incomparably more dangerous than that of wine.'[8]

That was the nub of it. Spirits weren't just stronger versions of wine or beer; they were different in kind, more destabilising, more dangerous. Beer and wine had been around for centuries. They were hallowed by tradition, ingrained in the woodwork; the tavern and alehouse reeked of them. Beer-drinkers raised their flagons in the same room where their grandfathers had drunk. When they broke into song, they didn't threaten the order of things; they were figures of fun. Falstaff was a cheery and familiar presence. By contrast, the new spirits were gaunt strangers in town. They took up residence in bare cellars and rooms behind shops; their devotees were vicious and unpredictable. Instead of good cheer and old drinking songs, spirits offered quick intoxication, then long oblivion.

Maybe the aura of magic never left distilling. Spirits would always reek of alchemy, of the dark arts. When English reformers came to revile spirit-drinking in the early eighteenth century, they saw gin not just as different in degree from beer, but worse, different in kind. 'Man,' wrote the campaigner Dr Stephen Hales in 1734, 'not contented with what his bountiful and munificent creator intend[ed] for his comfort . . . has unhappily found means to extract, from what God intended for his refreshment, a most pernicious and intoxicating liquor.'[9] The distiller was a second snake in the garden of Eden; gin-drinking was a second fall. Madam Geneva was not only unholy but unnatural as well, part whore and part witch.

By the time Dr Stephen Hales began his campaign, five million gallons of raw spirits were being distilled in London every year. The most common drink in the slums, flavoured with juniper berries, had once been called Geneva, after the Dutch name for juniper spirits. But by then it had 'by frequent use and the laconic spirit of the nation, from a word of middling length, shrunk into a monosyllable, intoxicating GIN.'[10]

# CHAPTER ONE

---

# THE GLORIOUS REVOLUTION

> Martial WILLIAM drank
> GENEVA, yet no age could ever boast
> A braver prince than he . . .[1]

Forty years after the Glorious Revolution, as Parliament passed the first act to control the scourge of gin-drinking, Alexander Blunt (pseudonym of Elias Bockett, a distiller) would write the first epistle to Geneva 'in verse sublime'. It didn't take long to develop into a paean to William of Orange, the King who 'with liberty restored, GENEVA introduced!'

Martial William may or may not have drunk Geneva himself. He certainly drank something. On his first Twelfth Night in London, while Mary spent the evening playing cards at Kensington with her sister, William entered into the spirit of things at Lord Shrewsbury's with Godolphin and the Duke of Marlborough. An onlooker recorded that in the end 'they all became so drunk that there was not a single one who did not lose consciousness.'[2]

Coming round, Marlborough managed to stagger back as far as Whitehall, where he passed out in the antechamber to the King's bedroom. The King himself fell asleep in a chair by the fire. Later, after Mary's death, William was said to indulge in drinking bouts with his old Dutch friend Augustus Keppel, by then Earl of Albemarle.

Whether it was gin William soaked in or not, to later writers the link between gin and the Glorious Revolution was an obvious one. William was Dutch; so was gin. 'Mother Gin was of Dutch parentage,' recorded a *Life of Mother Gin* published in 1736, 'but her father, who was a substantial trader in the city of Rotterdam . . . came to settle in London, where . . . he married an English woman, and obtained an Act of Parliament for his naturalization.' More importantly, it was William of Orange whose Acts of Parliament opened the floodgates to the cheap spirits that were soon being sold in cellars and garrets all over London, from barrows, out on the river, even in workshops. With the flight of James Stuart, all things French and Catholic were outlawed, and brandy went with them. Dutch Geneva became the spirit of the Glorious Revolution.

Until then, England had lagged behind the rest of Europe in the fashion for spirits. Dutch distillery manuals had been translated early in the sixteenth century, but most distilling took place in the farm kitchen, where country housewives used the still to prepare home remedies. Through most of the seventeenth century, professional interest stayed medical as well. When Charles I granted a monopoly of distilling to Sir William Brouncker in 1638, it was two distinguished physicians, Sir Theodore Turquet de Mayerne, a Huguenot and the King's doctor, and Sir Thomas Cademan, physician to the Queen, who joined him in setting up the Company of Distillers. Rivalry came from the apothecaries, not the brewers. When Samuel Pepys recorded his only encounter with Madam Geneva, on 10 October 1663, she was dressed up in nurse's uniform. Colleagues at work recommended 'strong water made of juniper' to cure constipation and pain in making water ('Whether that ... did it, I cannot tell, but I had a couple of stools forced after it and did break a fart or two').

All through the 1650s, while the French and Russians panicked about spirit-drinking, the puritan English stayed on their knees, sober and spiritless. The first change came with the return of the monarchy. 'Our drunkenness as a national vice takes its epoch at the Restoration,' Daniel Defoe wrote in 1726, 'anno 1661/2, or within a very few years after ... Very merry, and very mad, and very drunken, the people were, and grew more and more so every day.'[3] This time, there was more than beer for them to get drunk on. Brandy, outlawed in France, flooded across the Channel. Customs inspector and writer Charles Davenant soon noticed the 'considerable brandy retailers' in East Sussex, and all over Wiltshire, the 'abundance of brandy brought into every corner of this county.'[4] Brandy – from the Dutch 'brandewijn', burned (distilled) wine – was a generic for all spirits, but until the Glorious Revolution most of it did come from France and was made from wine. The best quality, fashionable at court, was often called Nantz, after the port it was shipped from.

Cheaper home-made spirits also started to make their appearance on the streets. Restoration London, Daniel Defoe recorded, 'began to abound in strong water-shops.' Defoe, born at the time of the Restoration, was an enthusiast for the Glorious Revolution, and would become London's most prolific journalist. For three decades he would also be the most ardent advocate of the distilling industry. 'These were a sort of petty distillers,' he recorded of the early days, 'who made up ... compound waters from such mixed and confused trash, as they could get to work from ... Till then there was very little distilling known in England, but for physical uses. The spirits they drew were foul and gross; but they mixed them up with such additions as they could get, to make them palatable, and so gave them in general, the name of Cordial Waters.'[5]

Distillers had been experimenting for generations with the flavourings that best masked the taste of cheap spirits. Juniper had been discovered early on – Augsburg had seen a petition against 'Cramatbeerwasser' back in 1613. In London it was aniseed – elsewhere the flavouring for spirits like raki and ouzo – that started out as the favourite. 'The quantity that was drunk of it was prodigious great,' Defoe recalled. 'The famous Aniseed Robin . . . was so well known in Leaden-Hall, and the Stocks-Market for his liquor, and his broad-brimmed hat, that it became proverbial, when we saw a man's hat hanging about his ears, to say, *he looks like Aniseed Robin*.' Defoe listed some of the other flavoured spirits that gained favour after the Restoration:

| | |
|---|---|
| Aqua Vitae | Aniseed Water |
| Aqua Mirabilis | Cinnamon Water |
| Aqua Solis | Clove Water |
| Aqua Dulcis | Plague Water . . . |

Colic Water, which in short was Geneva.

At this stage, though, the quantities didn't add up to much. As London recovered from plague and fire, no one was talking about a social problem, let alone a Gin Craze. The sudden explosion in spirit-drinking would only come when William of Orange crossed the sea from Holland, home of grain spirits, to ascend the English throne.

His first act was to declare war on France, and immediately measures were passed to ban trade with the new enemy. They made a point of singling out France's lucrative brandy exports. With French spirits out of the way, that left a gap in the market. And so Parliament opened the door to the English distilling industry.

In 1690 they passed 'An Act for encouraging the dis
brandy and spirits from corn,' and the industry was born. If
Parliaments wondered how the scourge of spirituous liquors had
taken root, they had only to look at their own statute book.

William was killing two birds with one stone. He wasn't
just hurting the French by banning brandy. A new British
distilling industry would lead, as the Act promised, to 'the greater
consumption of corn, and the advantage of tillage in this kingdom.'
Farming was Britain's key industry, and a distilling industry in
London meant a new market for English grain. The Act's main
beneficiaries were English farmers – and through their rents, the
landowners whose support the new King needed in Parliament.

To encourage distilling from corn (meaning any of the four
grain crops, wheat, barley, rye or oats) William's Act took advantage
of the manufacturing process for raw spirits. Distillers began their
work by fermenting a wash, much in the way that brewers made
beer. That wash could be made of almost anything – corn, wine,
fruit or molasses were favourites (reformers later hinted darkly at
human excrement and animal bones). When that weakly alcoholic
base was put into the still and heated for the first time, it wasn't
proof spirit that condensed out of the spout. The first run-off
produced coarse spirits, known as 'low wines', which were well
below proof strength. Low wines were distilled a second time to
make proof spirits, and it was these, in turn, which were sold on to
compound distillers to be flavoured as aniseed water, 'plague water'
or gin. Since Charles II's reign, there had been separate taxes on low
wines and on proof spirits. William's new legislation now tweaked
the rates on low wines so as to give a huge advantage to low wines
made from British corn. Distil most materials and you paid 12d a
gallon on the resulting low wines. Put malted British corn in your
vat, and your gallon of low wines paid just a penny of duty.

It was all a long way from 1638, when the Company of

Distillers had specifically outlawed 'working upon malt made of wheat or barley to the misexpense thereof.'[6] They had worried what people would say if corn went into their stills instead of to the bakers. They didn't want to be blamed for pushing up the price of bread. Now corn spirits would be distilled with official sanction.

The new Act filled London stills with cheap corn wash, but that wasn't the only boost William gave to the industry. The Company of Distillers' fifty-year-old monopoly was swept away. From now on there would be open season on distilling. Brewers and other drink manufacturers were still tied up in a web of regulations and duties. Most trades were burdened with controls. No one in London could make a shoe, sew a coat, plane a chair-leg or bake a loaf of bread unless they had paid their dues and gone through an expensive seven-year apprenticeship. But anyone who could afford a vat and a still could set up shop and make spirits.

The green light for the new spirits industry could hardly have shone brighter. Nothing would impede the flow from corn field to dram-shop. Beer-sellers carried a 200-year burden of legislation. By the 1680s, anyone who wanted to run an alehouse in Middlesex had to take out a magistrate's licence, attend church and take the sacrament, swear an oath of allegiance to the crown, and accept the expense of quartering troops. The numbers of alehouses were limited, opening times controlled. To run a dram-shop, by contrast, involved neither licences, costs, nor responsibilities. All the gin-seller needed was a cellar or garret – failing that, a wheelbarrow – and enough money to buy a stock of new, cheap British-made spirits.

If the aim was to get the English drinking corn spirits, William's legislation had to be rated a spectacular success. In 1690, English distillers paid duty on just over half a million gallons of spirits. By the end of the decade that figure had more than doubled.

Charles Davenant reported that 'since the breaking out of the first war, little brandies have been imported, in the room of which are come home-made spirits drawn from cider, molasses, wheat, and malt.'[7] It was nearly all happening in London, where Ned Ward, author of the satirical *London Spy*, was already, by the turn of the century, talking about the 'stinking fog that arose from . . . distillers' vats.'[8] In 1720, when more detailed figures become available, almost ninety per cent of English spirits were being distilled in London.[9] Farmers, meanwhile, benefited from the legislation as intended. It wasn't just that they had a new market for their corn. Distillers could make use of damaged corn which not even the brewers would buy. 'Great quantities of the worst sort of malted corn, not useful to the brewers,' a later Act affirmed, trumpeting the success of the new policy, 'hath been yearly consumed by those who set up works for that purpose.' For farmers and landowners, distilling was a godsend.

But William's legislation almost worked too well. From the start, the new industry turned out an unruly child. Within a year, Parliament was passing an 'Act for the better ordering . . . the duties on low wines . . . and preventing the abuses therein.' More legislation would soon follow. Distillers were supposed to use only corn which had been malted (maltsters soaked the grain until it started to sprout, then heated it to stop the growth; malted grain fermented more easily, but the process added fifty per cent to the cost of raw grain, and also attracted a tax). Now it turned out that distillers were cutting costs by mixing raw corn into their wash alongside the malt. They dodged duties by keeping hidden stills in back rooms, and tanks which they filled 'by private pipes and stop-cocks, and other private conveyances.' Hours for distilling soon had to be limited so that the Excise men could keep track.

It didn't make much difference. In this heady atmosphere of official encouragement, the distillers had the bit between their teeth. 'Compound distillers', who bought the raw spirits off the 'malt distillers' and added the flavours to them, became ever more inventive in their search for new products. Aniseed water remained popular. The taste for juniper-flavoured spirits – Geneva proper – was starting to gain ground. Many gallons of corn spirits were flavoured to counterfeit French Nantz. *Cerevisarii Comes* gushed in 1692 that 'our distillers . . . have various fantasies in the imitation of the flavours of brandy by rectifying from Bay Salt, Bay leaves; others from orrice, ginger, arsmart, pepperwort, pepper, clary, and many others, there being hardly a distiller but hath a different way to that of another.' Colour came, according to one recipe, from 'an infusion of prunes and burnt sugar.'[10] There were even stories of distillers shipping their counterfeit Nantz out to sea and landing it on the coast as if it had been smuggled from France.

Others stuck to clever marketing. Mr Baker, a bookseller, took out adverts in the papers for his 'Nectar and Ambrosia', sold 'inclosed in gilt frames, by the gallon, quart or two shilling bottle.'[11] Claims for the new drinks became as fantastical as the products themselves. In the *London Spy*, the landlady of the Widow's coffee-house declared that her 'Aqua Veneris' would 'restore an old man of threescore to the juvenility of thirty, or make a girl at fourteen, with drinking but one glass, as ripe as an old maid of twenty-four . . . a Puritan lust after the flesh, and a married man oblige his wife oftener in one night than without it he shall be able to do in seven.'[12]

The genie was well and truly out of the bottle. Government had declared free trade in a powerful new drug. It had done everything it could to promote its manufacture and sale. It had flooded London in spirits; now Londoners were only too happy to consume them. Coming out of St Paul's churchyard, Ned Ward and his companion 'went through [Covent Garden] market, where a parcel of jolly red-faced dames, in blue aprons and straw hats, sat selling their garden-ware, but they stunk so of brandy, strong drink and tobacco, that the fumes they belched up from their overcharged stomachs o'ercame the fragrance that arose from their sweet herbs and flowers.'[13] By 1703, Charles Davenant, for one, was starting to ring alarm bells about the new fad. ''Tis a growing vice among the common people,' he warned, 'and may, in time, prevail as much as opium with the Turks.' Everyone knew what had happened to the Turks. To opium, Davenant added gloomily, 'many attribute the scarcity of people in the East.'[14]

No one in authority was listening. There was a brief ban on corn distilling when the harvests failed in 1699, but distillers were compensated with cheaper duties on molasses – the readiest alternative to corn – and tax rebates for spirit exports. When the government did take a step towards restricting the trade, by requiring spirit-sellers to take out licences, the measure lasted no more than a year. William of Orange had usually been thought an abstemious man, at least by the standards of the age. No one ever called his successor abstemious. Saussure, shocked by the disrespect of Thames watermen, reported how 'my friends have told me that on the river Queen Anne was often called dram-shop because of her well-known liking for the bottle and spirituous liquors.'[15] Her reign opened with yet another 'Act for encouraging the consumption of malted corn,' meaning an Act to promote distilling. The brief experiment in spirit licensing, it declared, had proved 'a great hindrance to the consumption of English brandies.' ('Brandy' still covered all spirits.) From now on, common spirit-shops would still need retail licences, but distillers who sold their own spirits were let off the hook. There was an exemption, too, for 'anyone whose business was mainly in other goods' – in other words, for the corner-shops where most Londoners bought their staples. The only proviso was that spirit-sellers shouldn't 'permit tippling in . . . their houses.'

Along the way there had been sporadic attacks on spirit-drinkers by do-gooders, brewers and satirists. Brewers, in particular, were starting to worry. Outside London most spirits were sold in alehouses, so they made a direct hit on brewers' profits. It was no surprise when they started getting together petitions to have spirit duties put back up again. A 1700 *Satyr upon Brandy* warned off potential converts to spirits with the first description of a gin hangover:

> His skull, instead of brains, supplied with cinder,
> His nose turns all his handkerchiefs to tinder ...
> His stomach don't concoct, but bake his food,
> His liver even vitrefies his blood;
> His trembling hand scarce heaves his liquor in,
> His nerves all crackle under's parchment skin;
> His guts from nature's drudgery are freed,
> And in his bowels salamanders breed.

The authorities had yet to wake up to their own hangover. In thirty years, the only brief flurry of nerves for distillers came when the Peace of Utrecht ended war with France in 1713. The distilling industry had been set on its feet when the French brandy trade was shut off by William. Distillers now worried that peace would bring back competition. To make matters worse, the corn harvest looked bad. And Madam Geneva's enemies did their best to get a bandwagon rolling against her. One satirist published *The whole trial, indictment, arraignment, examination and condemnation of Madam Geneva ... taken in short-hand by Dorothy Addle-Brains, Fire-woman of the Jury*. At her mock-trial, Madam Geneva ('a gentlewoman born of Dutch parents in this nation') faced charges of plotting 'to make mad, and intoxicate the heads of ... journeymen taylors and shoemakers froes, tinkers and porters, doxies, butcher's wives, young strumpets, rotten bawds, tarpaulins and soldiers ... old basketwomen, and other honest and well-meaning people.' A succession of cobblers' wives and market-women testified to their own drunkenness, laziness, and neglect of their husbands. Sentenced to death, 'Madam Gin being made sensible of her heinous crimes by Mrs Prudence Pratapace, the independent Puritan Lady, she was conveyed to Tom Turdman's Fields ... where she bewailed her faults, and made open confession of her manifold crimes, with floods of tears, acknowledging herself guilty of death was turn'd off, and her body conveyed in a hurdle to Mumpers Hall, where her ... friends caused her to be embalmed, and laid ten days in state.'

But Madam Geneva's enemies had hired the funeral drapes too soon. Supporters like Daniel Defoe leapt to the defence. 'Our business,' he wrote in *The Review*, 'is to encourage every branch of trade by which our produce may find a vent, by which our people may find employment, our general commerce be increased, and the value and rent of lands kept up; and this, especially the last, the distilling of malt has so great a concern in, that it must for ever pass with me for a trade as profitable to the public as necessary to be supported, and as useful to be encouraged in proportion to its magnitude, as any trade in the nation.' To ram home his point he filled the paper with tales of woe from impoverished distillers.[16]

The distillers needn't have worried. Official support was as strong as ever. French brandy continued to be banned. The only new Act passed in 1713 went their way, putting an end to the Company of Distillers' backdoor attempt to win back their monopoly through Elizabethan charter legislation. And this time the law was unequivocal. 'Any person may distil brandy or spirits from British malt,' the Act declared, 'and such ... persons shall not be prosecuted for so doing.' Free trade in spirits stayed firmly in place.

*       *       *

By this time Geneva proper, spirits flavoured with juniper, were so popular that Geneva was starting to be used – at least by opponents – as a catch-all for cheap corn spirits. Corn spirits had been an import from Holland in the first place, and so was juniper flavouring. Holland had been a fertile source of new drinks over the years. The custom of hopping ale to make beer had been a Dutch one. Some even blamed the Dutch for Englishmen's habitual drunkenness. 'As the English returning from the wars in the Holy Land brought home the foul disease of leprosy,' was one assessment, 'so in our fathers' days the English returning from the service in the Netherlands brought with them the foul vice of drunkenness.'[17]

The English had suffered the strength of Dutch spirits in the wars of the mid-seventeenth century, when 'the captains of the Hollanders men of war usually set a hogshead of brandy abroach, afore the mast; and bid the men drink lusty, then they might fight lusty: and our poor seamen felt the force of the brandy, sometimes to their cost.' In the wars of William's and Anne's reigns, the Dutch were allies, and 'Dutch courage' was available to English soldiers as well. Into the army camps in Flanders, Daniel Defoe recorded, 'the Dutch sutlers carried . . . during the late long wars against France, a certain new distilled water called Geneva, being a good wholesome malt spirit, if rightly prepared, wrought up with juniper-berries.' It won some important endorsements. 'Nay, they tell us in Holland, that even the great Duke of Marlborough gave it a character . . . and that he recommended the (moderate) use of it . . . when they were going at any time to engage the enemy.'[18] Supporters would later chalk up victories like Blenheim in 1704 and Ramillies in 1706 to Madam Geneva's credit. It wasn't long before the common soldiers developed the taste. And it was the soldiers, according to Defoe, who 'tasting this liquor, brought the desire, as well as the fame of it, over with them at the ensuing peace; and our distillers preparing it as well here, as the Dutch abroad, they supply'd the people with it.'

The people didn't seem to need much encouragement. By 1713, when the wars ended, English distillers were already producing two million gallons of raw spirits a year. Some of those spirits were traded out to the country; some went abroad (Madam Geneva would play a walk-on role in the slave trade as part of a triangular route from London to West Africa); some went into medicines; and some appeared as counterfeit brandy to fool the rich. But the vast majority ended up on the streets of London. Gin was made sweetened or unsweetened, sometimes tinted to the colour of brandy, sometimes sold clear. It could be stirred into ale to make a popular drink called purl. More often, in the London brandy-shops, it was mixed two to one with water and sold in quarter-pint drams.

César de Saussure stumbled on one of those dram-shops when he visited London a decade later. By then, thirty years of unrestricted trade in spirits had had their effect. 'These taverns,' he reported, 'are almost always full of men and women, and even sometimes of children, who drink with so much enjoyment that they find it difficult to walk on going away, though these liquors are a sort of poison, and many people die from making too free a use of them.'[19]

But the poor, of course, weren't the only ones drinking too much in the decades after the Glorious Revolution. If they found it difficult to walk at the end of the evening, they were only copying their betters. 'It is not the lower populace alone that is addicted to drunkenness,' Saussure confirmed. 'Numbers of persons of high rank and even of distinction are over fond of liquor.'[20] Gamblers steadied their nerves with punch; long evenings in the coffee-house were lubricated by booze; young rakes reeled out of Tom King's into the Covent Garden dawn. To call the early eighteenth century a hard-drinking age would be something of an understatement.

*       *       *

Sir Robert Walpole learned to drink at his father's table at Houghton. 'Come, Robert,' his father was reputed to say, 'you shall drink twice while I drink once; for I will not permit the son in his sober senses to be witness of the intoxication of the father.'[21] The letter-writer Mrs Delaney recalled of Walpole's Tory opponent that, 'Bolingbroke, when in office, sat up whole nights drinking, and in the morning, having bound a wet napkin round his forehead and his eyes, to drive away the effects of his intemperance, he hastened without sleep to his official business.' As for John Carteret, who would eventually replace Walpole, 'The period of his ascendancy was known by the name of the Drunken Administration. His habits were extremely convivial; and champagne probably lent its aid to keep him in that state of joyous excitement in which his life was passed ... Driven from office, he retired laughing to his books and his bottle.'[22]

Hard drinking was barely even a vice. Samuel Johnson would recall that 'all the decent people of Litchfield got drunk every night, and were not the worse thought of.'[23]* Daniel Defoe, in 1702, thought that 'an honest drunken fellow is a character in a man's praise.' It was part of the age's clubbishness. All over London, men met in coffee-houses or rooms above pubs to drink, converse and do business. Drink was everywhere. Strike a business deal and you sealed it with a handshake and a dram. Go to the doctor and your medicine would be spiked with alcohol. Business meetings, magistrates' sessions, gatherings of old friends or wedding feasts; all were likely to be held in inns or taverns. There was nowhere else

* Dr Johnson himself had a complex relationship with the bottle. 'Sir,' he admitted, 'I have no objection to a man's drinking wine, if he can do it in moderation. I found myself apt to go to excess in it, and therefore ... thought it better not to return to it.' Elsewhere he confessed that he himself had drunk 'to get rid of myself, send myself away.'

# WH Smith
## Kings Cross

| | |
|---|---|
| THE MUCH-LAMENTED DE | 7.99 |
| NESTLE DOUBLE CREAM | 0.52 |
| | |
| TOTAL | 8.51 |
| Cash Payment | 10.00 |
| | |
| CHANGE | 1.49 |

Notified Terms and Conditions Apply
Thank you for shopping at
## WH Smith

06/05/03 14:32 Tn:2143370 Op:0242 4253/11

to congregate. Nor did Londoners only drink in their leisure time. Benjamin Franklin, apprenticed to a Lincoln's Inn Fields printer on his first visit to London in 1725 – later he would return as agent for the state of Pennsylvania and advocate of American Independence – recalled how 'my companion at press drank every day a pint between breakfast and dinner, a pint in the afternoon about 6 o'clock, and another pint when he had done his day's work.'[24]

And the thirsty Londoner with money in his pocket found he had an increasing range of drinks to choose from. Like so much else in London in the early decades of the eighteenth century, drink was being commercialised. The days of the independent alehouse-keeper brewing his own beer in the cellar were coming to an end. Robert Kirk, a Scot visiting London in 1690, remarked on the 'many strange kinds of drinks and liquors on sale.'[25] Not long afterwards there would be a craze for bottled beers: 'Beer of Dorchester . . . Burton Ale, Lincoln Ale, Derby Ale, Litchfield Ale, Yorkshire Ale, Yorkshire Stingo, Doncaster Ale, Basingstoke Beer, October Beer, Nottingham Ale, Boston Ale, Abingdon Beer, Newberry Beer, Chesterfield Ale, Welch Ale, Norwich Nogg, Amber Beer, Sir John Parson's Beer, Tamworth Ale, Dr Butler's Ale, Devonshire Beer, Plymouth White Ale, Oxford Ale, Sussex Beer . . . Jobson's Julep, or Lyon's Blood . . . Twankam . . . Coal Heaver's Cordial; and lastly plain humble Porter.'[26] Londoners were going mad for alcoholic novelty. 'The Ladies and gentlemen of quality and distinction,' Daniel Defoe remarked, 'not content with . . . French brandy, now treat with ratafia and citron, at a guinea a bottle. The punch drinkers of quality . . . not contented with French brandy in their bowls, must have Arrack at 16s to 18s per gallon. The wine drinkers of the better sort, not content with the Portugal and Barcelona Wines, must have high Country Margeaux, O Brian and Hermitage Clarets, at 5s to 6s per bottle; and after that Champagne and burgundy at 7s to 8s per bottle.'[27]

And it wasn't just the range of drinks that was increasing, or the amount that Londoners poured down their throats. Strength was on the way up as well. 'There has been for some years,' Defoe noted in 1726, 'a national gust or inclination to drinking stronger and higher priced liquors than formerly.' The well-off drank port or sherry ('and the Oporto and Lisbon whites, tho' very strong, are turned out of doors, for the yet stronger Mountain Malaga'). In the gambling-dens and coffee-houses, meanwhile, wits shunned wine and instead honed their punch-lines with vast bowls of arrack cocktail.

So when the ordinary Londoner spent his penny on a dram of gin, rather than a pot of ale, he was only following fashion. He didn't do it just to oblige English landowners and enrich the distilling industry. Thanks to Madam Geneva, he found that he, too, could afford a novelty drink; he, too, could buy something with a bit of kick to it. 'It seems to me,' as Defoe would point out, '[that the poor] have done . . . even what their superiors have seemed to lead them into just now, by a general example.'

And for the poor, gin offered something else as well. A cheap and powerful new drug was suddenly available to provide solace for desperately hard lives. One market-woman who gave evidence at the magistrates' Quarter Sessions in 1725 managed to put across something of what gin meant to her, and to other poor Londoners. 'We market-women are up early and late, and work hard for what we have,' she told the court. 'We stand all weathers and go thro' thick and thin. It's well known, that I was never the woman that spar'd my carcase; and if I spend three farthings now and then, in such simple stuff as poor souls are glad to drink, it's nothing but what's my own. I get it honestly, and I don't care who knows it; for if it were not for something to clear the spirits between whiles, and keep out the wet and cold; alackaday! it would never do! we should never be able to hold it; we should never go thorow-stitch with it, so as to keep body and soul together.'[28]

In the slums of St Giles-in-the-Fields and Saffron Hill a drifting population took dosshouse lodgings for tuppence a night. Stability meant a garret for a shilling a week. Work was seasonal. There were jobs on building sites when the rich were out of town for the summer, jobs in the fields at harvest time. The only god in the slums was Saint Monday, the day off to recover from the weekend. It was hardly surprising that Londoners turned to gin. For the poor man, Francis Place would later say, 'none but the animal sensations are left; to these his enjoyments are limited, and even these are frequently reduced to two – namely sexual intercourse and drinking.'[29] Drink seemed the better option to many; it cost less and lasted longer.

Gin had become ubiquitous; it was destructive and it was frightening. But far from being prohibited, it was still being promoted by the government. Gin was sold on every street corner. A man couldn't 'enter a tavern or an alehouse in which [spirits] will be denied him,' Earl Bathurst would complain during a later House of Lords debate on gin, 'or walk along the streets without being incited to drink them at every corner . . . and whoever walks in this great city, will find his way very frequently obstructed by those who are selling these pernicious liquors to the greedy populace, or by those who have drunk them until they are unable to move.'[30] Pushers soon added to the frenzy. 'Among the doting admirers of this liquid poison,' one reformer would soon warn, 'many of the meanest rank, from a sincere affection to the commodity itself, become dealers in it, and take delight to help others to what they love themselves.'[31]

By the 1720s it was hard to keep out of Madam Geneva's way. 'In the fag-end and out-parts of the town, and all places of the vilest resort,' the same writer went on, 'it is sold in some part or other of almost every house, frequently in cellars, and sometimes in the garret.' Chandlers, ubiquitous corner-shops of the poor, had all taken to selling gin. They didn't even need a licence to do it. The chandler, as Robert Campbell would explain in *The London Tradesman*, 'is partly cheesemonger, oilman, grocer.' His shop was where Londoners went to buy their staples. But it was the chandler's sideline as petty distiller, for Campbell, that 'brings him the greatest profit, and at the same time renders him the most obnoxious dealer in and about London. In these shops maid servants and the lower class of women learn the first rudiments of gin-drinking, a practice in which they soon become proficient, and load themselves with diseases, their families with poverty, and their posterity with want and infamy.'

Back in 1703, Charles Davenant had warned of trouble ahead. Three decades into William's project for a British distilling industry and a free market in spirits, all his warnings seemed to be coming true. London seemed to be floating in a lake of gin. 'Go along the streets,' wrote one critic, 'and you shall see every brandy shop swarming with scandalous wretches, swearing and drinking as if they had no notion of a future state. There they get drunk by daylight, and after that run up and down the streets swearing, cursing and talking beastliness like so many devils; setting ill examples and debauching our youth in general. Nay, to such a height are they arrived in their wickedness, that in a manner, they commit lewdness in the open streets. Young creatures, girls of 12 and 13 years of age, drink Geneva like fishes, and make themselves unfit to live in sober families; this damn'd bewitching liquor makes them shameless, and they talk enough to make a man shudder again; there is no passing the streets for 'em, so shameless are they grown . . . New oaths are coin'd every day; and little children swear before they can well speak . . . Geneva is now grown so general a liquor that there is not an ale-house . . . but can furnish you with a dram of Gin.'[32]

But it wasn't happening only because gin was cheap and easily accessible. The lives of the poor had always been hard. When they dreamed up a new market for English corn, no one had pictured dram-shops in every basement and Londoners sprawled drunk in the streets. Something else was going on. Something had changed in the city where Madam Geneva had made her home. London, brash, sprawling and chaotic, was fertile ground for her. The Glorious Revolution hadn't just shaken up the drinks trade. The changes which it triggered had created a chaotic and insecure city, vulnerable to a new drug, thirsty for gin.

# CHAPTER TWO

## LONDON

'O Molly! What shall I say of London?' gasped Win Jones, Tabitha Bramble's servant in Smollett's *Humphrey Clinker*, of her first glimpse of London. 'All the towns that ever I beheld in my born-days, are no more than Welsh barrows and crumlecks to this wonderful sitty! ... One would think there's no end of the streets but the land's end. Then there's such a power of people, going hurry skurry! Such a racket of coxes! Such a noise, and haliballoo! So many strange sites to be seen! O gracious! My poor Welsh brain has been spinning like a top ever since I came hither!'[1]

Even Londoners' heads spun as they looked at their city and watched its boundaries spread ever further from the old walls, transforming fields into elegant squares, villages into sprawling slums. 'If I stay here a fortnight, without going to town,' Horace Walpole would claim, 'I look about me to see if no new house is built since I went last.'[2] 'When I speak of London, now in the modern acceptation,' Daniel Defoe wrote in 1725, 'you expect I shall take in all that vast mass of buildings, reaching from Black-Wall in the east, to Tot-Hill Fields in the west; and extended in an unequal breadth, from the bridge, or river, in the south, to Islington north; and from Peterburgh House on the bank side in Westminster, to Cavendish Square.' Regarding this 'monstrous city,' he finished, 'how much further it may spread, who knows?'[3] Only two other towns in England at the time could claim populations above 20,000, while the metropolis teemed with 600,000 souls. Monstrously swollen, London in the decades after the Glorious Revolution filled Englishmen with a mixture of fascination and horror.

Mostly of fascination. The reformer Jonas Hanway later reckoned that 5,000 people a year flocked into London from the country. They left behind them a world of certainties and limited opportunities, a world of fixed social classes dominated by an *ancien régime* of gentry and church. London was their magnet. What drew them to the capital was the chance of 'betterment'. They were 'weary of restraint,' 'weary of country business'; they had 'an itching desire to see London.'[4] When the newcomers came over the hill at Highgate and caught their first glimpse of that 'vast mass of buildings,' they were staring down at a jungle of opportunities – and risks. Setting down from the coach in Holborn or tramping in across the last fields to the north of Clerkenwell, they found themselves in a place abounding in new possibilities.

London offered country people its own special alchemy. The country servant had hardly arrived, Daniel Defoe would lament, before 'her neat leathern shoes are . . . transformed into laced ones with light heels; her yarn stockings are turned into fine woollen ones . . . and her high wooden pattens are kicked away for leather clogs. She must have a hoop, too, as well as her mistress; and her poor scanty linsey-woolsey petticoat is changed into a good silk one . . . In short, plain country Joan is . . . turned into a fine London Madam, can drink tea, take snuff, and carry herself as high as the best.'[5] It was the old Dick Whittington fable, but in the heady decades after the Glorious Revolution it seemed more likely than ever to come true. London could transform nature; the philosopher's stone was hidden somewhere in its streets and alleys. The city had itself become a kind of still, and from a wash of half a million poor and struggling people, farm labourers, country girls, it distilled ersatz gentlemen and preening madams, gentlemen of the road, women of the town.

It may have been fool's gold but it kept tempting new arrivals to the metropolis. No one in the country could fake the estates and carriages that meant wealth. But in town, everyone could have aspirations. '[In London,] people . . . are generally honoured according to their clothes,' affirmed the satirist Bernard Mandeville in the 1720s. 'From the richness of them we judge their wealth . . . It is this which encourages every body, who is conscious of his little merit, if he is any ways able, to wear clothes above his rank.'[6] Clothes were easy enough to counterfeit; manners could be learnt. The important thing in London was to put on a show. And so one o'clock on a Saturday night saw 'would-be gentlemen, naked in back-garrets, boiling water in earthen chamberpots . . . to wash their sham necks, ruffled sleeves, and worn-out roll-up stockings, that they may make a genteel appearance in the public streets and walks at noon.'[7] Dolled up in their new finery, shopkeepers and apprentices headed out on their day off to preen and strut along St James's Park or the Mall. Satirists mocked the pretensions of the promenaders, spotting different kinds of gait: the 'Ludgate Hill Hobble', the 'Cheapside Swing', or the 'City Jolt and Wriggle'. Baron Pollnitz, visiting in 1733, was shocked that 'their Majesties . . . permit all persons without distinction of rank or character to walk there at the same time with them.'[8] 'The worthy gentlemen who chiefly frequent this sanctuary,' remarked the *London Spy* of the strollers on Duke Humphrey's Walk, 'would be very angry should you refuse to honour them with the title of Captain, though they never so much as trailed a pike towards the deserving it.'[9] Class in the countryside was set in stone; in London it softened and blurred. Even the all-important title of gentleman lost value. 'In our days,' sighed Nathaniel Bailey's *Dictionary* in 1730, 'all are accounted Gentlemen that have money.' Seeking a husband, Moll Flanders was 'not averse to a tradesman, but then I would have a tradesman, forsooth, that was something of a gentleman too.' Her target was 'this amphibious creature, this land water thing, called a gentleman-tradesman.'

There was no chance of such metamorphoses in the country. When, in *Tom Jones*, humble Molly Seagrim was seen in church in a cast-off lady's gown, 'such sneering, giggling, tittering, and laughing, ensued among the women, that Mr Allworthy was obliged to exert his authority to preserve any decency among them.'[10] But London was different. In 'large and populous cities,' as Bernard Mandeville put it, 'obscure men may hourly meet with fifty strangers to one acquaintance, and consequently have the pleasure of being esteemed by a vast majority, not as what they are, but what they appear to be.' London became a town of transformations, and its spas and parks, its theatres and coffee-houses, offered any number of opportunities for such alchemy to take effect. Its pleasure gardens were 'great scenes of rendezvous, where the nobleman and his tailor, the lady of quality and her tirewoman, meet together and form one common assembly.'[11] In Ranelagh, Horace Walpole reported that 'the company is universal . . . from his Grace the Duke of Grafton down to children out of the Foundling Hospital – from my Lady Townshend to the kitten.'[12]

A city of transformations was a city of insecurities, and insecurity was reason enough for any Londoner to turn to a new drug. But gin suited the mood of early eighteenth-century London in an even closer way. It offered an instant, heady transformation of its own. For a penny a dram, the poor man could fill his head with his own dreams; the market-woman could blank out the wet corner she sat on and fancy herself well-dressed, dry, and feasting at Vauxhall pleasure gardens.

Not all of London's transformations were illusory. There was real gold to go along with the dreams. Storms of change were not only raging across the surface; the very foundations of the city were being shaken as well.

A wave of speculative booms accompanied the Glorious Revolution. London, as Defoe put it, was gripped by a 'projecting humour'. Dozens of new patents were registered. In the traditional view of things, wealth was supposed to be inherited or earned by honest toil. But fortunes were soon being made in the City that dwarfed the estates of country squires, and which couldn't have been earned in a lifetime of hard work. Londoners of all ranks flocked to Exchange Alley. 'People have been drawn in and abused,' moaned one conservative after the crash of 1695, 'of all qualities, gentle and simple, wise and otherwise ... being allured with the hopes of gaining vast riches by this means.'[13] Speculation turned the dream of social metamorphosis into a reality, and traditionalists, of course, were appalled. 'We have seen a great part of the nation's money,' complained Jonathan Swift, 'got into the hands of those, who by their birth, education and merit, could pretend no higher than to wear our liveries.'[14]

But the new age was making new men who had no interest in wearing livery. ''Tis the principle of us Modern Whigs to get what we can, no matter how,' bragged Tom Double, Charles Davenant's 'got-rich-quick' satirical monster of the 1690s. 'Thanks to my industry I am now worth fifty thousand pound, and 14 years ago I had not shoes to my feet ... I can name fifty of our friends who have got much better fortunes since the Revolution, and from as poor beginnings ... I have my country-house, where I keep my whore as fine as an Empress ... I have my French cook and wax-candles; I drink nothing but Hermitage, Champagne and Burgundy; Cahors wine has hardly admittance to my side-board; my very footmen scorn French claret.'[15]

What was worse for traditionalists, the new government seemed intent on dragging England even further into the stormy seas of risk and uncertainty. Spiralling government debt was financed by City loans. The South Sea Bubble would originate in an attempt to convert £31m of public debt into South Sea stock. The government introduced public lotteries as well; a lottery office was built next to the Banqueting House, at the heart of Whitehall. A lottery win in 1712 gave £20,000 to a St Bride's widow who previously might have reckoned herself comfortable on a couple of hundred a year.[16]

'Stock-jobbing is play,' Daniel Defoe warned. 'A box and dice may be less dangerous, the nature of them are alike, a hazard.' But in the decades after the Glorious Revolution, London threw itself into a new age of risk. The mathematics of risk were newly discovered, and the language of risk was everywhere – at Lloyd's coffee-house, in the new insurance offices, even in the pulpit, where Isaac Barrow preached that through charity 'We ... lend our money to God, who repays with vast usury; an hundred to one is the rate he allows us at present, and about a hundred million to one he will render hereafter.'[17]

And risk had its sharpest edge of all at the gambling-table, where there were still more dangerous transformations to be made. The passion for gambling came from France after the Restoration, and it spread like wildfire. White's club opened in 1698; it wasn't long before Harley was dubbing it 'the bane of half the English nobility.' At Brooks's club, Horace Walpole would report, 'a thousand meadows and cornfields are staked at every throw, and as many villages lost as in the earthquakes that overwhelmed Herculaneum and Pompeii.'[18] By 1722, Covent Garden, centre of London's nightlife, had thirty gaming-houses, employing 'puffs' to draw in the innocent. Within them, wrote Henry Fielding, who had himself often enough 'fallen into the jaws of rattle-snakes', 'it would be tedious to relate all the freaks which fortune, or rather the dice, played in this her temple. Mountains of gold were in a few moments reduced to nothing at one part of the table, and rose as suddenly in another. The rich grew in a moment poor, and the poor as suddenly grew rich.'[19]

That was exactly what conservatives feared. Once again, Londoners were transforming themselves. And gambling spread through the whole town, from the Faro tables at White's to Holborn street corners where barrow-boys ran dice games on their counters, and shoeshines laid bets with their customers. The cards had no respect for rank. At the tables, Henry Fielding complained, 'sharpers of the lowest kind have frequently found there admission to their superiors, upon no other pretence or merit than that of a laced coat, and with no other stock than assurance.'[20] Gaming appealed to aristocrats because of its profligacy, its bravado, its carelessness of risk. Now any chancer with enough braggadocio could become a temporary aristocrat. Smollett's Roderick Random was assured by his friend Banter that 'there were a thousand ways of living in town without fortune, he himself having subsisted many years entirely by his wit.' He looked 'upon the gaming-table as a certain resource for a gentleman in want.'[21]

But the gambler was launched on a path of highs and lows which could only end in his own destruction. For Charles Cotton, author of *The Compleat Gamester* published in 1674, gambling was a kind of addiction, 'an itching disease . . . a paralytical distemper which drives the gamester's countenance, always in extremes, always in a storm, so that it threatens destruction to itself and others, and, as he is transported with joy when he wins, so, losing, is he tossed upon the billows of a high swelling passion, till he hath lost sight of both sense and reason.' Tom Brown described a gambler who 'had played away even his shirt and cravat, and all his clothes but his breeches. [He] stood shivering in a corner of the room ... And then fell a ranting, as if hell had broken loose that very moment.'[22]

The gambler was as self-destructive as the drinker, as random, as dangerous. Like any of Madam Geneva's devotees, he was intoxicated by possibilities, monomaniacal and carefree. He destabilised everything he touched. London was addicted to risk, hooked on the boom and bust of Exchange Alley, the highs and lows of the gaming-table. Some Londoners chased their dreams and nightmares at cards or the Exchange, or maybe in the arms of the Drury Lane prostitutes. Madam Geneva, with her instant kick and crushing hangover, offered her devotees the same cycle of dizzy euphoria and black despair.

London had become a city of risks, of glittering show masking uncertainty, a neurotic place. 'Is it to be wondered at,' the Bishop of London would ask, 'that [the people] should be indisposed to attend to anything serious, or that they grow sick of religion, which has no comforts for them; that they fly from the church and crowd to the playhouse. That they are tired of themselves, and their own thoughts, and want to lose themselves in company from morning to night? It is this unhappy, unsettled state of mind that has introduced a kind of general idleness among the people.'[23] 'The town of London is a kind of large forest of wild beasts,' growled another Londoner, 'where most of us range about at a venture, and are equally savage, and mutually destructive one of another. Observe the shops, and you'll see an universal discontent, and melancholy hanging in the faces of their respective occupiers.'[24]

It was a city of temptation and unsatisfied desire. Few could afford to buy the luxuries that filled the shops, but everyone could rub his nose against the glass. 'The four streets — The Strand, Fleet Street, Cheapside and Cornhill — are, I imagine, the finest in Europe,'[25] gasped Saussure in 1725. As with Londoners themselves, it was display which mattered as much as what was hidden inside. 'It is a modern custom,' Daniel Defoe complained, 'and wholly unknown to our ancestors to have tradesmen lay out two-thirds of their fortune in fitting up their shops . . . I do not mean furnishing their shops with wares and goods to sell; but in painting and gilding, fine shelves, shutters, boxes, glass doors, sashes and the like, in which, they tell us now, 'tis a small matter to lay out two or three hundred pounds.'[26]

Everything in London was on show. Everything was for sale. Passers-by hired spy-glasses for a halfpenny to see the heads of Jacobite traitors on Temple Bar. Hangman's rope was sold for 6d. Theatres thrived. Gardens like Vauxhall and Ranelagh sold pleasure to anyone who could afford the shilling entrance ticket. By the 1720s, race-tracks had appeared at Belsize and Finchley, Hampstead, Highgate, Kentish Town, and Tothill Fields. Spas like Islington and Bagnigge Wells drew Londoners to strut and preen on Sundays, to gamble and drink, show off their clothes and pick up whores.

For sex was on sale, as well. It was another kind of temptation for Londoners, another kind of unsatisfied desire. 'Women of the town . . . are more numerous than at Paris,' Grosley noted, 'and have more liberty and effrontery than at Rome itself. At nightfall they range themselves in a file in the footpaths of all the great streets, in companies of five or six . . . The low-taverns serve them as a retreat, to receive their gallants in.' Sex had been commercialised like everything else. There was even a list, the *New Atalantis*, 'of those [prostitutes] who are in any way eminent . . . [which] points out their places of abode, and gives the most circumstantial and exact detail of their features, their stations, and the several qualifications for which they are remarkable.'[27] The 'Folie' was a floating brothel moored in the river opposite Somerset House.

Prostitutes, known as 'punks', offered yet another instant high. But as with the gambling-table, as with the dram-shop, the price was to be paid next morning in shame and disgust, and the ever-present fear of venereal disease. For every high, there was a low. For every winner at the card-table, a loser staggered off into the dawn with his pockets empty. London's temptations were matched by its dangers. It wasn't just a city of opportunities; it was a city of risks. To start with, London devoured its own inhabitants. All through the years of the Gin Craze, more Londoners were buried than born in the city; if it wasn't for the eager newcomers flocking in from the countryside, the town would have dwindled away to nothing. Servants may have been able to strut around the town in smart clothes, but their lives were chronically insecure. One footman, John MacDonald, worked for twenty-eight masters in thirty years.[28] Tradesmen lived with the constant fear of bankruptcy. To Defoe, a youngster borrowing to set up in business was 'a man going into a house infected with the plague.' And debt meant summary arrest followed by indefinite imprisonment. London had many dangers, few safety nets. The eighteenth-century welfare system broke down in the sprawling slums of Middlesex. Poor people could claim support within their own parish, but the thousands who flocked into London could claim no parish and found no support.

Perhaps it wasn't surprising that London became not only a neurotic town, but a violent one as well. Violence was common in the streets, or at least was believed to be. In March 1712, rumours about random attacks by gangs of 'Mohocks' spread like wildfire. The gangs were said to drive sword-points randomly through sedan chairs, or give their victims 'lions' faces' by breaking their noses and poking out their eyes. At Hockley-in-the-Hole, near Clerkenwell, animals were set at each other, and bare-knuckle or sword fights staged between men and women. One advert promised 'a mad bull to be dressed up with fireworks, and turned loose. A dog to be dressed up with fireworks all over, and turned loose with the bull. Also a bear to be turned loose, and a cat to be tied to the bull's tail.' Saussure watched two women sword-fighters set about each other. Journalist and MP Richard Steele described the outcome of a sword-fight where 'the wound was exposed to the view of all who could delight in it, and sewed up on the stage.'[29] Huge crowds flocked to Tyburn to cheer as criminals were put to death in public.

And Londoners turned violence against themselves. Numerous tracts and enquiries, constant newspaper reports, testified to 'the English malady'. 'The list of suicides has been greatly swelled this last year,' wrote the *London Journal* early one December. 'Every week furnishes us with fresh instances of that kind. Since our last, James Milner esq, a Member of Parliament for Minehead, a gentleman well known in the Portugal trade, shot himself through the head, and died the same day; as did also Mr Ward, a fellow of Oriel College in Oxford.' 'A terrible malady of the mind,' Saussure agreed, 'is very frequent in London.'[30] And for the gambler, suicide was often the final throw of the dice. 'One day last week,' noted Lord Egmont in his diary in the 1740s, 'Mr Tryon, who married my Lady Mary Ferrers, cut both his arms below the elbows with design to bleed to death. . . . The cause is attributed to the inconveniences he had brought him under by gaming.'[31]

Londoners lived on a see-saw between triumph and disaster, glittering display and hopeless despair. The newspapers, proliferating from 1695, told stories of sensational crime and violent death, of novelties, of transformations. Choices abounded in every direction. Londoners could strut along the Strand as gentlemen for a day.

They could be ruined in an evening at cards. In the tarot pack of early eighteenth-century London, the city's emblematic figures were the gambler, the suicide and the self-made man, the foundling, the highwayman, the whore.

These were the years when the production of spirits rose from half a million gallons at the Glorious Revolution to two million gallons at the Peace of Utrecht. By 1720, on the eve of the South Sea crash, two and a half million gallons of proof spirit a year were being distilled in a city with a population of barely more than 600,000.

Madam Geneva had found London fertile ground on which to settle. Gin offered comfort and oblivion to a society which had yielded up certainties of identity for the new and heady terrors of an Age of Risk. Gin replicated the gambler's cycle of boom and bust, euphoria and despair. It counterfeited for drinkers, cheaply and immediately, the kind of transformation with which London seemed all at once to have become pregnant.

And it was on the poor, of course, that the town's risks weighed most heavily; for them its opportunities seemed all the more remote. When newcomers tramped the last few miles into London, they often found not wealth and fortune, but poverty, disease and hardship. They had left families far behind. Often they knew no one. George Burrington, looking at London's population in 1757, reckoned it 'very probable that two thirds of the grown persons at any time in London come from distant parts.'[32] A modern study has calculated that one in six of the British population spent at least part of their lives in the capital.[33]

Within the walls of the City, an older population, long-established, lived under a web of parish regulations, trades and guilds. But newcomers settled in the suburban sprawl of Middlesex, where labyrinthine courts and alleys mushroomed between the great squares of the West End. Where once there had been country parishes outside the walls, there now sprawled huge slums like Holborn or St Giles-in-the-Fields, where tenements and dosshouses were crowded with a fast-moving, anonymous population. 'Whoever ... considers the cities of London and Westminster,' Henry Fielding would later write, 'with the late vast addition of their suburbs, the great irregularity of their buildings, the immense number of lanes, alleys, courts, and bye-places; must think, that, had they been intended for the very purpose of concealment, they could scarce have been better contrived. Upon such a view the whole appears as a vast wood or forest, in which a thief may harbour with as much security as wild beasts do in the deserts of Africa or Arabia.'[34]

In this urban jungle Londoners lived anonymously, with no stable network of friends and family. They often drifted from one room to another, renting by the night. And to them, suddenly, a new and powerful drug was made available at a penny a dram. The novelty of spirits was part of their attraction, but also part of their danger. Madam Geneva was a new temptress. She beckoned to men and women living in a new world.

She beckoned to Robert Stafford one night in September 1720. He had already been 'merry-making'. In Chick Lane he saw a prostitute in a doorway and stopped. He pretended to ask the girl for directions; she got him into a brandy-shop nearby. Brandy, of course, still meant spirits of all kinds. According to Robert Stafford, that was where the girl stole his wallet. The prostitute, Elizabeth Ferrom, told the Old Bailey jury a different story. She faced death if they didn't believe her. She said Robert Stafford 'shoved her headlong into a brandy-shop, called for a quartern of brandy, then a bottle of china ale, then more brandy, and ale for 3 or 4 times one after another.' When another whore came in, the excitement proved all too much for him. That, she told the Old Bailey, who by this time were surely laughing at him, was when 'he called for a quartern of usquebaugh, let down his breeches, pulled up his shirt, and bid them see what he had got.'[35]

That was London in September 1720, the month when the South Sea Bubble finally burst. It was a city of temptations (the girl in the doorway, the drams sunk frantically, one after another); a city of risks (of disease, theft or worse). It was an anonymous place where no one who knew Robert Stafford was likely to see him or tell the tale. It offered both the crazy high which made Robert Stafford down a glass of spirits and pull his trousers down, and the hangover which awaited him next morning, when he woke up seven pounds the poorer and none the wiser. Robert Stafford's evening of highs and lows was a miniature version of what Londoners lived through again and again in the early decades of the eighteenth century, when life's possibilities and its risks both seemed to be expanding at the same dizzying rate.

This was the city where signboards outside dram-shops read 'Drunk for a Penny. Dead drunk for twopence. Straw for nothing.' The straw was for gin-drinkers to pass out on when they had taken their fill. It was the town where Anne Williams, a twelve-year-old prostitute, 'used to lie out o' nights frequently in Drury Lane and Covent Garden and . . . gentlemen used to give her sixpence and a dram.'[36]

Until 1720, hardly anyone had noticed what was happening in London's slums. The authorities had only seemed interested in counting the lighters of corn unloading at Bear Key market, and watching the distilling industry steadily expanding. All that was about to change. For 1720 was the year London's crazy merry-go-round finally took a spin too far. 1720 was the year the bubble burst.

# CHAPTER THREE

## SOUTH SEA MOUNTAIN

By the second day of September, when Robert Stafford had his adventure in Chick Lane, South Sea stock was in freefall. In late June it had been trading at over £1,000; by the end of August it was down past £750 and sinking. The Bubble that had sucked London into a frenzy of speculation had only weeks to run. The Sword Blade Company, bankers to the South Sea Company, would crash on 24 September. By mid-November Parliament would be demanding inquiries, and Robert Knight, the man who kept a green notebook of all the politicians he had bribed with South Sea Stock, would have fled abroad.

The wise had sold up in June, but not many in London had been wise. Even Alexander Pope, waspish critic of the new money men, had been seduced into speculation. 'Not to venture,' he had written to his stockbroker back in February, would be 'ignominious in this Age of Hope and Golden Mountains.'[1] London was in the grip of gambling mania. 'The great doses of opium that are swallowed by the stock-jobbers,' wrote Edward Harley to his father, who had established the South Sea Company in 1711, 'have intoxicated the whole town ... There are few in London that mind anything but the rising and falling of stocks.' 'The demon stock-jobbing is the genius of this place,' he would add a few months later. '[It] fills all hearts, tongues, and thoughts, and nothing is so like Bedlam as the present humour which has seized all parties ... No one is satisfied with even exorbitant gains, but every one thirsts for more, and all this is founded upon a machine of paper credit supported only by imagination.'[2]

It wasn't only the wealthy who thirsted for more. Even Billingsgate market-women had taken 'to a merry way of buying and selling South-Sea over a refreshing cup of Gin.'[3] There was a new name for gin: South Sea Mountain. A *South Sea Ballad,* one of many satires to be published that summer, mocked the motley crowd forging its way to the City in search of riches:

> Young Harlots too, from Drury Lane,
> Approach the 'Change in Coaches,
> To fool away the Gold they gain
> By their obscene Debauches.

Exchange Alley was filled with coaches, messengers and investors. Many had come just to watch the frenzy. A secure world was being turned upside-down before Londoners' eyes. *Mist's Journal* described 'rich farmers ... upon the roads from several parts of the Kingdom; all expecting no less than to ride home again, every man of them, in his coach and six.'[4] A Dutch paper reported more than a hundred ships for sale because 'the owners of capital prefer to speculate on shares than to work at their normal business.'[5] 'Our South-Sea equipages increase every day,' *Applebee's Original Weekly Journal* marvelled in August. 'The City ladies buy South-Sea jewels, hire South-Sea maids; and take new country South-Sea houses; the gentlemen set up South-Sea coaches, and buy South-Sea estates.'[6]

Rumours swept through the City. In Jonathan's and Garraway's coffee-houses, stock-jobbers crowded round tables to fight for deals. Prices were scrawled on scraps of paper, deals sealed with quick handshakes. At the height of the craze, Craggs, Secretary to the South Sea Company, wrote to Stanhope, junior Treasury Secretary, 'it is impossible to tell you what a rage prevails here for South Sea subscriptions at any price. The crowd . . . is so great that the Bank . . . has been forced to set tables with clerks in the street.'[7]

By autumn there were no tables out in the streets. When the crash came it swept away rich and poor alike. 'This town is in a very shattered condition,' wrote one sorry observer. 'Eleven out of the twelve judges are dipped in South Sea: Bishops, Deans and Doctors, in short everybody that had money. Some of the quality are quite broke. Coaches and equipages are laying down every day and 'tis expected that the Christmas Holidays will be very melancholy.'[8] More than a third of the banks in London were to go under. The millionaire Duke of Chandos lost £700,000. The South Sea Crash would leave a long shadow. As one onlooker put it, 'the fire of London or the plague ruin'd not the number that are now undone.'[9] By 1 October, South Sea Stock was down to £290, and still falling. 'Exchange Alley sounds no longer of thousands got in an instant,' reported the *Weekly Journal*, 'but, on the contrary, all corners of the town are filled with the groans of the afflicted.'[10] Daniel Defoe described South Sea investors as 'walking ghosts . . . [as if they] were all infected with the Plague.' 'Never men looked so wretchedly,' he went on. 'I shall remember a man with a South Sea face as long as I live.'[11]

A febrile atmosphere gripped London in the aftermath of the disaster. All winter the newspapers were full of rumours and recriminations. There were so many reports of investors taking their own lives that *Applebee's Original Weekly Journal* suggested, in January 1721, that South Sea suicides ought to be marked separately in the Bills of Mortality 'viz. Drowned herself (in the South Sea) at St Paul's Shadwell, one; Killed by a (South Sea) sword at St Margaret's Westminster, one; . . . Killed by excessive drinking of (South Sea) Geneva, five.' New terrors were imagined everywhere. In the spring a Royal Order in Council was issued, claiming that London was infested with 'scandalous clubs or societies of young persons who meet together and in the most impious and blasphemous manner insult the most sacred principles of our holy Religion, affront Almighty God himself, and corrupt the mind and morals of one another,'[12] and the magistrates of the County of Middlesex were charged to investigate.

But Londoners soon had more to worry about than scandalous societies. Early in autumn 1721, bubonic plague was reported in Marseilles. Old men could still remember 1665, and plague carts rumbling down the streets carrying the bodies of 70,000 Londoners. To zealots and fundamentalists – maybe to everybody, during that neurotic autumn – the South Sea Crash had demonstrated the folly of the age. For three decades, London had been the new Sodom, abandoned to pleasure, heedless of the future. Now it was reaping its reward; divine retribution was on the way. On 2 October, the *Daily Courant* published quarantine restrictions. Newspapers were full of adverts for patent plague medicines. 'The town was never known to be so thin within the memory of man,' commented the *Weekly Journal*. 'Not half of the members are come up, and we see a bill upon almost every door.' The court proclaimed 'a general fast, to be observed throughout Great Britain, in order to put up prayers to Almighty God to avert that dreadful calamity . . . from us.'[13]

Asked to look into 'scandalous clubs' back in April, the Middlesex magistrates had appointed a three-man committee to investigate. It was in the middle of the plague panic, on 13 October, that the committee delivered its report. The magistrates hadn't found any evidence of scandalous clubs. But under the shadow of the plague and divine wrath, they did take the opportunity to point out to the Lord Chancellor everything else that was wrong with the sprawling, vicious new metropolis.

One of the committee's members had known for a long time what was wrong with London. Sir John Gonson would turn out to be one of Madam Geneva's most implacable enemies. He was an enemy of sin in all its guises, a Christian zealot who would be at the heart of the growing evangelism of the 1730s. Only two pictures of Sir John Gonson survive. When Moll Hackabout is arrested by constables in Hogarth's *Harlot's Progress*, the magistrate creeping into her room to direct operations is Sir John Gonson. (Gonson never did have any time for whores; when Mother Needham, a notorious brothel-keeper, was arrested in 1731, he had her pilloried and the crowd treated her so harshly that she died.) The other picture of Sir John Gonson is scrawled on a prison wall in another Hogarth print. This time he is pictured the way prisoners wanted to see him — as a stick figure with a noose around his neck.

The town was out of control, so Sir John Gonson and his Middlesex colleagues thought. Middlesex meant London outside the walls of the old City and north of the river. It meant the sprawling alleys and tenements of St Giles, dosshouses and drinking dens, whores on the Strand, Holborn and Clerkenwell. It meant rural parishes which had suddenly turned into urban jungles. It meant Irish migrant labourers, poor people from the country, epidemics and street crime. It meant gin.

For men like Sir John Gonson, it meant everything that had gone wrong with London since the Glorious Revolution. His report thundered against masquerades and gaming-houses, playhouses and public houses — all the symbols of the new age. But one kind of public house was singled out for special attention. 'Your committee,' he advised, 'are to take notice of the great destruction made by Brandy and Geneva shops whose owners retail their liquors to the poorer sort of people and do suffer them to sit tippling in their shops, by which practice they are . . . rendered incapable of labour to get an honest living.'[14] In St Giles, one building in seven was said to house a gin-seller.

Madam Geneva had had her own way in the slums for thirty years. Now, under the shadow of the plague, she was in the frame for all the evils of the age. If the Gin Craze, as disapproving later historians would dub it, started in 1690 with William III's deregulation of the distilling industry, then the South Sea Crash marked the start of its alter ego, the Gin Panic. From then on, Gin Craze and Gin Panic would be Siamese twins, joined at the neck. We know about the Gin Craze, of course, mainly through the voices of those who were panicking about it. The poor of St Giles left few records. We have to reconstruct London's gutters mostly through the shocked expressions on the faces of passers-by.

Newspapers leapt on the bandwagon. The *London Journal* started running stories of gin-drinking alongside its usual fare of robberies, curiosities, child abuse and highwaymen. On Wednesday 29 November, 'an unhappy accident happened in the passage from Petty-France to Bedlam, where a poor woman was burnt in her chamber. Some attribute her inability to save herself to Geneva.' A couple of weeks later, 'one of the keepers of Bridewell at Dartford in Kent, killed himself on the spot with drinking Geneva, and some of his infantry have been in the like danger, by drinking the same liquor in solemn festival for his death.' The same issue carried a report that 'a porter that plied near Chequer-Inn in Holborn, drank so plentifully of Geneva, with his wife, that he died upon the spot, and she is like to follow him; 'tis said that they drank three pints apiece, in a little more than an hour.'

For Sir John Gonson, evangelist, Madam Geneva had more than a couple of dead porters on her conscience. If the plague came back, he had no doubt that it would be her fault. All through the report, it was unclear whether he was talking about infection or sin. The plague ran through every line, weaving and mingling with the evils of the age. By sitting in gin-shops, drinkers didn't just make themselves unable to work, 'but (by their bodies being kept in a continued heat) are thereby more liable to receive infection.' He turned his fire on beggars ('loose idle people ... with distorted limbs or otherwise distempered ... [who] may conduce to the spreading of infection among us ...'), on the crowded, insanitary gaols, on the animals kept in filthy sheds in back alleys ('the great number of hogs ... kept by brewers, distillers, starch-makers and other persons ... must be very dangerous if God Almighty should visit us with any contagious distemper'). He shone a first light on the filthy dosshouses of Holborn and St Giles ('where 'tis frequent for fifteen, twenty or more to lie in a small room, where it sometimes happens that poor wretches are found dead, and the corps have lain many days among the living before the parish officers have been prevailed on to put them into the ground').

Sir John Gonson had lifted the curtain on life in the slums, and found nothing but depravity and vice. He wasn't the only one to blame that depravity for all London's woes. There were many who thought the city reeling down from the South Sea Mountain was paying the price for its theatres and pleasure gardens, its dram-shops and brothels, for its obsession with display, its hunger for wealth.

Not everyone, after all, had spent the last thirty years gambling, drinking and speculating on the stock market. Some had tried to cling on to old values. For them, the changes associated with the Glorious Revolution were a catastrophe and a sin, an affront to God, a threat to the very survival of society.

Just two years after William III signed his 1690 Act 'for encouraging the distilling of brandy and spirits from corn', the court issued a proclamation against blasphemy, profane swearing, cursing, drunkenness, lewdness, Sabbath-breaking, and 'any other dissolute, immoral or disorderly practice.'[15] The decade that witnessed stockmarket boom and bust, national lotteries and White's gaming-house also saw the emergence of the Societies for the Reformation of Manners.

Josiah Woodward, one of their pioneers, traced the roots of the Societies back 'about two and thirty years,' which would link them to fire, plague, and the puritan generation of Praise-God Barebones. Their first meeting took place a year after the Glorious Revolution, when a pious group in Tower Hamlets agreed to meet monthly to 'resolve upon the best methods for putting the laws in execution against houses of lewdness and debauchery and also against drunkenness, swearing and cursing, and profanation of the Lord's day.'[16]

The best method, they decided, was to use informers. Neighbours, servants and apprentices, London's moral majority, would point the finger at sinners and have them dragged off to the courts for punishment. Right-thinking citizens were exhorted by reformers like Woodward to 'do all that you regularly can, towards the suppression of abounding vice, and the reviving of languishing religion, that this our good [country] may not be as Sodom, first in sin, and then in desolation . . . Will you be discouraged from this,' he asked them, 'because some vain people will call it fanaticism?'[17] They wouldn't. By 1725, 90,000 sinners had been informed against, taken to court by the Societies and prosecuted.

Sex came top of the Societies' agenda, then Sabbath-breaking, then swearing. Drink, back at the turn of the century, hadn't yet been tagged as the root of all evil. But the Societies for Reformation of Manners weren't short of targets. It wasn't only one sin they were attacking; it was the whole new order of things in London. Wherever they looked they saw nothing but 'delight in idleness, excessive vanity, revellings, luxury, wantonness, lasciviousness, whoredoms.'[18] They were shocked by clothes, shocked by theatres, shocked by all the novelties of the times. In an age whose 'deplorable distinction . . . is an avowed scorn of religion in some and a growing disregard of it in the generality,'[19] the Societies clung to pungent Old Testament fundamentalism. The age was rushing forward into risk and change. The Societies preached a return to dry land.

Fundamentalists weren't the only ones to shake their heads over stock-jobbers, gamblers and preening servants. But others found different ground on which to launch their assault. Writers like Swift and Pope fled from Exchange Alley and Covent Garden into the timeless pastoral idyll of Vergil and Horace. The past was a Golden Age, the town a symbol of everything that had gone wrong with it. For the Augustans, the wise man had only one option: to wish the 'dear, damn'd, distracting Town, farewell!'[20] (as most of them didn't) and bury himself in country solitude. Dr Johnson, who reached London in 1737, would castigate town life as Juvenal had, and look back to the golden reigns of Alfred and Elizabeth,

> 'Ere masquerades debauch'd, excise oppress'd,
> Or English honour grew a standing jest.[21]

Dr Thomas Short, analysing London's death rate in 1750, would still see the rural life as 'the first state of mankind, and . . . the healthiest . . . For there . . . still remains such vestiges of virtue, sobriety, regularity, plainness, and simplicity of diet, &c. as bears some small image or resemblance of the primeval state.'[22]

London, for these romantic conservatives, was unnatural and destructive. Its values were corroding the country's traditional virtues. The terrible example was ancient Rome, where a free republic had sacrificed freedom to tyranny, strength to luxury, and all had ended in ruin.

Adapting this vision to their own circumstances, the Tories

and independent Whigs who adopted this viewpoint recast the Hanoverian succession as the start of tyranny and the beginning of England's decline and fall. England, the 'happy seat of liberty,' was 'yet running perhaps, the same course, which Rome itself had run before it; from virtuous industry to wealth; from wealth to luxury; from luxury to an impatience of discipline and corruption of morals; till, by a total degeneracy and loss of virtue . . . it falls a prey . . . to some hardy oppressor, and, with the loss of liberty . . . sinks gradually again into its original barbarism.'[23]

This 'country' vision deplored the vices of the town and the corruption of the court. It looked back to a time before speculation; a time when power was vested in landowners, not in 'usurers and stockjobbers,' and land was owned by those who were born to it; a time of tradition not novelty, frugality not luxury. 'Luxury and the love of riches came into Rome,' warned the *Craftsman*, the newspaper which gave strongest voice to this idea, 'and that poverty and temperance, which had form'd so many great captains, fell into contempt.'[24] Luxury, of course, meant shop windows and the leisure industry. It meant gentlemen-tradesmen. It meant the poor coveting goods and clothes above their station.

Speculation had long been a target of these conservatives, and the South Sea disaster confirmed all their worst fears. 'What advantage,' asked the authors of *Cato's Letters*, a prolonged 'country' attack on the government in the years after the bubble burst, 'ever has, or ever can, accrue to the publick by raising stocks to an imaginary value, beyond what they are really worth? . . . It enriches the worst men, and ruins the innocent . . . It has changed honest commerce into bubbling; our traders into projectors, industry into tricking, and applause is earned, when the pillory is deserved.'[25]

William Hogarth's satirical print of the South Sea Bubble showed speculators on a merry-go-round. To Christians and conservatives, that was how the whole of London seemed: a top spinning out of control, with disaster the only possible outcome. When the South Sea Bubble burst, that disaster had finally arrived. Speculation had ended in ruin; fortunes had been lost; the crowds who flocked into Jonathan's had been clutching at fool's gold. The state would be dragged down as well, for the whole mad scheme of the South Sea Company was supposed to finance government loans and the wrong-headed new idea that a state should live on credit and borrow to pay for standing armies and foreign wars. Honest tradesmen would be bankrupt when their bills went unpaid. London stared ruin in the face.

God stayed his hand; the plague stopped at Marseilles. But the atmosphere of panic remained.

Panic at the financial collapse (and the corruption it uncovered) and panic about the plague were followed by a panic about crime. 'So many ... robberies happen daily that 'tis almost incredible,' declared *Applebee's Original Weekly Journal* in February 1722. The *Weekly Journal* reported highway robberies on the Clapham road ten nights in a row. As the panic spread, the carts rumbling towards Tyburn became ever more heavily laden. One court recorder opposed pardons for highwaymen 'especially at this juncture when so many notorious offenders are daily and nightly robbing the open streets in a most flagrant manner with violence and arms and terrifying His Majesty's innocent subjects.'[26] But neither executions nor rewards seemed to solve the problem. 'Footpads are met with especially in and around London,' worried Saussure soon afterwards. 'Should they meet any well-dressed person at night in some unfrequented spot they will collar him, put the muzzle of a pistol to his throat and threaten to kill him if he makes the slightest movement or calls for help ... Pickpockets are legion.'[27]

The newspapers didn't help. 'The apparent increase of thieves,' the *Daily Journal* scaremongered, 'has not been known in the memory of man, or within the reach of history.'[28] The papers fostered the idea that the crime wave was the work of organised gangs. 'There are advertisements in the Gazette of Saturday last,' reported the *London Journal*, 'of no less than twenty robberies, which have been committed within these three months . . . by a gang of highwaymen, who are at present in Newgate.' Egged on by lurid reports, Londoners became obsessed with crime. They queued for the publications of the Newgate 'Ordinaries' which described hangings, confessions, and the final hours of condemned men. They followed the exploits of Jack Sheppard, who broke his apprentice's bonds and went on the road in spring 1723. After he was hanged, on 16 November, they shivered at the name of the man who took him, Jonathan Wild, self-proclaimed 'Thief-taker General', who took rewards for the thieves he managed himself, sending them to the gallows after he had profited from their crimes.

But it wasn't only crimes in the streets they worried about. There was crime in the corridors of power as well. The South Sea Bubble had uncovered massive corruption among ministers. Then, within months of Jack Sheppard's execution, Lord Macclesfield, the Lord Chancellor, was impeached for selling Masterships in Chancery. The court seemed to be rotten to the very core. 'Hear her black trumpet through the land proclaim,' Pope would write,

> That 'Not to be corrupted is the Shame.' . . .
> See, all our Nobles begging to be Slaves!
> See, all our Fools aspiring to be Knaves!
> The Wit of Cheats, the Courage of a Whore,
> Are what ten thousand envy and adore.[29]

John Gay's *Beggar's Opera*, the satire which broke all records at Lincoln's Inn Fields in 1728, would liken Robert Walpole, the manipulative Prime Minister, to a common gang leader.

In the panicky 1720s, the streets seemed to be infested with footpads, the ministries with thieves. Your lifetime's savings could disappear overnight; your walk home could end in robbery and murder. Defoe's *Moll Flanders*, a publishing sensation on its appearance in 1722, exactly caught the mood of the moment with its tale of a random life driven through highs and lows by every whim of fortune. Panic was in the air. The same year brought a Jacobite scare with the revelation of a plot led by Bishop Atterbury. And with panic came panic reactions. The Atterbury plot was followed by the suspension of habeas corpus, troops in Hyde Park and fines for Catholics. 1722 saw prosecutions by the Societies for Reformation of Manners peak at over 7,000. The Workhouse Test Acts allowed parishes to refuse poor relief if the poor wouldn't work. The Black Act of 1723 came up with yet more hanging offences to send petty criminals on the grim journey to Tyburn.

Madam Geneva was caught up in the flood. Maybe it wasn't surprising that in this wave of recrimination and soul-searching reformers of all stamps should round on her. After all, she had had her own way in the slums for thirty years. She was bound to attract attention sooner or later.

For Christians, Josiah Woodward had sounded the key note back in 1711 in his *Dissuasive from the Sin of Drunkenness*. 'When the dog turns to his vomit,' he sorrowed, 'or the swine wallows in the mire, they do but act according to their nature. But for the noble creature, man, that is made after the image of God ... for this wise and noble creature to part with his reason, his conscience, his Heaven, his God, for a little drink more than he needs ... is a most desperate pitch of sin and folly.' For reformers of the 'country' school, the Golden Age wasn't just a time before speculation and corruption, it was a time before gin. In the good old days, 'the labourer perform[ed] an honest day's work for his wages, and his wife and children would be fed at home with wholesome meat and drink; the butcher, the baker, and the brewer would take his money instead of the distiller, his family would be decently cloathed, his landlord have his rent duly paid; the man would enjoy his health, his strength and his senses, his wife a good husband, himself a plentiful issue, with strong and healthful children; and his prince reap the fruits of their labours, in the increase of his subjects, as well as the riches of his people.'[30]

And when they did, at last, focus their sights on gin, reformers found plenty to worry about. It wasn't just vice and immorality; Madam Geneva was ruining the economy. One reform publication, *The Occasional Monitor*, would complain of tradesmen 'not daring to employ dram-drinkers, because they have not half the strength and capacity they ought to have to do their business; besides the many fatal instances we meet with of day-labourers falling off houses, and other the like accidents thro' drunkenness.' Drinkers lost their strength. They shirked hard work. And for early eighteenth-century economists, that wasn't just their funeral; it spelled ruin for everyone. Conventional economic wisdom said that the more a nation produced, the more it could sell. Economic activity depended on supply, not demand. 'The trade of this or any other country,' as the *London Magazine* would later explain, 'depends chiefly upon the number of natural born subjects employed in producing, manufacturing, conveying, or transporting any commodity.'[31] So every active working man had a value to the nation (Braddon, a solicitor to the wine Excise board, reckoned a poor child at £15 a year).[32] But if the working man was slumped in the doorway of a dram-shop, the whole system went wrong. Reformers produced streams of complaints about the idleness of the labouring classes. 'If a person can get sufficient in four days, to support himself for seven days,' one commentator sighed, 'he will keep holiday the other three, that is he will live in riot and debauchery.'[33] 'Labour,' Bishop

Sherlock proclaimed, 'is the business and employment of the poor: it is the work which God has given him to do.'[34] Unfortunately, in St Giles-in-the-Fields, God came a poor third after Madam Geneva and Saint Monday.

In the aftermath of the South Sea Crash, everything became clear to reformers. Sir John Gonson had found his scapegoat. Gin suddenly crystallised as the root cause of all London's woes. For the poor, it was the start of the slippery slope. In brandy-shops, warned one magistrate, servants and apprentices 'learn gaming; lose their money; then rob and pilfer from their masters and parents to recruit; and by quick progressions, at last come to the gallows.'[35] When they attacked gin, reformers wanted to halt not just the chemistry of the still, but the stockmarket's alchemy which transformed poor into rich, the masquerade that turned your serving maid into a sexual equal, a whole town which could magic highwaymen into heroes, country girls into preening sluts. But when it came to the poor, gin was the key. In an age whose nerve-ends always jangled at the threat of disrespect, Madam Geneva was the siren voice leading the poor away from their duty. She was, as the Middlesex magistrates put it, 'the principal cause . . . of all the vice & debauchery committed among the inferior sort of people, as well as of the felonies & other disorders committed in & about this town.'[36]

Even after thirty years, Madam Geneva still had the reek of the alchemist's laboratory about her. A dangerous magic had been unleashed; something unholy and unnatural was at large in the slums. Madam Geneva was the unacceptable face of the Age of Risk. She had corrupted London, and reformers wanted her out of town.

CHAPTER FOUR

# THE MAGISTRATES

The Middlesex magistrates may have identified Madam Geneva as the villain and handed out wanted posters. They may have warned that 'in some of the larger parishes' – they meant St Giles – 'every seventh house at least sells one sort or other of these liquors.'[1] There still remained the question of how to deal with it all. Distilling was a privileged industry, after all. Madam Geneva had friends in high places and a string of Acts to protect her.

There were plenty of Londoners, if it came to that, who weren't sure the magistrates were the right men to cope with Madam Geneva in the first place.

Magistrates didn't just sit in judgement. They were there to investigate crimes as well, to take evidence and call witnesses. Their business didn't even end with crime. It extended from street repairs to the price of bread, from neighbour disputes to blasphemy. It was the magistrate who would chastise a shopkeeper for blocking a street, the magistrate who would direct a raid on a brothel – quite often in person. Magistrates were police chiefs, local council, social services and highways agency all rolled into one. If some new vice reared its head on the streets, it was the job of magistrates to alert the higher authorities by 'presenting' it at Quarter Sessions. If the King issued a proclamation against gambling-houses or brothels, it was the magistrate who found himself interviewing drunken young rakes at three in the morning.

To make the life of magistrates even harder, there was a constant risk of being sued for mistakes, and the bureaucracy was nightmarish. London was divided into separate jurisdictions. The City of London took care of its own affairs; the Lord Mayor and Aldermen formed its 'Commission of Peace'. Across the river, Southwark counted as the City ward of Bridge Without, but the rest of south London fell under the jurisdiction of Surrey. The eastern suburbs were run by the justices of Tower Hamlets. Everything to the west and north fell into Middlesex. The City of Westminster, meanwhile – an island within Middlesex – had its own Commission of Peace, and was usually taken as a kind of junior partner to Middlesex. Most magistrates ended up sitting on two or three different Commissions of Peace just to make sense of it all.

They had no training. Nobody paid them a stipend. Magistrates were supposed to be independent gentlemen, endowed with private means that lifted them beyond corruption or partiality. The trouble was that few gentlemen in London wanted the job. John Evelyn was approached to join the Surrey Commission back in 1666, but refused because of 'the perpetual trouble thereof in these numerous parishes.'[2] There was an income threshold of £300 – to keep out undesirables – but in 1732 that would have to be cut back to £100. Anyone with an income of £300 could find better things to do in London than sit up till all hours being abused by drunken streetwalkers.

The result was that the London Commissions of Peace were taken up not only by altruistic gentry, but by men who saw yet another chance to make money out of the city's teeming streets. When the writer Henry Fielding took his place as Westminster's senior magistrate in 1749, he complained that 'a predecessor of mine used to boast that he made one thousand pounds a year in his office.'[3] A thousand pounds a year put the canny magistrate in the bracket of the most successful doctors and top businessmen. There were plenty of ways for a 'trading justice' to wring money out of the bench. The trick with whores was simple. 'The plan used to be to issue warrants,' as a House of Commons committee was told, 'and take up all the poor devils in the streets, and then there was the bailing them, 2/4, which the magistrate had; and taking up a hundred girls, that would make, at 2/4, £11.13.4.'[4] In January 1726, Westminster JPs had to put out a warrant against their own clerk, Simon Parry, 'for extorting money from victuallers & pretending to renew their licences.'[5]

So it was a disparate group of zealots and cynics, trading justices and reformers, hard-working public servants and bumbling amateurs that took the burden of controlling all the crime and chaos of Middlesex in the 1720s. It wasn't surprising that their pronouncements should be greeted with a certain amount of scepticism. Nor was it surprising that within the Commission of Peace, Sir John Gonson and some like-minded zealots should decide to form themselves into a tightly knit cabal. A couple of years later, after a campaign against gambling, the Westminster Order Book would record the magistrates who 'entered into a society to suppress gaming houses in . . . Westminster & . . . Middlesex in the year 1723 . . . who call themselves a convention.'[6] Sir John Gonson headed that list of twenty-six names. It was the same group that decided to put Madam Geneva on the rack.

The trouble was the magistrates didn't have the powers they needed to deal with her. They had pointed the finger. They had complained that 'brandy shops are . . . the cause of more mischief

& inconveniences to this town, than all other publick houses joined together.'7 But when they set to work, it turned out there was almost nothing they could do to run Madam Geneva out of town.

She was protected by law. When the Middlesex magistrates met to consider Sir John's report on 13 October 1721, they resolved 'to suppress all houses, shops and other places where these sorts of liquors are retailed without licence.'8 But most gin-sellers didn't need a licence anyway. Under the Act of 1701, distillers and chandlers' shops were exempt. Even if the magistrates found an unlicensed dram-shop and tried to shut it down, they ended up gagging on red tape. 'The certificate of conviction,' they complained to the Lord Chancellor, 'amounts to above threescore sheets of paper writ copywise, and the expense attending them, which no person or parish is obliged to disburse, in effect renders this method impractical & encourages the offenders to continue selling liquors without licences.'9 With the very first action of their campaign, the magistrates had run up against a brick wall.

The licensing exemption was bad enough, but there was more than that to make a reformer's blood boil. Sir John Gonson soon spotted another legal loophole. Troops in the early eighteenth century were billeted on public houses. It was one of the constant laments of alehouse-keepers and victuallers; the billet filled their houses with unruly soldiers, and always ended up costing them money. But the Mutiny Act – which was passed each year to regulate such matters – exempted distillers' shops and chandlers from having to house soldiers. It was based on the Licensing Act. So drink-sellers had only to buy a still and they could laugh at the billeting officer who turned up with six hulking soldiers in search of a home.

The law was actively encouraging the spread of back-room stills. '[Brandy-shops] distil small quantities only,' complained a letter which the magistrates fired off to the Secretary at War the day they approved Sir John's report, '& yet insist they are thereby distillers within this exception, and as such to be exempted from quartering soldiers & taking licences, the two greatest inconveniences which attend those who keep any kind of publick house.'[10] To make matters worse, the powerful malt distillers were throwing their weight behind gin-shops. 'Almost all that sell brandy or Geneva shelter themselves from quartering of soldiers,' the letter went on, '& on all occasion threaten the Justice & Constables with actions, if they quarter upon them, wherein they [claim] to be supported by those ... distillers, of whom they buy the waters they sell.' Threatened with legal action, constables backed down.

And for the moment, that was where the magistrates had to back down as well. There was nothing else they could do but write angry letters. All the 1721 campaign achieved was to highlight the charmed circle in which Madam Geneva lived. No action could be taken against her until the law was changed. The campaign of the zealots was over almost before it had begun.

Not everybody in London was sorry about that. For many, Sir John Gonson and his 'convention' sounded too much like the Societies for Reformation of Manners. The zealots' 'busy care and officious instruction' were criticised in the London Journal. 'Every man must carry his own conscience,' the paper warned. 'Neither has the magistrate a right to direct the private behaviour of men; nor has the magistrate, or any body else, any manner of power to model people's speculations, any more than their dreams.'[11]

Others had already complained about the way reformers of Sir John's stamp picked on the poor. After all, it wasn't only the poor who drank and gambled. 'Your annual lists of criminals appear,' had been Defoe's early riposte to the Societies for Reformation of Manners. 'But no Sir Harry or Sir Charles is here.'[12] A Poor Man's Plea in 1703 had been that 'We don't find the rich drunkard carried before my Lord Mayor, nor a swearing, lewd merchant punished.'[13]

In any case, not everyone in London joined the backlash when the South Sea Mountain erupted; a good number set off for the alehouse instead. Porter, a draught rival to bottled imports, was invented in Shoreditch in autumn 1722. Much stronger than ordinary beer, it sold for 3d a 'pot', or quart. The same year saw growth in spirits production hit a new peak. While the ink was drying on Sir John Gonson's report, output of raw spirits was going up by twenty per cent a year. More than three and a quarter million gallons of spirits were distilled in England in 1723, four-fifths of them in London. And those were just raw spirits — turning them into gin increased the volume by a third. Not all of London's spirits were being compounded into gin, of course, nor drunk in London. But for that matter, official figures didn't pick up what the distillers managed to hide from Excise men, and left out imports from Holland. It all meant that by 1723 each man, woman, child, market-woman and magistrate in London was getting through something like a pint of gin a week.

All that was bad enough for reformers. Worse was to come. In 1723, the Grand Jury of Middlesex furiously proscribed a poem by the little-known doctor and writer, Bernard Mandeville. The poem, *The Fable of the Bees*, had first been published back in 1714 but had attracted little notice, possibly because no one could see what Mandeville (Man-Devil, he was soon being dubbed) was getting at. Reissued in 1723 with copious explanatory notes, it caused a storm. The book was sub-titled *Public Vices and Private Benefits,* and Mandeville's subversive notion was that national prosperity might come not from frugal living and hard work, but from the very vices, fashions and luxuries that reformers abhorred. Whores made work for seamstresses (and doctors). The consumer society had found its first apologist. When it came to gin, the 'large catalogue of solid blessings that accrue from . . . [this] evil' included 'the rents that are received, the ground that is tilled, the tools that are made, the cattle that are employed, and, above all, the multitude of poor that are maintained, by the variety of labour, required in husbandry, in malting, in carriage, and distillation.'[14] It was bad enough that Madam Geneva should be tolerated in London at all. Now she was being held up as a pillar of the economy.

Maybe that was what stung Sir John and his convention of magistrates back into action, or maybe they were inspired by a 1724 sermon against strong-water shops by Dr Chandler, Bishop of Litchfield (the occasion had been the annual address preached to the Societies for Reformation of Manners). Either way, when Westminster Quarter Sessions met in February 1725, the magistrates returned to the attack. They started by ordering their constables out onto the streets to make a tally of shops which sold gin.[15] But this time Sir John Gonson and his colleagues knew what they were after. To clamp down on unlicensed gin-shops wasn't enough. This time they wanted a change in the law.

Before the Westminster report could be written, the magistrates' campaign widened to the whole of Middlesex. 'The cry of [this] wickedness,' proclaimed Sir Daniel Dolins, Chair of Middlesex Quarter Sessions, in October 1725, 'I mean excessive drinking gin, and other pernicious spirits; is become so great, so loud, so importunate; and the growing mischiefs from it so many, so great, so destructive to the lives, families, trades and business of such multitudes, especially of the lower, poorer sort of people; that I can no longer doubt, but it must soon reach the ears of our legislators in parliament assembled; and there meet with . . . effectual redress.'[16]

The survey of gin-shops was also widened to cover the whole district. Constables tramped up and down the alleys of Middlesex, noting down names, asking questions. Some of the constables scribbled their notes on rough scraps of paper ('a list of the Chandler shops that sell drams in Suffolk Street Ward by John Cameron Constable'). Others embellished their returns with pompous flourishes ('Civitas et Libertas Westm. in Com Middx. The Returns of Rich Dew Constable of Exchange Ward in the Parish of St Martins in the Fields in the Liberty & County aforesaid, of all those that sells Geneva'). There were scatter-brained officers who scrawled down a rough list of householders, and more meticulous types who added trades, addresses and shop signs. The constables struggled with foreign names. They were jeered at when they went into brandy-shops. The pompous Richard Dew left Church Lane laughing up their sleeves the day he was taken in by 'Will Wildgoose, victualler.'[17]

But the numbers were serious enough. On 13 January 1726, the Middlesex committee delivered its report. In Westminster and Middlesex alone – leaving out the whole of Southwark and the City of London – there were 6,187 properties where gin was sold. In St Giles-in-the-Fields, you could buy a dram in every fifth house.

That sounded bad enough, but the shops and houses in the constables' returns were just the tip of the iceberg. 'Altho' this number is exceeding great,' the report went on, 'we have great reason to believe, it is very short of the true number ... [for] 'tis known there are many others who sell by retail ... in the streets ... some on bulks and stalls set up for that purpose, and others in wheelbarrows ... and many more who sell privately in garrets, cellars, back rooms, and other places.'

The message of the report was that it was impossible for Londoners to stay out of Madam Geneva's way. Gin was being sold in brandy-shops and alehouses, by landladies, by street-corner vendors who owned nothing but a tray, a bottle and a couple of dirty glasses. Londoners couldn't 'go anywhere, without being drawn in, either by those who sell [gin], or by their acquaintance they meet with in the streets, who generally begin with inviting them to a dram, which is everywhere near at hand.' Gin-sellers didn't even wait for the customers to come to them. 'All arts are used to tempt and invite [them].' Pushers seemed to stand on every street corner. Chandlers would 'tempt and press [people] to drink, and even . . . give them drams of this liquor.' There was no refuge even in the workplace. Gin, by 1726, was being sold by 'dyers, carpenters, gardiners, barbers [and] shoemakers.' In Bethnal Green there were forty weavers who sold it to their own employees. That was the most damaging habit of all. Workers, the report complained, 'having always this liquor ready at hand, are easily tempted to drink freely of it, especially as they may drink the whole week upon score, and perhaps without minding how fast the score rises upon them, whereby at the week's end they find themselves without any surplusage to carry home to their families.' Even when the worker dropped out of employment, hit rock bottom and ended up on social security, he would still have access to gin. Workhouses were awash with the stuff. In Holborn, 'notwithstanding all the care that has been taken, Geneva is clandestinely brought in among the poor there . . . [Inmates] will suffer any punishment or inconvenience rather than live without it, tho' they cannot avoid seeing its fatal effects by the death of those amongst them, who had drank most freely of it.'

After thirty-five years of free trade in spirits, the report revealed how deep gin had put down its roots in London. And turning to the results, the magistrates found social damage wherever they looked. Gin robbed its devotees of 'money, time, health and understanding;' it caused street-fights; it 'never fails to produce a strong aversion to work and labour.' Families were devastated by the new drug. 'Among . . . women . . . it has this further effect, by inflaming their blood, and stupifying their senses, to expose them as easy prey to the attacks of vicious men; and yet many of them are so blind to these dismal consequences, that they are often seen to give it to their youngest children, even to such whom they carry in their arms.' Children suffered most of all. 'Whilst the husband, and perhaps his wife also, are drinking and spending their money in Geneva shops, their children are starv'd and naked at home, without bread to eat or clothes to put on, and either become a burden to their parishes, or being suffer'd to ramble about the streets, are forced to beg while they are children, and learn as they grow up to pilfer and steal.'

The magistrates looked at all the problems which festered in London's slums and every single one was traced back to gin. Gin was bound up with prostitution and crime. It was implicated in the abuse of social security – gin-drinkers sold clothes given them by the parish 'and cheat . . . by all the ways and means they can devise, to get money to spend in this destructive liquor, which generally ends in the husband's being thrown into a jail, and his whole family on the parish.' Gin, the Committee reported, was 'one of the principal causes of the great increase of beggars and parish poor.'

The report pulled no punches. It wasn't intended to. It was intended to provoke legislation. In fact, the figures for gin-shops were no worse than they had been fifteen years earlier. Back in 1711, when spirits went through a minor crisis towards the end of the French wars, magistrates had asked for a count of gin-shops, and in many wards there had been even more then than in 1726.[18] What had changed, five years after the South Sea disaster, was the mood in London.

In 1726, for the first time, a bandwagon started to roll against gin-drinking. The brewers leapt on board with a satirical tract published just a week after the Middlesex report. The tract pitted a brewer called Swell-Gut against Mr Scorch-Gut, a distiller, in a violent tavern quarrel. It was a one-sided encounter. The distiller 'was Scorch-gut by name, and Scorch-gut by nature; for that his damn'd devil's piss, burnt out the entrails of three fourths of the King's subjects.' South Sea Mountain made the poor 'unfit for business, and at the same time fills 'em with all manner of diseases, and throws them on the parish.' Getting personal,

Swell-gut jeered that gin 'make[s] people piss with a vengeance, when you put so much turpentine in it,' whereas beer was 'nourishing and strengthening . . . balsamic to the bowels, and gently laxative.'[19]

The support of brewers was hardly surprising. More significant was the help the magistrates received from the medical world. It wasn't the first time doctors had worried about spirit-drinking. Three years earlier a medical assessment of 'tobacco, tea, coffee, chocolate, and drams' had warned that spirits could lead to depression, and were addictive.[20] Now, timing its announcement to coincide with the magistrates' report, the College of Physicians announced 'that we have with concern observed, for some years past, the fatal effects of the frequent use of several sorts of distilled spirituous liquors upon great numbers of both sexes.' Gin-drinking made them 'diseas'd, not fit for business, poor, and a burthen to themselves and neighbours, and too often the cause of weak, feeble, and distemper'd children, who must be, instead of an advantage and strength, a charge to their country.'[21]

Back in 1721, magistrates had shone the spotlight on Madam Geneva, and had discovered that it was no use working with existing laws. Westminster had tried another clamp-down on unlicensed houses in 1725, and it had 'proved of no effect, having only served to drive those who before were used to these liquors, into greater shops, which are now to be seen full of poor people from morning to night.' But this time the magistrates were calling for a change in the law, and they had powerful voices to support them. It was time for Madam Geneva's friends to start worrying.

The Company of Distillers spearheaded the fightback. The Company hadn't disappeared when their monopoly was taken away in 1690. They had turned, instead, into a comfortable society of medium-sized, well-established compounders. On previous occasions they had lobbied against the brewers, and against smuggling. They were respectable businessmen. They wanted to make a good living, and they didn't want to be blamed for what was happening in St Giles's. But if harsh action was taken against the distilling industry, they would suffer along with the rest. That was reason enough for them to lead the campaign against legislation.

The other reason was that somehow they had got wind of what Sir John Gonson and the magistrates were planning.

On 5 January 1725, a month before the Westminster campaign was even launched, the Company of Distillers met to discuss the crisis. Their answer was a pre-emptive campaign of lobbying in Parliament. They 'ordered that so soon as any matter relating to the Company be moved in Parliament, that the Master and Wardens cause that the Court of Assistants be summon'd to meet them . . . And that . . . such . . . as shall then meet . . . be deemed a Committee to have a full power to act in the Company's Affairs in this present Parliament.'[22] Nothing, as it turned out, would reach Parliament in 1725. But the distillers were prepared. And a year later, with the temperature rising, their Quarterly General Court was ready to address the threat of legislation again.

Parliamentary lobbying didn't come cheap. At the next meeting, the Warden was ordered to 'pay to Mr Warden Palmer forty pounds on account of what he hath disbursed for the Company's affair.' By July, Palmer had paid out another £44. And by then the Committee had decided they needed a professional lobbyist on their books as well. On 12 July it was 'ordered that Mr Warden Roberts do pay to Mr Kenn, the Company's Sollicitor in Parliament, twelve pounds fifteen shillings for business done & moneys disbursed on the Company's affairs & do also pay him twenty guineas for his extraordinary trouble.'[23] In seven months, the Distillers' Company had paid out more than £100.

It was money well spent, though. And if the Company needed an advocate for the distilling industry, they knew exactly where to turn. Daniel Defoe had been the distillers' champion in all their battles before. Now in his mid-sixties, he was London's most famous journalist, and the successes of *Robinson Crusoe* and *Moll Flanders* had turned him into a literary phenomenon. The Company of Distillers paid out £84.4.10 in the early part of 1726, besides what they gave Mr Kenn. And at the height of the crisis, Daniel Defoe went into print with *A Brief Case of the Distillers and the Distilling Trade in England, shewing how far it is in the interest of England to encourage the said trade*. The tract was 'humbly recommended to the Lords and Commons of Great Britain, in the present parliament assembled.'

Defoe's new tract wasn't particularly brief. In fact, it rambled. As well as a long discourse on the history of spirit-drinking, Defoe went to town on the benefits of the industry. His theme was an old one. 'The distilling trade, considered in its present magnitude,' he wrote, 'is one of the greatest improvements, and the most to the advantage of the publick, of any business now carried on in England.'[24] Distilling was essential to the landed interest because it ate up corn. The poor needed it for employment. The shipping industry depended on it for cargoes.

As for the accusations piled up by zealots at Madam Geneva's door, Daniel Defoe swept them aside with all the panache a celebrated elderly journalist could command: 'As for the excesses and intemperances of the people, and their drinking immoderate quantities of malt spirits, the distillers are not concern'd in it at all; their business is to prepare a spirit wholesome and good. If the people will destroy themselves by their own excesses ... 'tis the magistrate's business to help that, not the distillers.' Beer and wine, after all, were just as open to abuse, and no one was campaigning against them.

Other voices were raised in Madam Geneva's defence as well. To many, Sir John Gonson's campaign smacked too much of the Societies for Reformation of Manners, of puritans, preachers and curtain-twitchers. Responding to the Middlesex report in February 1726, the *Daily Journal* took a clear swipe at his 'convention'. The paper had no 'doubt, but that His Majesty's Bench of Justices had all that great and good Work of Reforming our Manners in their view, when they appointed their Committee.'[25] It criticised the magistrates for blaming everything on gin, and for focusing only on the poor, 'as if the disease lay nowhere but among the beggars and labourers; and that nothing requir'd their inspection, but the low-priced debaucheries of the chandlery shop.' As for the physicians, 'it is not many years ago,' the paper scoffed, 'since this very destructive liquor called Geneva, was esteemed medicinal, and cordial, and has been administered as physick.' If it came to that, it wasn't so long since spirits had been prescribed by doctors to cure the plague.

Maybe it was Daniel Defoe's eloquence that carried the day. Maybe MPs had enough else on their plate in 1726. Perhaps the Middlesex magistrates took their eye off the ball. At April Quarter Sessions, Sir Daniel Dolins had switched his fire to homosexuals, attacking crime 'of that enormous, flagrant, horrid nature, that I had much rather not mention it . . . I mean, vile, detestable sodomy, and abominable sodomitical practices.' He didn't mention gin. The Middlesex magistrates were a large and disparate body and not all of them backed Sir John Gonson and the zealots. Maybe reformers didn't yet have the power to force a sustained campaign through the bench.

Either way, there would be no change in the law in 1726. The reformers had led a charge on Parliament and been repulsed. The Company of Distillers glowed with triumph. The danger to Madam Geneva was over.

But only for the moment. London in 1726 was still jittering over crime, worrying about vice. And the reformers had, at least, laid the groundwork. Madam Geneva's face was now firmly associated with social breakdown and moral decay. She had kept her privileges for the moment, but her reputation was in tatters. Next time she would be fighting for her life.

## CHAPTER FIVE

————◆————

# THE FIRST GIN ACT

S uddenly everything went wrong for Madam Geneva. Maybe the pressure was bound to get to her sooner or later. She was too conspicuous. She'd ruled unchallenged in the slums for too long.

In 1727, an anonymous reformer wrote *A Dissertation upon Drunkenness* setting out to show 'to what an intolerable pitch that vice is arriv'd at in this kingdom, together with the astonishing number of taverns, coffee-houses, alehouses, brandy-shops &c. now extant in London, the like not to be paralleled by any other city in the Christian world.' Its warning was stark. 'If this drinking spirit does not soon abate, all our arts, sciences, trade, and manufactures will be entirely lost, and the island become nothing but a brewery or distillery, and the inhabitants all drunkards.'

That was only the start of the distillers' woes. At the same time, Daniel Defoe, their most eloquent supporter, began to wobble. The second volume of *The Complete English Tradesman*, published in 1727, still expanded on the importance of the distilling industry, but there were warning signs. 'I must confess,' Defoe added, 'that the advice to the Complete Tradesman ought to have bestowed a little pains upon these gentlemen called strong-water men, whose share in ruining the people's morals, as well as their health, is too great ... Let them take this gentle hint, they know how to reform it.'

The trouble with Defoe as an ally was that if he changed his mind, he didn't keep quiet about it. He was a journalist. His opinions might fluctuate, but he always knew how to express them. By 1728, his U-turn was complete. *Augusta Triumphans* was subtitled 'the way to make London the most flourishing City in the Universe.' One way was 'to save our lower class of people from utter ruin, and rendering them useful by preventing the immoderate use of Geneva.'

If 1727 had been bad for the distillers, 1728 was even worse. Sir John Gonson was chair of Quarter Sessions in both Westminster and Tower Hamlets at the same time, and with a platform like that he saw no reason to mince his words. Drunkenness, for Sir John, was the root of 'blood-shed, stabbing, murder, swearing, fornication [and] adultery ... the overthrow of many good arts and manual trades, the disabling of divers workmen, and the general impoverishment of many good subjects, abusively wasting the good creatures of God.'[1]

Worst of all, in 1728 the door of Parliament finally swung open to reformers. On 8 October the new King, George II, issued yet another proclamation against the evils of London. And by now the work of Sir John Gonson and his colleagues had had its effect. After seven years of campaigning, Madam Geneva was squarely in the frame for the city's ills. In a follow-up letter to the magistrates, Viscount Townshend, the Secretary of State, was already talking about 'the shops where Geneva, and other spirits and strong liquors are drunk to excess,' and instructing the Middlesex magistrates to proceed against them.[2]

The reformers took up the battle exactly where they had left off. Sir John Gonson was on the committee established in response to the royal proclamation, and the magistrates immediately recommended new legislation. They had already pointed out the problem with the existing laws. They had done what they could; extra petty sessions had been held to suppress unlicensed houses. What they needed was a change in the law.

Reformers had been calling for a Gin Act for years; this time they were going all the way to Parliament. But that didn't mean that new laws were a foregone conclusion. Parliament in 1729 didn't have much appetite for social issues, or much of a track record with them. For early eighteenth-century legislators, domestic issues came a poor third to foreign policy and the serious business of raising revenue.

Back in Elizabeth's reign, Parliament had produced the Poor Laws, it was true, and later the Acts of Settlement. It had set up Houses of Correction late in the sixteenth century, and workhouses more recently. In a way, those all tackled social issues. But the only social agenda for a 1720s Parliament was to maintain the status quo. There was no notion of progress, no idea that social change was desirable, or that it might be engineered by legislation. All parts of the constitution were supposed to operate in balance, like the organs of a healthy body. Change was a symptom of sickness. Then again, gin-drinking was a new problem, and Parliament wasn't good at novelty. It didn't have the statistical tools to get to grips with new problems, or social theories to cope with them. There was no Civil Service to go out and rustle up data. Vice was the church's problem, not theirs; the poor should be dealt with by magistrates.

There were practical difficulties as well. Parliamentary time was limited. There was a single session which ran, in 1729, from January to May. Parliament was dominated by parties, but parties were not interested in social policy. Sir Robert Walpole, Parliament's master, reckoned himself 'no Saint, no Spartan, no reformer.' If a 'social' initiative was brought in, it was usually introduced by a private member, and survived only if he was particularly energetic or influential. Without parties throwing their weight behind reform, it was hard ever to break through the logjam of different interest groups of which Parliament was made up. The result was that when Parliament did address 'social' matters, it did so piecemeal – a plethora of lighting acts, a separate private bill to repair every stretch of broken highway in the country. Like the little Dutch boy, Parliament stuck its finger into every leak that appeared; it didn't think of rebuilding the dyke.

As it happened, the session of 1729 almost managed to crack the mould. In 1729 the House of Commons was presented not only with Madam Geneva bound and gagged, but with a rare example of a social issue around which MPs could unite: prisons.

Prisons, like everything else in London, were a business. In 1713 John Huggins bought the wardenship of the Fleet jail for £5,000. It was a lucrative asset. Prisoners could be blackmailed to improve their accommodation; concessions could be sold for food and drink. In 1728 Huggins sold the wardenship to his deputy, Thomas Bambridge. It didn't take long for rumours about conditions in the Fleet to start leaking out. Sir William Rich, unable to pay for better conditions in the jail, was threatened with a poker, then shackled and thrown into a freezing hole above an open sewer. Robert Castell, scholarly author of *The Villas of the Ancients Illustrated*, was forced to sleep in a sponging-house where smallpox was rife, even though he begged the Warden for mercy. He died.

In the ensuing outcry, a parliamentary Committee was appointed to investigate what was going on in the Fleet. The Committee laid before the House a catalogue of brutality, incompetence and corruption. Huggins admitted 'that so many prisoners had escaped, during the time he was warden, that it was impossible to enumerate them.'[3] Healthy women had been forced into smallpox wards; casual cruelty was an everyday occurrence. When the Committee moved on to look at the Marshalsea and King's Bench, they found the same thing. Investigating the overall management of London's prisons, they uncovered a Byzantine web of lets and sub-lets, transfers of ownership and corrupt charities.

During the session of 1729 some energetic MPs started to take an interest in reform. On 27 February the Prisons Committee had been painted at the Fleet by a rising young artist called William Hogarth. Hogarth's sketch caught the moment when Bambridge was brought face to face with his accusers. Ranged around the table in front of him were William Pulteney, who would lead the Whig opposition to Walpole, and share power in the government that replaced him, Henry Pelham, who would be Walpole's anointed successor, and several MPs who would take an active part in reform over the next thirty years.

But the most colourful and energetic of all the Prisons Committee was its Chair. Major-General James Oglethorpe wasn't just a soldier, adventurer, Jacobite and bully. He was also an evangelical Christian, friend of Sir John Gonson and sworn enemy of Madam Geneva.

After meeting him for dinner in 1755, Dr Johnson urged Oglethorpe, then almost sixty, to write his autobiography. He even offered to write it himself. He told Boswell that he knew 'no man whose life would be more interesting.' It did turn out to be quite a life. In 1722, when he became an MP, Oglethorpe was only in his mid-twenties and already had a military career behind him. That year he wounded another MP in a fight. Three years later he killed a linkman when he got caught up in a brawl at a London brothel. Following his work on the Prisons Committee, Oglethorpe would move to America to found the colony of Georgia as a Christian refuge for the poor of England and the persecuted Protestants of Europe – it was Oglethorpe who persuaded the young John Wesley to go there. He would be a leading member of the Society for Promoting Christian Knowledge. Along the way, he would campaign against gin and in favour of Protestant minorities, prison inmates and the rights of lower deck sailors. When the *General Magazine* ran a competition for poems on 'The Christian Hero', the prize was a gold medal engraved with James Oglethorpe's head.

The reports of Oglethorpe's Committee held Parliament spell-bound all through the 1729 session. Reform was in the air. For once, MPs were having their faces rubbed in London's seamy side. They were mesmerised; but despite the horrific descriptions of torture and brutality they took no action. Not even the Prisons Committee could break the inertia of the House of Commons. The hours of evidence and cross-examination, the long reports to Parliament and stories in the press, still didn't result in a Prison Reform Act.

If prison campaigners couldn't win legislation from the House of Commons, there seemed little chance for the enemies of Madam Geneva. Luckily for the gin reformers, though, the Gin Act wasn't going to have much to do with reform in any case. Madam Geneva was about to become embroiled with interests far closer to Parliament's heart: money and power.

Two issues dominated the parliamentary session. The first was Sir Robert Walpole's need to secure his position with a new monarch. The second was the likely collapse of the sixteen-year peace which had lasted since the Treaty of Utrecht. When he came to the throne in 1727, George II had tried to replace Walpole with the colourless Sir Spencer Compton. Walpole, showing his usual combination of charm, ruthlessness and brains, had quickly outmanoeuvred his rival. He had survived a general election. But he still needed to consolidate his position with a monarch who had got on badly with his father, and saw Walpole as his father's creature.

Understanding that kings, like everyone else, have their price, Walpole had immediately proposed to increase the Civil List, which covered the King's own expenses. Even this settlement, though, hadn't been enough to secure his position. Eighteen months later, George II was complaining about arrears in the Civil List payments. No one took it very seriously. In private, Walpole had always held out against any reimbursement. But that had suddenly become risky. As Lord Hervey recorded, 'the King ... intimated to him, if he could not or would not do it, his Majesty would find those who were both able and willing.'[4] The King was preparing to sell the ministry to the highest bidder.

Madam Geneva was exactly the woman Walpole needed. By this time drinkers were getting through 4,750,000 gallons of spirits a year, and on most of it they paid less than fivepence a gallon in tax. On 4 February Sir James Oglethorpe put forward a proposal that distillers should pay sixpence a bushel when they worked with unmalted corn. If that didn't bring gin to the Prime Minister's attention, it would certainly have caught his eye a week later. That was when the Grand Jury of Middlesex laid before the House a representation against 'the number of shops or houses selling a liquor called Geneva, in and about this city.'

Sir Robert Walpole had no interest in reform, but he did need money, and was soon weighing up options for raising it. The Excise Office had already sent through statistics for spirit production over the last ten years. He now asked them to work out 'an estimate of what may be raised by an additional duty of 2d per gallon on low wines from foreign materials, 1d per gallon on low wines from malted corn, 1d per gallon on spirits.' A new 'still-head' tax, to be imposed on spirit production at source, would, they calculated, raise nearly £39,000 a year.[5]

It wasn't a bad scheme, but there was a snag. The problem was the malt distillers.

By 1729 there was a clear split in the London distilling industry. The compound distillers – who bought proof spirits and turned them into gin – were everywhere. It didn't cost much to buy a small still, and making gin wasn't rocket science. One calculation reckoned there were 1,500 of them in London, with most owning less than a hundred pounds' worth of equipment. If you believed Sir John Gonson, every chandler's shop and alehouse had a still set up on the kitchen table. Making raw spirits, though, was a different matter. With vats and stills, sheds and bulk corn buying, the set up costs alone could come to over £4,000. That made malt or corn distilling one of the most costly investments in London. By 1729 the industry was dominated by no more than a couple of dozen large operators. But the rewards were equally inflated. Fifteen years later, Lord Hervey would reckon 'that [distilling] is the most profitable trade of any now exercised in the kingdom, except that of being broker to a prime minister.'[6]

The malt distillers (they were called malt distillers even when they used unmalted corn) were wealthy, and they used that wealth to control the whole industry. 'The smallness of their number,' complained a compound distiller in 1733, 'makes them easily capable of combining together, and they neglect not the advantage; this union is facilitated among them by their meeting at Bear Key, on market days for corn, three times a week, where they . . . arbitrarily settle the prices of spirits.' If anyone new tried to break in, they squeezed them out by a spirits price war, or by pushing up the price of corn. Nor was it only the distilling industry they controlled. As one of the major purchasers on the London corn market, they could 'oblige the factor to take what price they please for their corn . . . Every factor in Bear Key knows their power, knows they make their own prices, and destroy all that would be a check upon their proceeding.'[7]

There had been plenty of signs already of how far the malt distillers would go. The Middlesex magistrates had seen them threatening constables and protecting their customers from prosecution. Others blamed them for the whole Gin Craze. The malt distillers, it was rumoured, 'supplied [an agent] with means to open warehouses for the sale of spirituous liquors in every part of the town, underselling the compounders.' That was what 'brought the prices of spirituous liquors to that vile price as has ... made them the bane of the vulgar.'

They certainly weren't above bringing their power to bear in Parliament. When more detailed plans were presented to the Commons on 15 April, the 'still-head' duty on spirit production had mysteriously been dropped. Malt distillers would not be taxed. They would be hit by any fall in consumption, of course, but at least the tax wouldn't come out of their own pockets. Instead, the proposed Gin Act would target London's thousands of small compound distillers and gin-sellers. There would be no extra costs for anyone who drank French brandy or punch. Madam Geneva and her devotees stood in the dock alone.

The Company of Distillers had coped with Sir John Gonson, but Robert Walpole on the hunt for cash was a different matter. The Company had a clerk waiting to rush them a draft of the Bill as soon as it was published. What they read was about as bad as it could have been. They embarked on a pamphlet campaign, but it was never more than a rearguard action. The trouble was that by now Sir John Gonson had managed to link Madam Geneva and public disorder inextricably in the public mind. And the Company of Distillers couldn't, in any case, deny what was going on in Rag Fair and Drury Lane. Nor was there any hiding the fact that spirits production had doubled in the last ten years. The Company had to make the best of a bad case. They tried to make out that respectable compounders were on the side of reform. They were 'very desirous the excessive use of any of the said liquors, that enervate and debauch the common people, may, in the most effectual manner, be prevented.'[8] They supported moderate restrictions,[9] and reminded MPs that it was Parliament who had encouraged the trade in the first place. They had coopers lobby the Commons as an example of the other trades which would be hit by a distilling slump. Then they played their strongest card – the quantities of corn the industry bought from landowners – for all it was worth.

But they suffered from a shortage of fire-power. They didn't have Daniel Defoe on their side in 1729. The best they could manage was 'Alexander Blunt, Distiller', who droned on about William of Orange, and addressed his poem, *Geneva*, 'to the Right Honourable Sir R— W—.' 'O may I live to hail the day!' he exhorted the Prime Minister, 'when thou . . .'

> (Suspending the fatigue of state affairs)
> Shalt make the city tour, and condescend
> To visit my poor mansion, and, beneath
> Its humble roof, take a reviving glass
> Of anodyne GENEVA!

Unfortunately for the distillers, it was going to take more than a glass of gin to win over Sir Robert Walpole. The Prime Minister was looking for enough cash to buy off a king. A week after the Gin Act got its first reading, on 23 April, the ministry proposed to a shocked House of Commons that they offer George II the lump sum of £115,000 on account of Civil List arrears. Sir Robert had done his calculations. For gin-sellers there was a new retail licence for £20 a year, which was as much as many of them earned. And 'for every gallon of mixed or compound . . . spirits, commonly called Gin,' the new Act decreed an additional duty of five shillings a gallon, payable by the compounders. The excise duty on a gallon of gin had just been increased by 1,400 per cent.

If only half of English spirits were compounded and paid the new duty, the Gin Act would give Sir Robert £400,000 a year. That was enough to make even a Hanoverian king smile. Not everybody was expecting the same thing out of the first Gin Act, of course. Sir John Gonson assumed that the distillery would slump, and the manners of the poor be reformed. Parliament had, to his joy, overturned forty years of promoting the distillers; it had taken action for the first time against the scourge of spirit-drinking.

But it had also hooked itself up to a drip-feed of new revenue from gin. The unholy trinity of drug abuse, tax revenues, and powerful industry was complete. It wasn't only the poor of St Giles who could get hooked on gin. Governments could as well.

CHAPTER SIX

# CORN

The Company of Distillers didn't waste time crying over spilt milk. They paid their lobbying bills and thanked the MPs who had supported them. They had an advert published in the papers 'to signify the Company's good inclination to prevent the excessive drinking of any distilled liquors to the damage of the common people.' They fired off a memo to the Commissioners of Excise to get various points in the new act clarified.[1]

The 1729 lobbying campaign had been expensive. Kenn, the political lobbyist, put in a bill for £56. The House of Commons doormen had needed their palms greased. The campaign accounts also explained, at last, how the Company of Distillers always seemed to know what the magistrates were planning. They included a payment, 'to satisfy Mr Justice Robe ... for [his] expences in relation to the Company's affairs last session in Parliament.'[2] Thomas Robe had written tracts for the distillers under the pen-name of Eboranos. He also happened to be a magistrate for the County of Middlesex. He had even been on the committee which drew up the 1726 magistrates' report.

It was time to count up Madam Geneva's friends. Top of the list were Sir John Barnard and Micaiah Perry, influential MPs for the City of London. The City was less affected by the social problems of gin-drinking than Middlesex, and more concerned about business. It was a promising ally. To reinforce the link, the Company sent a memo to the Court of Aldermen to underline their own 'dislike of . . . the scandalous practice of tippling.'

It was time, too, to come up with a strategy for the fight-back. A committee was quickly appointed 'to consider of the present state of the Company & report their opinion.'[3] First priority was to make sure everyone knew how much the distillers were suffering. A petition to George II bewailed 'the miserable and deplorable condition to which we are brought,' and tugged the royal heartstrings on behalf of apprentices whose families had 'bestowed their all in giving them a trade by which they thought to have enabled them to lead their lives comfortably.'[4] Old friends weighed in to help. 'Not long ago I knew the day,' lamented a familiar voice,

> When I could rent and taxes pay:
> Each morning with my wife drink tea,
> And who so happy then as we! . . .
> And whence this wretched change? In fact,
> It comes from the GENEVA Act.

In case Walpole, the subject of this call for repeal, was wondering who the author was, he didn't have long to wait.

> 'Do it I say,' ended the poem, 'and don't affront,

The muse of
Your old friend,
A Blunt.'[5]

Next, the Company did all it could to persuade the world that respectable distillers were part of the solution to gin-drinking, not part of the problem. There was a subtext. The Company of Distillers had never stopped grieving for its lost monopoly. Now they argued that if Parliament would only put the industry back in their hands, they could drive out the crooks and cowboys and back-room distillers. That was what lay behind their request to the crown, 'that we may be made an incorporated body.'

But the distillers knew all along what was their strongest card. The industry had, after all, been established in the first place 'for the greater consumption of corn, and the advantage of tillage in this kingdom.' Their best hope for repeal of the Gin Act was to get the farmers back on their side and, through them, the landed interest.

Farming had gone through changes of its own in the years since the Glorious Revolution. Once, the prices of bread and beer had been fixed by the authorities. But farming was being commercialised, like so much else. Traditionalists complained that ancient corn markets stood deserted. 'Where . . . there us'd to come to town upon a day, one, two, perhaps three, and in some boroughs, four hundred loads of corn,' sighed one writer, 'now grass grows in the market-place.' Instead of honest trading, 'badgers' – grain merchants – met in inns to strike deals over 'parcels of corn in a bag or handkerchief, which are called samples.'[6] They were middlemen. This was business, not subsistence. Small farmers who couldn't hang on for the best prices after harvest were squeezed out.

Agriculture had a regular problem of over-production. 'Nothing is more certain,' Daniel Defoe wrote in 1713, 'than that the ordinary produce of corn in England is much greater than the numbers of our own people or cattle can consume.'[7] But grain was hard to store and expensive to transport. A bad year could cause famine. Then, twelve months on, farmers could be scrabbling desperately around to sell off their surplus.

That was the thinking behind William III's package for farming in the 1690s. Find a new market for excess corn and the surplus in good years would be soaked up. Encourage over-capacity and there was less chance of famine after a bad harvest. He had started, in 1689, by reviving 'bounties' — subsidies — for corn exports. Setting up the distilling industry had followed the same logic. It wasn't just that William had found a new market for English corn. Both policies had, as Daniel Defoe pointed out, the added advantage that 'if at any time a scarcity happens, this trade can halt for a year, and not be lost entirely.'

Neither went down well with the general public (apart from gin-drinkers). There were stories of dealers picking up the export bounties and then dumping corn at sea. Most people assumed that if distillers were fixing prices at Bear Key, their loaf of bread probably cost more than it needed to. For landowners, though — and eighteenth-century Parliaments were particularly alive to the problems of landowners — the policies were a godsend. Without subsidies, English farmers could never have competed with farmers abroad. As for the distilling industry, to Daniel Defoe it was 'one of the most essential things to support the landed interest, that any branch of trade can help us to; and therefore especially to be preserved, and tenderly used.'

So it wasn't surprising that farmers had offered support to the distillers in the past. Back in 1702, when the brewers had promoted a bill against distilling, it was the 'farmers and maltsters of the counties of Middlesex, Surrey, Essex, Kent, Sussex, Suffolk and Norfolk' who weighed in with a petition to get it crushed. By 1714, distillers claimed they bought 'above one hundred thousand quarters of malt yearly.' By the time the first Gin Act came in, claims of 300,000 quarters were being bandied around. They were exaggerations, of course, but only by about fifty per cent. It took thirteen quarters of grain to make a tun of spirits, and 15,500 tuns were distilled in London the year before the Act came in.[8] That meant 200,000 quarters of corn passing through the London grain market at Bear Key.

In the great scheme of things that didn't exactly transform English agriculture. Over the whole country farmers produced more than thirteen million quarters of grain a year. But the distilling industry didn't affect the whole country. It changed things for some farmers in some places. The key factors were what kind of grain the distillers bought, and where it came from.

Four corn crops were cultivated in England on a big scale – wheat, barley, rye and oats. But down in the south of England, for brewers, bakers and distillers, the ones that mattered were wheat and barley. Wheat fetched much the better price. Wheat flour was what London bakers wanted for bread; often it cost almost twice as much as barley. But wheat couldn't be sown in the same field year after year. Thomas Coke's tenants in Norfolk were allowed to plant three corn crops every six years. But two of those had to be barley, not wheat. The economics of eighteenth-century farming only worked if a market could be found for an awful lot of extra barley.

In the past, that had meant selling it to the brewers. But since 1690, the distilling industry had opened a whole new outlet. 'The tenants of this kingdom,' reckoned one parliamentarian in 1743, 'pay their rents by their barley: and if we had no distillery our barley would be worth little.'[9] Reformers soon twigged that 'to suppress the distillery at home will raise great clamour from ... the country gentlemen upon account of its taking barley.'[10] The distillers wouldn't just buy barley; they would buy bad barley, and bad malt as well. 'What would become of our corn injured by bad harvests, were it not for distilling?' asked one writer in 1736.[11] The arrival of the distillers had been 'sensibly felt by our farmers,' according to another supporter, 'because it opened to them a market for spoilt and coarse sorts of corn, which they never before could make anything of.'[12] Often that meant barley which was damaged by rain, or which hadn't fully ripened. But it could also mean barley from poor soil which had never in the past produced a marketable crop. 'This,' as Defoe put it, 'is visible in the northern and eastern counties and coasts of England, where a very great quantity of poor and unimproveable lands, which formerly lay waste, are now plow'd and sow'd.'[13] The eastern counties and coasts were the key. The 200,000 quarters of grain distillers bought was a drop in the ocean of overall grain output. It didn't amount to all that much against the four million quarters of barley which England produced every year. But set it against the barley output of those counties which had cheap and ready access to London, and suddenly the malt distillers at Bear Key meant business.

That was why the farmers and maltsters 'of the counties of Middlesex, Surrey, Essex, Kent, Sussex, Suffolk and Norfolk' had stood up for distillers when the brewers were lobbying against them in 1702. It cost a lot to transport corn without roads or railways. Only the counties around London could compete at Bear Key. Hertfordshire was one big malting centre, buying 'all the barley they can get out of the counties of Essex, Cambridge, Bedford, Huntingdon, and even as far as Suffolk.'[14] They sent it on down the river Lea, or else along the turnpike road to London. But even from as close as Bedford, road transport added 3/6 a quarter to the price of corn. Sea transport, at two shillings a quarter, was always a better bet. For barley farmers, that had to mean the coasts of Sussex or East Anglia. Hence the 'many ships or vessels,' seen by one commentator, 'loaded in Sussex, Suffolk, Norfolk, and other ports bound for Bear-Key Market, London, with 200 quarters of barley in each ship.'[15]

Landowners in East Anglia had done well out of William's agricultural reforms. They were the ones who benefited most from the export subsidies as well. Ships from Great Yarmouth could sail to Holland, where the Baltic grain fleets loaded, and the Rhine flowed in from central Europe, and the Jenever distillers – there were 121 of them in Schiedam by 1730[16] – were always hungry for cheap barley and malt. In 1728, 96 per cent of England's 200,000-odd quarters of malt and barley exports left from Norfolk ports.[17] Add in the barley they could sell to London distillers, and East Anglian farming was transformed. Between them, the export trade and the corn distillery would soak up nearly a million quarters of corn a year, on average, for the two decades after 1730, and by far the biggest share came from the eastern counties. East Anglian landowners – men like Sir Robert Walpole* and Viscount Townshend** – suddenly found themselves in a whole new agricultural world.

It was 'the great consumption of corn . . . in the distillery,' for a distillery supporter looking back from 1760, that 'first induced the farmer and landholder, to increase his tillage . . . Without [a regular market], many of the great and valuable improvements of land, in this kingdom, by tillage, must be greatly diminished . . . for, if the farmer cannot dispose of his grain . . . at such a price as will enable him to pay his rent . . . he must of course lay down his tillage, and these improvements cease.'[18] Contemplating the 1690 Distillery Act, *The Farmer Restored* would celebrate in 1739 'what a great and extensive effect had this law, by encouraging the farmers to grub and break up immense numbers of acres of

* First Lord of the Treasury, 1721–1742.
** Brother-in-law of the above. Secretary of State 1721–1730.

wood-lands and warrens, cultivating and sowing great quantities of other poor land, to the great advantage of the landed interest.'

In the past, over-production had been the farmer's curse; now there was a market for the surplus. In the past, crop rotation had been an impossibility – it produced too much barley. Suddenly it was a money-spinner. In East Anglia, where the new markets had the biggest impact, the effects went a long way. After his resignation in 1730, 'Turnip' Townshend retired to Norfolk to improve his estates through crop rotation. A *Gentleman's Magazine* feature on Norfolk farming tabulated the Norfolk rotation of turnips – barley – wheat – barley – clover – clover.[19] 'In Norfolk,' commented Miller's *Gardener's Dictionary* of 1733, 'they cultivate great quantities of turnips . . . [w]hereby they procure a good dressing for their land, so that they have extraordinary good crops of barley.' The 'agricultural revolution' was under way.

'Government must certainly draw from [Norfolk] a much greater portion of revenue than from any other,' wrote Nathaniel Kent at the end of the century. 'The return which [barley] must make when traced through the malthouse, brewhouse and distillery, will be found to amount to a sum almost incredible.'[20] It would never have worked without a market for all that barley. For a 'farmer' writing to support the distillery in 1736, it was 'the goodness and certainty of our market at Bear-Key' which had led to 'good husbandry . . . and the improvement of turnips.'[21]

Madam Geneva wore many disguises in her career. She was the avenging angel of the slums, and the comforter of the poor; she was the curse of London and the friend of market-women. But her most unlikely role was as agricultural reformer, out in the windswept Norfolk fields where barley was sowed and harvested, and loaded in ships bound for Schiedam and London to be made into gin.

\*    \*    \*

All of that might have been reason enough for farmers and landowners to flock to the defence of Madam Geneva. But in 1729 they needed her more than ever. Farming was heading into recession. People in towns dreaded bad harvests because the price of bread went up. For farmers, it was the opposite. Farmers were 'always more afraid of a good year than a bad one.'[22] Good years hit farmers from both sides. The price they got for their corn dropped, but it cost them more to take a big harvest in because agricultural wages went up. And that double whammy was about to hit them hard. 'All history,' as Wimpey would write in 1775, 'cannot furnish twenty such years of fertility and abundance as from 1730 to 1750.'[23] Between 1729 and 1732 the price of a loaf of bread in London fell below fourpence halfpenny for the first time in more than a decade. Rents were on their way down from 1730 onwards; even so, tenants fell into arrears. And when a farm was abandoned, landlords had to invest in improvements to pull new tenants in. 'The interests of our British landholders has been declining several years last past,' reported William Allen in 1736. 'It has been a general observation, that rents have been sinking, and tenants as unable to make as good payments as formerly ... Innumerable are the distresses of our farmers.'[24] The worst year of all was 1732–3, when one landowner found a tenth of the income on his estate – nearly £2,000 – to be in arrears.[25] By 1734, farmers were producing so much excess corn that they were exporting five times as much as they had in 1728. That corn glut just happened to coincide with the brief, inglorious career of the first Gin Act.

Distillers' attempts to whip up support in the cornfields hit a raw nerve among reformers straightaway. Reformers were perfectly well aware how strong the farming lobby was. 'The distillers make it their business,' one tract seethed, 'to persuade and influence the farmers ... for forty or fifty miles about London, that if the late Act of Parliament to restrain them from distilling gin ... be not repealed, all their grain and other produce . . . will come to so low a market, that they will not be able to pay their rents.'[26] The distillers, it seemed, had been asking farmers to lobby landowners for action in Parliament. 'Nay . . . the farmers publickly declare in the markets thro' the adjacent counties about London, that they will not give their votes again to any representative who will not promise them to get the distillers such a law made as may enable them to buy all their . . . corn . . . as usually.' That was 1731, and by then reformers were on the back foot.

But it wasn't just because of the farmers. By then everybody could see that the Gin Act hadn't worked.

In fact, it never had a prayer. The Excise men had a hard enough time keeping tabs on a couple of dozen malt distillers. The 1729 Gin Act expected them to track down thousands of compound distillers and gin-sellers scattered all over London's attics and cellars, its sheds and back rooms. There were 6,187 gin-sellers in Middlesex alone, as the magistrates kept telling everybody. And because compound spirits had never been liable to duty before – duties were paid further up the supply line, by the malt distillers – most compound distillers had never been registered before. The Excise men were starting from scratch.

That wasn't the only trouble with the Gin Act. There was a problem of definitions as well. Everyone knew what gin was, but it was more difficult to pin it down in law. The Act defined it as spirits to which had been added 'juniper berries, or other fruit, spices, or ingredients.'[27] Out in the streets of St Giles, the answer was blindingly obvious: don't add the juniper berries.

The public 'got drunk as frequently as ever,' Carteret remembered during a debate in 1743, 'with that nauseous . . . spirit, which, in derision of the authority of the legislature, they called Parliamentary Brandy.'[28] Parliamentary Brandy was gin without the juniper. It was dirty spirit, pure hooch, and it fell outside the

Gin Act. Londoners preferred their dram to taste of juniper (failing that, turpentine) but they weren't going to make a fuss about it. If they couldn't drink gin, they were perfectly happy to drink raw spirit instead. 'Who,' asked the compound distiller John Brown in disgust, 'could imagine that the most abandoned would continue to swallow down burning spirit, prohibited by law from having any salutary ingredient in its composition?' The answer was thousands of Londoners. Spirit output dipped briefly in 1729, but it was back up to 4.3 million gallons within a year. Poor John Brown had to conclude, more in sorrow than anger, that 'the vulgar have no joy in drinking these spirits but to be intoxicated and inflamed.'[29]

Intoxicated and inflamed, and possibly crippled as well. Drinking raw spirits was dangerous. Drams of Parliamentary Brandy, as the *Occasional Monitor* pointed out in 1731, 'not only kill, which would be some charity to the public, but . . . maim and disable the drinkers thereof, so as to be only fit for hospitals, alms-houses, and Bedlam itself.' Even the Excise Office could see the Act wasn't working. As early as March 1731 they had preliminary meetings with the Treasury to discuss a 'Bill intended to be brought into Parliament for new modelling the duties on spirits drawn from corn.' The Company of Distillers had been bombarding them with suggestions ever since the Gin Act was passed. One which found its way into the draft bill was a subsidy for spirit exports. If London distillers could prosper while the social problems of spirit-drinking were sold abroad, then everybody would be happy. There was talk of offering distillers as much as nine shillings a gallon to export gin.[30]

The main goal for the Company of Distillers, though, was to get the Gin Act repealed. And that took time. 1731 went by without repeal. The Company of Distillers was only a small organisation; for the past eight years it had been punching above its weight.

Now they were running out of cash. Mr Kenn, the parliamentary lobbyist, kept presenting his bills. There was another guinea apiece to be paid 'to Mr Hollinshead & Mr Bradshaw, doorkeepers of the House of Commons.'[31] Then there were the printer's bills for all their tracts. Ten years earlier, Daniel Defoe had been the distillers' champion; two decades later, Henry Fielding would spearhead the campaign against gin and Tobias Smollett would weigh in on the same side. It was ironic that the Company of Distillers' bills for tracts against the first Gin Act would come from the other great novelist of the mid-century, 'Mr Richardson, printer.'

To cut costs, they even had to agree, in January 1732, 'that during the next Sessions of Parliament the expense of the dinner of the Committee during their attendance there shall not exceed forty shillings in any one day.'[32] Even so, in 1733 the Company's lobbying bill would again top £100. But by then the prize of repeal was almost within their grasp. They only failed to get it through in 1732 because the measure ran out of parliamentary time. In 1733, repeal of the Gin Act was top of the agenda. The House wasted no time in meeting 'to consider of methods for encouraging the making and exporting of . . . spirits distilled from British grain.'[33]

That was quite a turnaround for a Parliament which four years before had proclaimed that 'the drinking of spirits . . . is become very common among the people of inferior rank, and the constant and excessive use thereof tends greatly to the destruction of their healths, enervating them, and rendering them unfit for useful labour and service, intoxicating them, and debauching their morals, and driving them into all manner of vices and wickedness.'[34]

But Sir Robert Walpole had been as disappointed by the Gin Act as everyone else. It had never produced a fraction of what he had hoped. It was Sir Robert's brother, Horatio, who signalled the U-turn with the announcement, on 9 March, that 'we are now in a committee for encouraging home-made spirits.' MPs agreed that the Gin Act had been 'a discouragement to the distilling of spirits from corn in Great Britain, and therefore ought to be repealed.' A petition was brought in by some Essex farmers. Outside the House, meanwhile, Thomas Robe was arguing in the Post-Boy that 'there is nothing that ever more required the care of the legislature, than the preserving and improving the British distillery.' The distilling industry, Robe argued implausibly, 'is of more value to the kingdom in general, than the mines of Potosi to the King of Spain.'[35] Madam Geneva was back in favour again.

The five-shilling duty on compound spirits was discarded and nothing brought in to replace it. Subsidies were offered for exports. For reformers, the only crumbs of comfort were that distillers and chandlers would still need retail licences, and there would be a ban on spirit-selling in the streets. Street-hawkers couldn't afford a parliamentary lobby.

It was hardly enough to cheer up Sir John Gonson. To make matters worse, the new Act squeezed its way through Parliament only just in time. Two days after the House approved it, Sir Robert Walpole plunged into the Excise Affair, the worst crisis of his political career.

The celebrations were left to Madam Geneva's new poet laureate. Stephen Buck's *Geneva, A Poem in Blank Verse*, was dedicated 'to all gin-drinkers in Great-Britain and Ireland.' If Stephen Buck had wanted to turn the knife in Sir John's wounds, he could hardly have done better. The thing conservatives hated most about drink was the transformation it offered; the way it broke down traditional barriers. That was what they hated most about the whole age. Now Stephen Buck asked,

What can impart such solace to mankind,
As this most powerful dram, which levels all
The different ranks in this unequal world?
The poor plebeian, elevate by Gin,
Fancies himself a King.

# CHAPTER SEVEN

# THE CHRISTIANS

Landowners sought new markets in a corn glut; politicians argued and reformers preached; businessmen squabbled, and agriculture strode forward; but nothing much changed for gin addicts in the London slums.

Judith Defour was a poor girl. She worked at a throwster's, but earned only two or three shillings a week. She had a child, a little girl called Mary, born after a fling two years before. Judith wasn't in touch with the father. Her own mother helped out, but money was always short. For the last few weeks Mary had lived at the parish workhouse.

On a Sunday morning late in January 1734, Judith Defour went to collect Mary for a day out. Bethnal Green workhouse was out in open fields, ten minutes' walk across footpaths from the top end of Brick Lane. Judith Defour arrived early, but the matron, Jane Prig, stopped her from taking Mary away. 'I would not let her,' she recalled, 'without an order from the church wardens; so she went away, and came again in half an hour, and brought a note, as from the church warden, and upon that I let her have the child out.'[1] Judith exclaimed over her daughter's smart clothes. Just a few days before, the parish had given the child a new petticoat and stockings, and a coat to go over them. Judith Defour took Mary and promised to bring her back in the early afternoon. She was on shift that night. It was about ten o'clock in the morning when Jane Prig saw her set off across the fields, with the little girl clinging to her neck.

At half past seven the same evening, Judith appeared for work as normal. Her workmates didn't notice anything strange. She was a bit drunk, but Judith Defour was quite often a bit drunk. A lot of the women had the taste for gin and came to work topsey-frizey, as they used to say, particularly after a Sunday off.

They settled down to the shift. Susan Jones asked Judith if she'd taken Mary back to the workhouse. Judith said it was her mother who had taken the little girl back. They didn't talk much after that. The work was hard and boring, but slowly the hours went by. About one in the morning, Judith Defour sent out for a dram of gin. There was nothing strange about that. The women could always send out for gin if they wanted it. Their boss had an arrangement with a local dram-shop, and deducted it from their wages at the end of the week. That night, after her first dram, Judith Defour would have sent out for another, but Susan Jones stopped her. She could see the girl had had enough already. Instead, Susan remembered, 'she desired a penny to buy a roll and cheese. I gave her a penny, but instead of fetching a roll and cheese, she brought in a roll and a ha'porth of gin.' With another dram inside her, something in Judith Defour seemed to give way. Susan Jones remembered her looking blearily around the room full of workbenches. Then, out of the blue, 'she said, she had done something that deserved Newgate.' Susan Jones was shocked. She and another of the women, Elizabeth Scot, clustered round Judith Defour's bench to find out what she was talking about. 'I hoped she had not wrong'd my mistress,' Susan Jones told her. Maybe that was when Susan realised what a state Judith Defour was in. 'She said it was no such thing as that,' she recalled. It was far worse. '[She said] she had left her child all night in the field. *What?* says I, *in such a dismal cold night? How can you be so cruel?*' It wasn't her fault, Judith Defour said; it was another woman who had made her do it, a girl called Sukey.

But the two older women weren't interested in that. It was January, and outside the night was freezing. And a child was lying out there somewhere in the fields.

Shocked, Susan 'bid Elizabeth Scot take a piece of bread and butter, and go with me and [Judith] to fetch the child.' It must have been getting on for three in the morning by the time the women left the workshop. Stumbling a little from the gin she had drunk, Judith Defour led the others up Hare Street. They passed the wall of a market garden, and headed along a footpath towards the George public house. It was cold; out in the open fields, when the houses fell away, it felt colder still. Judith Defour led them through the darkness towards a rundown little shack out in the open. That was where she stopped. She seemed numbed by something, maybe by gin. Susan Jones would never forget what she saw when she looked down. In the uncertain glimmer of the moon, she could make out a little child 'stript and lying dead in a ditch, with a linen rag tied hard about its poor neck.'

John Wolveridge lived in another hut out in the fields, near Bethnal Green. On the morning of Monday 30 January he was woken by shouting outside. At Judith Defour's trial, a month later, he remembered hearing the outcry, 'that a child was murder'd in the field. I went to the place and found a child dead; it appear'd to be upwards of two year old. I found a black circle about the neck, and a mark like the print of a thumb, under the right ear.' A crowd had gathered by then. 'Some gentlemen told me, they had seen three women coming from the place where the child lay.' That was Susan Jones and Elizabeth Scot, hurrying Judith Defour off to get help. A doctor, Job London, was one of the first to arrive. Mary was lying in a shallow ditch that ran along one side of a field. She had been stripped naked except for the linen handkerchief tied round her neck. 'About the fore-part of the child's neck,' the surgeon observed, was 'part of a black circle, like that in executed persons, and I believe the violence it was done with, was the cause of her death.' By then Susan Jones and Elizabeth Scot had raised the parish wardens, and Judith Defour had been brought back to the scene. John Wolveridge couldn't help going up to her. He 'ask'd her, how she could be so barbarous as to murder her own infant? She said she had only stripp'd it about seven at night, and laid it naked in the ditch; and this was all I could get out of her for a pretty while; but at last, in a violent agony of grief, she said, *Then, sir, I will tell you how I did it; but there was a vagabond creature, one Sukey, that persuaded me to it; and was equally concern'd with me. On Sunday night we took the child into the fields, and stripp'd it, and ty'd a linen handkerchief hard about its neck to keep it from crying, and then laid it in a ditch. And after that, we went together, and sold the coat and stay for a shilling, and the petticoat and stockings for a groat. We parted the money, and join'd for a quartern of Gin.*'

It all came out at the trial. Judith Defour had forged the workhouse release note. She had collected Mary and then, 'kept [the child] with her, till about 6 or 7 a clock in the evening.' By that time she was with a woman called Susanna, or Sukey; Judith Defour didn't know her surname. They had been drinking, but had run out of money. It was Susanna, Judith Defour said, 'who persuaded her . . . to sell the child's clothes and carry it into the fields and leave it there.' She didn't know why she agreed. She was drunk. 'They went both of them together into a field near Joan Harding's [shack], where they stripp'd the said child.' She admitted all that. They were planning simply to abandon Mary. Maybe someone would find her and take care of her. But every time Judith walked away, her daughter started to cry. That was when the two women decided they had to silence her. They 'ty'd a linen rag very hard about the child's neck, to prevent its crying out, which strangled her, and . . . afterwards, they went together, leaving the child dead.'

Stumbling away through the fields, they were carrying the clothes the workhouse had given Mary four days before, the petticoat and stockings and the new coat. They went 'to one Mary Witts, who lives in Swan Yard, in the parish of St Leonard Shoreditch, and sold the clothes.' They got sixteen pence for them, and split the money between them. And they spent what they got on gin.

At the hearing in the great Old Bailey courtroom, open to the elements, with lawyers and onlookers crowded into the yard outside to hear the child-killer speak, Judith Defour testified that it was the woman called Susanna who had talked her into it. 'I did not think to do anything to the child,' she pleaded, 'but that wicked creature Sukey seduced me to it.' Judith Defour would 'plead her belly' to escape punishment. But a jury of matrons decided she wasn't pregnant. In the end it was her mother who had the last word on the short and tragic life of Judith Defour. Her daughter had never been right in the head, she testified on the witness stand; she 'never was in her right mind, but was always roving.'

For disappointed reformers in 1734, Judith Defour's case became something of a rallying point. Maybe it was an isolated incident, murder in the slums, the tragedy of a single mother who had never been 'in her right mind.' But to Madam Geneva's enemies, the Defour story had all the ingredients they had warned about: addiction, violence, even the abuse of welfare. It summed up everything that the Gin Craze led to: the irresponsibility of the poor, the failure of a mother, the death of a child.

And reformers needed something to rally around. The repeal of the first Gin Act had left them on the ropes. Eight years of campaigning had come to nothing. When push came to shove, Parliament was as solid for the distilling industry and the farmers as ever. And in St Giles and Clerkenwell, all over Middlesex, the evils of gin-drinking were getting worse every year.

It wasn't only horror stories like the Judith Defour case which reignited the reform campaign in the mid-1730s. There was new blood coming into the reform movement as well. The Societies for Reformation of Manners were winding down. Prosecutions had peaked in 1722. Twelve years later they had dwindled almost to nothing. The Societies had set out to save the world, but all they'd done was to make themselves unpopular. Quite early on, the high church maverick Henry Sacheverell had criticised the Societies' campaigns as 'the unwarranted effects of an idle, incroaching, impertinent, and medling curiosity . . . the base product of ill-nature, spiritual pride, censoriousness and sanctified spleen.'[2] No one ever loved an informer. It was time for a new approach.

The Society for Promoting Christian Knowledge had been founded not long after the first Societies, in 1699, but it had moved in a quite different direction. Its founder was Thomas Bray, evangelical vicar of St Botolph-without-Aldgate. He had decided that 'the growth of vice and immorality is greatly owing to the gross ignorance of the principles of the Christian religion.' The SPCK wouldn't spy on sinners, berate blasphemers or drag drunkards to the courts. Instead, they would promote Christianity through charity schools and improving literature, and the results would speak for themselves.

In 1732 they had their first major success. Thomas Bray was dead by then, but before his death he had been entrusted with a charitable legacy and established a group of SPCK members — 'The Associates of Dr Bray' — to administer it. The result was the foundation of the Georgia Colony, chartered by Act of Parliament in 1732, to assist the poor of England and the persecuted Protestants of Europe. Its first governor was Major James Oglethorpe.

Every week, a dedicated group of Christian reformers met at the SPCK headquarters in Bartlett's Buildings. Many were Trustees of the Georgia Colony; all were devoted to the promotion of Christian principles. They included James Oglethorpe, Lord Egmont, retired sea-captain Thomas Coram, and the distinguished scientist and churchman Dr Stephen Hales. It was from this group that the next blow would be struck against Madam Geneva. There was nothing surprising in that. Another member was that tireless campaigner and zealous magistrate, Sir John Gonson.

It came a year after repeal of the first Gin Act, when the taste of Parliamentary Brandy was almost forgotten and Judith Defour was the talk of London. In 1734, Dr Stephen Hales published *A Friendly Admonition to the Drinkers of Brandy, and other distilled spirituous liquors.*

It could hardly have been a friendlier admonition. Dr Stephen Hales never did anything unfriendly in his life. Even Alexander Pope, who could find a bad word for most people, called him 'plain Parson Hale,' and added 'I ... always love to see him; he is so worthy and so good a man.'[3] Horace Walpole remembered him later as 'the old philosopher, a poor, good primitive creature.' As a scientist, Hales roved widely. His *Vegetable Staticks* of 1727 explored the physiology of plants. He came up with ventilators, through which 'great quantities of fresh air [were] conveyed into mines, gaols, hospitals, work-houses and ships, in exchange for their noxious air.' He busied himself with fire-fighting, food preservation and wholemeal bread. He invented airholes to ventilate floor joists, and pumps for fish tanks. There was something of the mad professor in Stephen Hales. A friend walked into his house one afternoon to find him dissecting a frog on the dining-room table. 'His whole mind,' as Gilbert White put it, 'seemed replete with experiment, which of course gave a tincture, and turn to his conversation, often somewhat peculiar, but always interesting.' Taking tea at Leicester House, he asked the Princess of Wales to look in her cup for mineral sediments.[4] Talking politics, he would calculate out loud the amount of air breathed in an hour by the Members of the House of Commons.

Stephen Hales ended up a celebrity and pillar of the establishment. He would even be talked of as a possible tutor for the future George III. But in his own mind, there was one achievement which overshadowed all his publications and prizes, all the professional acclaim. It was his campaign against gin, he told Bishop Hildesley in 1758, '[over] 30 years, in eleven different books or newspapers' that gave him the greatest satisfaction of his entire life.[5]

In publishing his *Friendly Admonition,* Hales wasn't only bringing a scientific reputation to the reform campaign. For the first time he built a detailed medical case against the abuse of spirits. In an age that loved bowing to the marvels of science, Stephen Hales attacked Madam Geneva with medical argument backed up by experiment. Hales found that spirits 'coagulate and thicken the blood, [and] also contract and narrow the blood-vessels.' He discovered this 'by experiments purposely made, with brandy, on the blood and blood-vessels of animals.'[6] The experiments had probably been carried out on Hales' dining-room table. The result for gin-drinkers? 'Obstructions and stoppages in the liver; whence the jaundice, dropsy, and many other fatal diseases.' That wasn't the only effect of gin. Spirits caused problems with circulation, brain damage ('whereby they spoil the memory and intellectual faculties') and heart disease. Gin was so addictive that 'when men had got a habit of it, they would go on, though they saw

Hell-fire burning before them.' Stephen Hales' experiments may have been quaint and his explanations curious, but his diagnosis was accurate enough. It even went as far as advice for pregnant women and breast-feeding mothers. 'We have too frequent instances,' he warned, 'where the unhappy mothers habituate themselves to these distill'd liquors, whose children, when first born, are often either of a diminutive, pygmy, size, or look withered and old, as if they had numbered many years, when they have not, as yet, alas! attained to the evening of the first day. How many more instances are there of children, who, tho born with good constitutions, have unhappily sucked in the deadly spirituous poison with their nurse's milk?'

Gin hadn't gone away. More was being drunk than ever. In the London tenements, Madam Geneva's trail of broken hearts and ruined families, of crime and violence, was longer than ever. Stephen Hales' *Friendly Admonition* opened a new front in the battle. The bandwagon against Madam Geneva was rolling again.

But Stephen Hales was no politician. If progress was to be made, the campaign needed a very different kind of champion. It needed someone with a genius for publicity, a man of energy and ambition, someone who had the cunning to guide legislation through a fickle Parliament. And it so happened that a couple of years earlier a young churchman called Thomas Wilson had landed at Bristol on his way to build a career in London. Thomas Wilson had no shortage of energy, cunning or ambition, and in his pocket he was carrying a letter of introduction to Dr Stephen Hales. Madam Geneva was about to meet her most dangerous enemy.

The eighteenth-century Church of England was accused of many things, from sloth to venality, corruption to greed. But at least there was one sin it never had on its conscience. It never made Thomas Wilson a bishop. Horace Walpole described Thomas Wilson in old age as 'that dirty disappointed hunter of a mitre.' He came from an impeccable church background. His father was the venerated Bishop of Sodor and Man. Thomas Wilson senior was an Old Testament prophet, a harsh and unrelenting holy man who kept the Isle of Man in the grip of Bible law. Under Bishop Wilson, prostitutes were dragged through the sea behind boats, and adulterers stood at crossroads holding lists of their crimes. Maybe it wasn't surprising that Thomas Wilson decided to make his own career elsewhere.

In London, aged twenty-eight, he wasted no time in searching for a good living. He entered a little vow in his diary 'that I may make no indirect methods to gain preferment.'[7] That was one promise Thomas Wilson never broke. His schemes for getting on in the world were anything but indirect.

Church livings were only available when someone died. So for the next six years Thomas Wilson's diary became a roll-call of the sick and dying of the Church of England. When death knocked, Thomas Wilson was sure to be lurking somewhere near the rectory door. In August 1735 he noted 'that Dr. Brampston, Prebendary of Worcester and Rector of St. Christopher's and Vicar of Mortlake died at Worcester. Aged 80.' In October 'Mr Fynch was very ill and . . . Dr Sharp was in a declining state of health at Bath.' The death of a Bishop created the best openings of all. When the Bishop of St Asaph expired, Thomas Wilson 'waited upon Sir Robt. W[alpole] [and] told him that the Bishop . . . died Sunday night between 8 and 9 . . . He told me that he would do what he could for me.' Another time he heard a rumour that the Canon of Christ Church had passed away. 'Wrote to Lady Sundon about it,' he recorded, 'and to Mr Phillips to speak to Sir Robt. W.' He only stopped to check the rumour afterwards, when he added the exultant note, 'Knipe . . . certainly dead.' His web of information didn't often let him down. Once someone told him the Bishop of Durham had passed on. Hurrying to the Bishop's home, Thomas Wilson 'found it was a mistake,

he being in very good health.' Shamefaced, he 'returned home
to dinner.'

Meanwhile he did everything he could to make contacts. And
his father's letters of introduction led him straight to the SPCK
offices at Bartlett's Buildings. There, within weeks of his arrival in
London, Thomas Wilson had met not only Dr Stephen Hales,
but gin's oldest enemy, Sir John Gonson.

The SPCK was a tight-knit group. The wealthy philanthropist
Sir John Phillips and his son Erasmus were regulars at the weekly
meetings, as was the hellfire evangelist, John Thorold. Thomas
Wilson turned Bartlett's Buildings into a virtual home from
home. Hales and Gonson weren't the only gin-haters he met
there. James Vernon, an Excise Commissioner, was another regular. James Oglethorpe was in frequent contact from Georgia
(his first act on taking charge of the colony was to distribute a hundred copies of Stephen Hales' *Friendly Admonition*).
And in January 1735, Thomas Wilson would be present when
'The Revd Dr Maddox, Dean of Wells ... [and] the Right
Revd Thomas Secker Rector of St James, now Lord Bishop
Elect of Bristol ... were chosen ... members.' Isaac Maddox,
later Bishop of Worcester, would spearhead the 1751 campaign
against gin, while Thomas Secker, as Bishop of Oxford, would
speak passionately against spirits in the 1743 House of Lords
debate. And on 29 April 1735, the SPCK welcomed another
new member who would play a vital part in the fight against
Madam Geneva. Thomas Wilson and Dr Stephen Hales were
both present that evening to watch Sir John Gonson introduce Thomas Lane, one of the most senior magistrates on the
Middlesex bench.[8]

Gin wasn't on the formal agenda at SPCK meetings. It was,
as one member sniffily put it, 'foreign to [our] proper business.'[9]
But there was little doubt what the campaigners talked about as

summer 1735 drew on. In June, Thomas Secker's parish of St James's ordered officials to count up gin-shops in the parish and denounce them to the magistrates.[10] The new campaign was under way, and from then on the reformers moved at lightning speed. The Queen had been spotted as a possible ally, and Thomas Secker joined a deputation to win her support. Goaded on by Gonson and Lane, the Middlesex magistrates passed a resolution to suppress gin-shops.

And this time there was no doubt in reformers' minds what they were after. Half-measures were not enough. The first Gin Act had been a fiasco; now they wanted complete prohibition of all spirits. Madam Geneva had come back from the dead once. This time they wanted her six foot under with a stake through her heart.

They had even found the man they needed to steer prohibition through Parliament. Sir Joseph Jekyll was sixty-eight years old and had been Master of the Rolls for nearly two decades. He wasn't exactly popular, but he could certainly pull strings. At last the campaigners had a parliamentary heavyweight on their side.

It was easy enough to poke fun at Sir Joseph Jekyll. Lord Hervey, who could always find everyone's bad side, reckoned him 'an impractical old fellow of four score.' The Master of the Rolls had 'no great natural perspicuity of understanding and had, instead of lightening that natural cloud, only gilded it with knowledge, reading and learning, and made it more shining but not less thick.' But even Hervey had to admit he had the ear of the House. Politically, Sir Joseph was a Whig, but he prided himself on his independence. He liked to boast that he came to the House 'undetermined, and resolved so to remain, till I am fully informed by other gentlemen . . . of all the facts which ought to be known.' For Hervey, that was just flannel. Jekyll 'argued on both sides and voted for neither.' There was one thing, though, that the Master of the Rolls was certain about. In the words of Sir Arthur Onslow, long-standing Speaker of the House, he 'had much dislike of Sir Robert Walpole.'[11]

Jekyll spent much of his time at his estate at Bell Bar, north of London. He disinherited his only son, who was blind. There was no evidence for the rumour that he hated Madam Geneva because his own wife had taken to drink. It might have been Thomas Sherlock, Bishop of Salisbury, who first got him interested in gin. Back in April, Jekyll had been present as President of the Westminster Infirmary when Sherlock preached a hellfire sermon against Madam Geneva. By June, Jekyll was firmly enough on board to join the deputation to the Queen.

It was James Oglethorpe who introduced Thomas Wilson to the Master of the Rolls. In London on a visit from Georgia, he met Wilson at the Cheapside Coffee House, the two men 'talked about the Affair of Gin,' and Oglethorpe took him up to Bell Bar a few days later.[12] For the ambitious young cleric, that meeting was a dream come true.

Thomas Wilson had come to a decision. Madam Geneva was going to make his name. Others drowned in spirits; he was going to build a career on them. Through the reform campaign he would meet movers and shakers, senior politicians, men who could dispense livings. 'The Master of the Rolls and his lady received us very kindly,' he gushed into his diary after the visit to Bell Bar. He had presented Sir Joseph with a draft of his new anti-gin pamphlet. He had spent all weekend finishing it off; the working title was *Distilled Spirituous Liquors the Bane of the Nation*. Within days, Thomas Wilson was settling happily into a new role as the campaign's chief co-ordinator. He ran a message from Jekyll down to Thomas Lane, went on to see James Oglethorpe, then took a letter from the Master of the Rolls to Sir John Barnard, the new Lord Mayor. A couple of weeks later he was back at Bell Bar for a meeting between Jekyll and Lane. Thomas Wilson was going places. 'Sir Robt. W.,' he confided to his diary on 12 October, 'told Mr Oglethorpe that I stood as fair as any man in England for preferment in the Church.'

The pieces of the new anti-gin campaign were starting to come together. The aim was to present a Bill in the session of 1736, and by early September preparations were well advanced. The trigger for legislation would be another tirade from the Middlesex magistrates (hence the meeting between Jekyll and Thomas Lane in early September). Quarter Sessions – the last before Parliament met – came round in late September. In a carefully orchestrated move, the Grand Juries of the City of London, Middlesex and Tower Hamlets all issued simultaneous presentments against gin. In Tower Hamlets, where Sir John Gonson was Chair of Sessions, the text was particularly eloquent. 'How often,' Gonson asked, 'do we see women . . . lying in the very channels and corners of streets like dead carcasses, generally without cloaths to protect them from the inclemency of the weather, or cover their nakedness and shame? How many breaches of the peace, dangerous assaults, and often murders have been occasion'd by this deluge of debauchery?'[13] 'Men and women servants,' added the Middlesex magistrates, 'nay even children, are enticed and seduced, to taste, like and approve of those pernicious liquors sold for such small sums of money, whereby they are daily intoxicated and get drunk, and are frequently seen in our streets, in a condition abhorrent to reasonable creatures.'[14] Thomas Lane chaired the committee of magistrates set up on 18 October to take the campaign forward. By the time he met Isaac Maddox at the SPCK ten days later, and went on to dinner with Thomas Wilson afterwards, the constables were already out in the alleys of Middlesex, knocking on the dram-shop doors, counting gin-sellers.[15]

Meanwhile, it was time to work out political strategy. On

17 November, Thomas Wilson dined with Stephen Hales at the Thames Ditton home of the Speaker, Arthur Onslow. With Stephen Hales at the dinner table, conversation was always erratic. They had to talk mathematical experiments and the immateriality of the soul before they could get on to Madam Geneva. But when they 'began upon the Gin Affair,' everyone was in complete agreement. 'Heartily for suppression,' Thomas Wilson recorded in his diary. 'All spirituous liquors the highest calamity there are before a nation.' The campaigners were sure enough about that, but they could also see the opposition that lay ahead. 'To suppress the distillery at home,' Thomas Wilson minuted in his diary, 'will raise great clamour from . . . the country gentlemen upon account of its taking barley.'

So far, though, nothing had been heard from the country gentlemen, or from the distillers. Madam Geneva seemed to have gone to ground. The prohibitionists were having it all their own way. Speed and co-ordination had given their campaign an unstoppable momentum.

Things could hardly have gone better. The brewers had been persuaded to stump up printing costs for the campaign. On 11 December, Joseph Jekyll told Thomas Wilson 'that he had seen the Queen, who seemed to be an hearty enemy to distilled and spirituous liquors. [She] said she had seen a great deal of bestialities and indecencies as she has gone by in the streets.' ('The Master,' Thomas Wilson added, 'took the opportunity of recommending me strongly for preferment.') Parliament was due to meet in mid-January; the Queen was going to ask George II to mention gin in his speech.

The report of the Middlesex magistrates was due to come out as the MPs gathered. Thomas Wilson's own tract, *Distilled Spirituous Liquors the Bane of the Nation*, would follow immediately afterwards. He spent the Christmas holidays adding the finishing touches. If he heard the noise of revelry in the streets, he comforted himself with the thought that it was the last time the mob would toast the New Year in gin. Two weeks later, the King opened the 1736 session of Parliament.

# CHAPTER EIGHT

---

# PROHIBITION

A frightening new statistic awaited MPs as they gathered for the new session on 15 January in St Stephen's chapel. The same number was being read in the *London Evening Post* in coffee-houses all over London. In the last ten years, almost a thousand new gin-shops had opened in Middlesex.

The Middlesex magistrates, led by Thomas Lane, had published their report. There were now 7,022 gin-sellers in Middlesex alone. And even that statistic came with a word of caution. It wasn't just that constables had left out street-hawkers and old ladies in attics. 'Upon enquiry into the respective trade and callings of the several constables,' the report admitted, 'it appears to us, that over half of those employ'd in this enquiry are retailers of those liquors themselves.'[1]

Apart from that, the report told the same dismal story of social decay that the magistrates had revealed ten years earlier. If anything, Madam Geneva's grip on the slums had tightened. Now, even more than in 1726, it was 'scarce possible for persons in low life to go anywhere, or to be anywhere without being drawn in to taste, and by degrees to like and approve this pernicious liquor.' But if gin was responsible for all the ills of the age – in the opinion of men like Thomas Lane – now, at least, they knew how to put the age to rights. Prohibition had become their panacea. Banish Madam Geneva and the nation would return to sanity. 'In consequence of this remedy,' the magistrates promised, 'trade must increase with the labours of the poor, our soldiers will still be renowned for their strength and real courage, servants will be more obedient, honest and faithful, and all sorts of persons in low life will become more strong & robust, better inclined to industry and labour, and be less induced to rob & commit murders and outrages ... In time our morals will be better secured, and we may, with great reason, hope once more to see religion, sobriety and industry flourish once more among us.'

A fortnight later, the reformers unleashed their second broadside against Madam Geneva's defences. It was Thomas Wilson's big day. Just before publication, he had shown the final manuscript of *Distilled Spirituous Liquors the Bane of the Nation* to his new patron. The Master of the Rolls had approved it, only asking 'that its moral reflections might be kept to the last and not intermixt in the body of the treatise.'[2] Not even Sir Joseph Jekyll could stomach Thomas Wilson's moral reflections. All the same, Wilson couldn't help feeling pleased with himself. He had heard from the Bishop of Durham that Sir Joseph had been singing his praises, and had 'said that if he had £500 a year he would give it me.'[3] Sir Joseph had even agreed to underwrite printing costs for the pamphlet, so Thomas Wilson had the printer, Rivington, run off a thousand, including '100 in large paper and sticht in Marble Covers.' He spent Thursday 5 February delivering them around town. Any young cleric would have felt pleased with himself as he looked down the list of subscribers. As well as SPCK stalwarts like James Vernon and John Thorold, Thomas Wilson could count no fewer than ten bishops, including not only the Archbishop of York but Edmund Gibson, influential Bishop of London. The Bishop of Durham had signed up, as had Thomas Secker, Thomas Sherlock and Benjamin Hoadly, Bishop of Winchester. The Master of the Rolls had signed for six copies, and Arthur Onslow, Speaker of the House, for one. Philip Hardwicke, the Lord Chancellor, must have added his name when Thomas Wilson met him just before Christmas. Lord Egmont recorded in his own diary that 'in the evening Dr Wilson, son to the Bishop of Man, came and presented me his book against the baneful spirituous liquor called gin.' Thomas Wilson had some news to spread round, as well as his tract. 'He told me,' Egmont added, 'Sir Joseph Jekyll has a Bill to discourage the drinking it, which he brings this day sennit into the House.'[4]

For once, Thomas Wilson had good reason to feel pleased with himself. He was no fool. *Distilled Spirituous Liquors the Bane of the Nation* was the most sustained and damaging attack on gin-drinking so far.

He had gone right to the heart of the problem. Reformers had to break up the love affair between distillers and the landed interest. So Thomas Wilson's tract, taking no prisoners, would comprise 'Considerations humbly offer'd to the Hon. the House of Commons, by which it will appear that the Landed Interest suffers greatly by the distilling of spirituous liquors.'

Arthur Onslow had given him some pointers the day the reformers dined at Thames Ditton. The Speaker had been full of good ideas about beer production, the cost of social security, and figures for child mortality. He had also suggested that gin-drinking could be shown to harm farmers 'if it be considered [that] fewer cloths are worn and much less coarse meat eat [by gin-drinkers] than formerly.' Thomas Wilson used this slender idea to turn the farming argument on its head. Citing Judith Defour, he claimed that gin-drinkers sold their clothes rather than buy new ones, which meant gin damaged the wool industry. Gin-drinkers ate less as well. 'Those that keep large numbers of cows near the town, will tell you, that they have not had near the demand for their milk, and have been forced to sell off some part of their stock; which they attribute to mothers and nurses giving their children gin.' If London's Gin Craze continued, the result could only be ruin for farmers, for everyone depended on London. The distillers had never been slow to wheel out figures for the amount of grain eaten up by the London distillery. Thomas Wilson set out to beat them at their own game. Starting with Dr Cheyne's calculations for how much an average man ate in a day, he was soon reckoning that each gin-drinker, his appetite gone, his earning-power diminished, and his cash spent on booze, cost the landlords threepence a day. If there were 10,000 gin-shops around London and each gin-shop had forty customers, the Gin Craze in London cost farmers nearly a million pounds a year.

It was quite a performance. Thomas Wilson was impassioned ('War, plague and pestilence rage for a while, and then they cease; but this merciless destroyer threatens misery, sickness, and want, for generations that are yet . . . to come'). He invoked his readers' worst demons: high wages, shortage of cheap labour, beggars, street-robbers and housebreakers. He played on country mistrust of London, which sucked in honest countrymen and turned them into gin addicts. Gin was the cause of crime. Gin debilitated the army and left the nation defenceless. Gin added to the burden of social security. Thomas Wilson lifted medical arguments from Stephen Hales' *Friendly Admonition*. And looking to the future of a gin-sodden England, he pointed out the awful example of Rome: 'It was thrift, sobriety and virtue that laid at first and continued so long the grandeur of the Roman Empire; when they lost their first simplicity, and sunk into effeminacy and luxury, they soon became a prey to the most barbarous nations.'

*Distilled Spirituous Liquors the Bane of the Nation* was an instant success. Its timing was right. The gin issue had been brought to the boil just as Parliament met. The reformers had mixed up a powerful brew of statistics, moral outrage, family values and patriotism. But they had had it their own way for too long. Madam Geneva's friends weren't going to stand and watch while the zealots dragged her off to the stake. The gin war of 1736 would be fought in tract and counter-tract. As Parliament met to consider prohibition, a paper fusillade broke out.

*An Impartial Enquiry into the Present State of the British Distillery* argued for 'a proper regulation in the home-consumption of this manufacture without the total prohibition of it.' For Thomas Wilson's statistics its author traded an equally unreliable calculation that had the distillery employing 10,000 people and 3,000 tons of shipping. There was a healthy dose of abuse for 'the manifest absurdities and gross impositions [of] a printed pamphlet entitled Distilled Spirituous Liquors the Bane of the Nation.' Thomas Wilson's reasoning was lampooned ('He [observes] that more children die under three years old since the use of spirituous liquors than before . . . He might with equal certainty have said, that such increase of deaths happened since the use of narrow-brim'd hats, which therefore was the cause'). He poured doubt on Wilson's claim that gin-drinkers had died like flies in the recent 'flu epidemic. 'What were these persons?' he asked. 'What hospitals did they die in? Where is the public attestation of the physicians or surgeons attending them?'

Thomas Wilson was always thin-skinned. The counter-tract stung him into a revised edition, including a graphic description of conditions in the back-alleys of Middlesex. 'In one place not far from East Smithfield,' he reported, 'a trader has a large empty room backwards, where as his wretched guests get intoxicated, they are laid together in heaps promiscuously, men, women, and children, till they recover their senses, when they proceed to drink on, or, having spent all they had, go out to find wherewithal to return to the same dreadful pursuit; and how they acquire more money the sessions papers too often acquaint us.'

That, of course, only inspired *A Supplement to the Impartial Enquiry . . . in a letter to the Reverend Author*, which launched into Thomas Wilson's 'insuperable pride and vanity, that officious ill-nature and inclination to be busy at any expence, so well known to govern you in every past station of your life.' But by now Thomas Wilson and his tormentor no longer had the field to themselves. General pamphlet war had broken out and the air was thick with accusations. *The Trial of the Spirits*, attacking gin, was countered by *A Proper Reply to a Scandalous Libel intituled The Trial of the Spirits*, which only provoked a *Vindication* of the first tract. The gloves were off. A 'Farmer of Kent' read *Distilled Spirituous Liquors* with some friends 'and we agreed one and all, that the Gentleman who took so much pains to write it, was certainly mad.'⁵ The 'farmer's' enemies then published an advert in the *Daily Journal* unmasking him as a distiller's servant. ''Tis almost as difficult a task,' the *Daily Post* sighed, 'to methodise and reconcile the arguments of a mad author . . . as to bring him back to his senses; nevertheless, as I have begun an examination of the TRIAL OF THE SPIRITS, I shall endeavour to go through it.'⁶ That author took to the pages of the *Daily Journal* to denounce his tormentor as 'some little imp formed out of the dregs of Gin as you do Phosphorus from Piss.'⁷

The newspapers split over the gin issue. The *Daily Gazetteer* and *London Daily Post* espoused the cause of prohibition. The *Daily Post* published an impassioned series of leaders against prohibition in late March. The news columns filled up with sensational cuttings about gin-drinkers. Just one day before Joseph Jekyll launched his campaign in Parliament, the *Daily Gazetteer* came up with another horrific account of a drunken childminder: 'Mary Estwick came home on Tuesday last about two in the afternoon, quite intoxicated with Gin, sate down before the fire, and, it is supposed, had the child in her lap, which fell out of it on the hearth, and the fire catched hold of the child's clothes and burnt it to death. People heard the child cry and run into Estwick's room, and found the child in the hearth burnt to death, and the fire catching hold of the old woman . . . When the people that came in had put the fire out, they attempted to rouse Estwick; but she was so intoxicated, she knew nothing of what had been done.'[8]

There was a spate of stories about deaths from hard drinking. The *Gentleman's Magazine* reported that 'four persons drinking Geneva together in an alley near Holbourn Bridge, died next day, and about 10 more were mentioned in the newspapers of this month, to have kill'd themselves in the same manner.'[9] The *London Daily Post* fleshed out the details: 'On Friday in the evening, Fosset a cobbler in Field Lane, and a person known by the name of Joss the Glazier . . . with one Summers a bricklayer in that neighbourhood, and a carman, who plies at Holbourn Bridge, and two or three others, met accidentally at a Gin shop in Field Lane, where they drank gin in half pint glasses, without intermission, to so great an excess, that Joss the Glazier fell backward with the eleventh half pint in his hand, and died on the spot about 8 o'clock at night; Fosset died in the same shop about 3 o'clock the next morning; the others, by advice of Mr Lee a surgeon in the neighbourhood, had oil and warm water poured down their throats, which set them a vomiting, tho one is said to be dead since.'[10]

Other stories of gin drinkers were more salacious. Few of the papers could resist the one about Jane Andrews, 'servant maid to Mr William Bird, a brewer at Kensington Gore.' When her master went on a journey, 'she shut up his doors, and went to Kensington Town to a Gin shop she usually frequented, and there found a drummer of the guards of her acquaintance, a chimney-sweeper, and a woman traveller. She invited this guest [sic] home to her master's house where they drank plentifully from ten in the morning till four in the afternoon, when Jane Andrews proposed to the company . . . they, and she, should all go to bed together; and thereupon they shut up the doors and windows, and tho twas but about four o'clock in the afternoon, they stript, and all four went into one bed together (as the Maid called it *to ring changes*) and lay there till a mob, hearing of this affair, surrounded the door, and disturbed the happy pairs.'[11]

But one thing was clear from all the tracts and column inches. Supporters of Madam Geneva were on the back foot. The speed of the reform campaign had caught them by surprise. Just three years before, Parliament had sat as 'a committee for encouraging home-made spirits.' In the space of seven months, the reformers had shifted the agenda all the way to prohibition.

The press hadn't helped. 'As to the many frightful stories which have been published in the newspapers,' complained the author of the *Impartial Enquiry*, 'they are generally exaggerated far beyond the truth, and oftentimes invented by those whose interest it is to inflame the nation . . . or by the runners employed to pick up domestick news, who are obliged to bring every day a number of fresh paragraphs, and coin and adapt these to the prejudiced belief and opinion of the public.' He even claimed that the notorious signboard promising customers they could be drunk for a penny and dead drunk for twopence was a myth. 'On the most diligent enquiry,' the writer declared, 'I cannot find any reason to believe there ever was such a sign.'

The Company of Distillers shared his mood of frustration. Their parliamentary committee had failed, for once, to anticipate the reform campaign. Maybe they couldn't afford a full-scale counter-attack. There were rumours of vast payments being made by distillers to MPs – there was talk that one member had been given £5,000[12] – but sums like that weren't coming from the Company of Distillers. Only at the last moment did they come up with *The Case of the Distillers Company and Proposals for Better Regulating the Trade*, but the argument it made (back-street drinking was caused by distillers 'of mean fortune, and worse character;'[13] give the Company back its monopoly and it would control the trade) was the wrong line at the wrong time. No one was handing out monopolies in 1736.

For the reformers, there had been only one disappointment. Despite, or maybe because of, his wife's interest, the King had refused to mention gin in his opening speech to Parliament. Apart from that, everything had gone according to plan. A week after the session opened, the Middlesex magistrates put in their formal petition calling for legislation.

That was the easy part. 'Whatever difficulties may be stated,' wrote the author of a prohibitionist tract published a few days later, 'the greatest . . . is Parliamentary Faith.'[14] It hadn't got any easier to push legislation through the House. At least one person, though, was confident. Thomas Wilson dined with Sir Joseph Jekyll the weekend before it all started. The Secretary to the Treasury was against their Bill, Sir Joseph told him, 'but he does not doubt carrying it.'[15]

It was the Master of the Rolls himself who opened the two-day committee debate on the 'total suppression of all distilled spirituous liquors.' Thomas Wilson was in the gallery to hear him. Few voices were raised against prohibition. Micaiah Perry, member for the City of London, supported the Company of Distillers (as he had before) and worried about smuggling. But Jekyll had no trouble in winning the four resolutions he put before the House: that the root of the problem was the low price of spirits; that the price should be raised drastically by duties; that gin-selling should be restricted to brandy-shops, alehouses and victuallers; and that such vendors should be forced to take out an expensive licence.

Only a few of the sharper members might have noticed what was missing from the list. Back in 1729 Walpole had considered taxing the malt distillers at the first point of spirits production, but had backed off. In 1733 the same idea had been trailed as the obvious way to bring Madam Geneva under control. When Sir Joseph Jekyll first unveiled his own plans to Thomas Wilson, in August 1735, Wilson had noted in his diary that 'I believe it will be by laying on a greater duty.'[16] Now the Master of the Rolls had backed off as well. The malt distillers were still too powerful to touch.

Instead, Sir Joseph had decided to target the other end of the spirit chain: not tuns of raw spirit but drams of gin. His final proposal, put to the House on 8 March, was for a massive new retail duty applying to spirits sold in small quantities. With twenty shillings a gallon added to their price, a dram of gin would cost the same as a week's lodging. On top of that there would be an annual licence for spirit retailers costing £50. Most Londoners didn't earn that much in a year. On paper it could hardly have looked more convincing. No one doubted that Sir Joseph's plan added up to prohibition.

Only a few MPs heard alarm bells ringing. William Pulteney had been an ally of Walpole, once, but they had fallen out in 1725. Pulteney agreed that gin-drinking 'has of late years grown to a monstrous height.' There didn't seem to be anyone in London who disputed that. But he couldn't persuade himself to make the leap from that to 'a total prohibition upon the retail of such liquors.' It seemed unfair to ban spirits all of a sudden, when successive governments had encouraged the distilling industry for so long. 'Likewise,' he went on, 'the retail of them has been so much encouraged, or at least connived at, [that] there is not now an inn, an alehouse, or a coffee house in the kingdom, but what owes a great part of its profits to the retail of such liquors.'[17] He was worried about sugar imports, and about employment. He thought reformers were probably exaggerating the problem. He couldn't understand why they were dodging the obvious solution of a still-head duty on the malt distillers.

And, alone in the House, William Pulteney also stopped, just for a moment, to wonder how people were likely to react to prohibition. 'I foresee [they] will raise great dissatisfaction to the present government,' he warned, 'and may produce such riots and tumults, as may endanger our present establishment.' Alone in the House, he was struck by the injustice of a wealthy Parliament legislating to curb the habits of the poor: 'A poor journeyman or labourer shall not have a dram . . . whereas if a man is rich enough to lay out eight or ten shillings at a time, or profligate enough to pawn his coat . . . he may drink as much . . . as he pleases . . . If spirituous liquors . . . are of such a pernicious nature, that they ought never to be tasted without the advice and prescription of a physician, we ought to take care of the rich, as well as of the poor . . . I can see no reason for our making any such invidious distinction.'

None of that worried the reformers. And on the evening of 8 March, with Jekyll's four resolutions in the bag, they began their celebrations. Lord Egmont recorded that, 'Dr Hales, minister of Teddington, who dined with me, had tears in his eyes for joy.'[18] Within a few days newspapers noted that, 'all manner of grain fell at Bear Key, and distiller's barley bore no price at all.'[19] Thomas Wilson published the second edition of *Distilled Spirituous Liquors* a week later, and sent a copy to every MP. He had a celebratory dinner with Stephen Hales, who 'liked my pamphlet very well.'[20]

But they had let off the fireworks too soon. They should have been paying attention to Sir Robert Walpole. Sir Robert was no reformer. He wasn't interested in Madam Geneva's looks or her morals, only in her fortune.

In the very first debate the Prime Minister had quietly wondered what would happen to royal revenues if the distillery was closed down. 'If the House . . . intended it as a total Prohibition . . . he hoped they would seriously consider of replacing this duty in some other way.'[21] He had reckoned the loss as high as £292,000 a year, but the House hardly noticed. 'Flushed with success,' as Pulteney recalled in a letter he published later that year against the Gin Act, 'and not being opposed in this first righteous essay, they thought it impossible that there should be any fallibility in any part of so well-intended a scheme.'[22] As business moved to a close on 8 March, Sir Robert raised his hand again. 'The Chairman of the Committee being about to make a report of the . . . resolutions to the House,' reported Chandler's *Proceedings*, 'Sir Robert Walpole stood up.' The Prime Minister moved 'that the Committee might sit again before any report was made to the House.' He was worried about revenues. 'As the duties proposed to be laid upon spirituous liquors would certainly very much diminish the consumption of such spirits, it was not to be expected that the duties upon such spirits would produce so much yearly as they had formerly done.' He asked for a committee 'to consider of ways and means to make good the deficiencies.'

Most MPs still hadn't noticed, but – timing his move with his usual care – Sir Robert Walpole had just hijacked prohibition.

The plan became clearer a week later. The Prime Minister had been doing some calculations. Spirit duties, according to his figures, had raised £70,000 a year for the Civil List. Prohibition was going to leave the crown short. Walpole knew exactly when to bore the House. His speech was, as Pulteney recorded drily, 'a long, laborious account, full of infinite knowledge.' But William Pulteney, for one, could see exactly what was going on. Buried within the speech was not only a covert raid on the sinking fund which was supposed to be paying off the nation's debts, but another free gift for the Civil List.

When realisation dawned on the House what Walpole was up to, it immediately 'put a stop to the unanimity, which had long reign'd upon this subject . . . open'd the eyes of many, and made the bill to be consider'd entirely in a different light.' The move to ban gin, backed by almost the entire House, had suddenly turned into a political flashpoint. Walpole had used Jekyll and the reformers as a front for his own political game – a plan to increase revenues and profit the crown. 'I am fully convinced,' a Pulteney supporter wrote, that the Master of the Rolls 'had no share in, nor knew anything of [these] designs.'[23] Jekyll had been duped. The 'grant of . . . a large annual sum to the Civil List was the chief, tho the secret and conceal'd . . . motive' of the Ministry all along.[24]

The Gin Bill was no longer about gin. It was 1729 all over again; it was about money and power. The opposition were too weak to stop Sir Robert Walpole, but they could delay a second reading, and that delay gave the distillers time to fight a rear-guard action. The American sugar planters came in with a petition and a tract, and the sugar ports of Bristol and Liverpool backed them up. Early in April, 'such of the Distillers as are of the Younger Branch of the Trade' produced a pamphlet bemoaning the plight of those who 'have taken long leases of houses, shops, and warehouses . . . at advanced rents . . . and have also laid out great sums of money in fitting up the same,' and asked Parliament for compensation. One amendment got the definition of small quantities – which attracted the new retail duty – reduced from five gallons to two. Another allowed distillers to pursue other trades without going through apprenticeship. The introduction of the Act was put back from June until Michaelmas – 29 September.

But those were rearguard victories. They didn't stop prohibition, any more than the opposition could stop Walpole's Civil List gambit. On 10 April the committee debate ended, and 'it was observable,' *Read's Weekly Journal* noted, 'that the distillers of this city and suburbs, who on Wednesday swarmed in the courts of request and lobby of the House of Commons went away under a very visible mortification.' The Act for Laying a Duty upon the Retailers of Spirituous Liquors had become law.

The Act's severity didn't just show in the twenty-shilling duty on gallons of gin sold in small quantities, or the £50 retail licence. It was in the penalties for anyone who evaded the Act. There was a £100 fine for unlicensed retailers, and a £10 fine for anyone selling gin 'about the streets, highways, or fields, in any wheelbarrow or basket . . . on any bulk or bulks, stall or stalls, or in any shed or sheds.' Magistrates had the right of summary conviction and could summon Excise men at will to help secure a conviction. A hawker who defaulted on the fine made himself liable to two months' hard labour.

For William Pulteney, prohibition was 'one of the boldest experiments in politics that was ever made in a free country: and seems as if intended to try the submission and obedience of our people.' He had no doubt 'that before next session it will be found necessary to alter the whole scheme of this Bill, and to contrive some new method for preventing the excessive use of spirituous liquors among our common people.'[25] But William Pulteney was wrong. It would be seven long years before prohibition was repealed.

In 1743, considering the achievement of Sir Joseph Jekyll — who had been dead for five years by then — the Earl of Chesterfield would tell the House of Lords, 'If the promoter of the Bill against gin had not been known to be a very sober man, I should have suspected him to be an excessive gin-drinker; because when all the world were crying out for a law to put a stop to that abominable vice, he, in order to stifle that cry, contrived a law which evidently appeared to be inexecutable.' In the same debate, the Earl of Ilay exactly caught the odd, symbiotic relationship of the Gin Craze and the Gin Panic. 'The law ... was passed in a sort of mad fit, and has been an affront to our government ever since it was passed. Every man that could foresee any thing, foresaw, that it was such a law as could not be executed. But as the poor had run gin-mad, the rich had run anti-gin-mad, and in this fit of madness, no one would give ear to reason.'[26]

Both were speaking with the benefit of hindsight. When the parliamentary session closed, no one knew how the public would react to prohibition. The Gin Act would come into force at Michaelmas, 29 September. The mood in the country was uncertain. The King might have had the gift of foresight when he told the assembled Houses of Parliament in May, 'It is a great concern to me, to see such seeds of dissension sown among my good people, as, if not timely prevented, may prove very prejudicial to the peace and quiet of my kingdoms.'

Two months later, in a protest against the Gin Act, Jacobite terrorists exploded a bomb in Westminster Hall.

# CHAPTER NINE

## SUMMER RIOTS

I t wasn't much of a bomb. There was a loud bang and some smoke, and then Westminster Hall was filled with fluttering sheets of paper. It happened between one and two o'clock on a Wednesday afternoon, and the hall was crowded. In 1736, the Courts of Chancery and King's Bench and the Court of Common Pleas all sat there, in open-plan wooden booths. Uffenbach, who visited in 1710, commented on the general chaos of people walking up and down, and the 'stalls on both sides, where books and all kinds of wares are sold.'[1] The bomb had been hidden under the Counsels' bench in the Court of Chancery.

As with the Gin Craze, the resulting panic caused as much damage as the explosion itself. The Duke of Newcastle, Secretary of State with ultimate responsibility for the affairs of Middlesex, reported that 'the noise . . . and smoke created a great consternation in the hall.'[2] In his memoirs, Lord Hervey described 'such a loud report from a discharge of gunpowder, that the whole Hall was in a moment in the utmost confusion; and everybody concluding it was a plot to blow up the Hall, the judges started from the benches, the lawyers were all running over one another's backs to make their escape, some losing part of their gowns, others their periwigs, in the scuffle.'[3]

The date was 14 July, not that there was any significance in that. It would be another fifty-three years before the Bastille went up in smoke. When the initial panic had subsided, someone picked up one of the sheets of paper and took it to Lord Chancellor Hardwicke, sitting in the Court of King's Bench. Blurrily printed on cheap paper, the bomber's calling card read as a kind of proclamation:

> By a general consent of the citizens and tradesmen of London, Westminster, and the Borough of Southwark, this being the last day of term, were publickly burnt, between the hours of twelve and two, at the Royal Exchange, Cornhill, at Westminster Hall ... and at Margaret's Hill, Southwark, as destructive of the product, trade and manufacture of this kingdom and the plantations thereunto belonging, and tending to the utter subversion of the liberties and properties thereof, the five following printed books, or libels, called Acts of Parliament.

The Gin Act came top of the list. Parliament's other 'libels' were the Mortmain Act, which had outraged church leaders by limiting charitable bequests, the Act for Westminster Bridge, bitterly opposed by Thames watermen, the Smuggler's Act which had further restricted the right to carry arms, and Walpole's £600,000 raid on the sinking fund on behalf of George II, derided in the paper as a 'foreign prince'. When the bomber signed off 'God Save the King!' he left no one in doubt that he was referring to the king across the water.

Somehow, the Jacobites had managed to strike a blow at the

Hanoverian establishment in the very heart of Westminster Hall. It was only smoke and paper, but as a publicity stunt it could hardly have had more effect. Lord Hervey afterwards commented that the affair was 'as much talked of for a time as any I have mentioned.' For Newcastle, it was 'a very extraordinary insult . . . a wicked and traitorous design,' for the London Daily Post, 'the most impudent and daring insult.'⁴

For Samuel Killingbeck, waiting in an alehouse nearby, it was a triumph, but he still couldn't stop his hands from shaking. A few years before, Samuel Killingbeck had been introduced to a clergyman called Robert Nixon. Nixon was a 'non-juror', one of the hardliners who refused to take the oath of allegiance to the Hanoverian régime. Like Killingbeck, he was a Jacobite. They used to meet quite often to talk about the Pretender, across the water in Paris, and discuss the chances of a restoration.

But a fortnight before, that idle talk had suddenly turned serious. Robert Nixon had asked Samuel Killingbeck to come for a walk out on St George's Fields. Usually they met at one of the pubs in the Borough. Killingbeck had thought Nixon wanted to be out of doors just because it was a hot day. It was only when they were out in the Fields that he realised there was another reason. What Nixon had to say could see both of them hanged.

Robert Nixon had had enough of idle talk. He announced that he had a plan to blow up a parcel bomb in Westminster Hall. To start with, Samuel Killingbeck simply didn't believe it was possible. Much later, when he'd been caught, and questioned, and had broken down, he described the conversation to his examiner. They had had a friend with them, another Jacobite called William Spittell. Spittell and Nixon explained how it could be done. The clergyman had been carrying out some experiments. 'Nixon . . . knew how to make papers burn of themselves without being visibly set fire to . . . [and Spittell] himself had seen the experiment made.'⁵

Killingbeck was still unsure. It wasn't just the danger. He replied that 'he was an unbelieving Thomas and must see the experiment himself before he would believe it.'

A few days later he found himself standing on the Falcon Stairs, waiting with William Spittell for a boat to take them across the Thames to Fleet market. To Samuel Killingbeck, the whole plot had suddenly become frighteningly real. He had even seen a proof of the paper Nixon was planning to put in his parcel. The printer who had typeset it was waiting with them now, carrying two rollers and a portable chase. A boatman pulled up to the steps. In silence they crossed the river to Blackfriars. In silence they walked through the streets to Nixon's house near Hatton Gardens.

Samuel Killingbeck was nervous. Once inside he 'desired the experiment . . . might be made, because he was desirous to be gone.' Robert Nixon put a sheet of paper on his hand, '[and] poured out of a small vial a few [grains] of a powder.' There was a sudden fizz, and the paper burst into flame. Shocked, Killingbeck 'threw it out of his hand.' But the clergyman hadn't finished. Nixon 'made a second experiment, namely he laid upon the hearth a piece of the said prepared paper, and upon a part of that paper laid a little gunpowder, and upon these he laid some papers, then putting a little of his powder out of the vial upon the said prepared paper, it took fire and spread, and when the fire reached the gunpowder, it blew up and scattered the papers laid over it.'

The little parlour in Nixon's house was full of smoke and the reek of chemicals. The powder in the vial was phosphorus.

After that demonstration Killingbeck needed no more persuasion. The three men worked fast. They made up three parcels, each packed with copies of the five Acts and the paper denouncing them. The plan was to detonate all three at different times in different places around London. Westminster Hall would be the first target.

They agreed final arrangements as they walked towards

Westminster. Killingbeck would stand in front of Nixon to cover him while he fumbled with the phosphorus. 'Nixon would signal to Killingbeck when to move off, 'touching him on the back or side and saying let us be going or words to that effect.' Spittell, meanwhile, would 'stay at Westminster Hall Gate until the explosion should be over, and then they were all three to meet at a certain alehouse not far from Westminster Hall.'

The Courts of Chancery and King's Bench were at the far end of the hall, separated by a flight of steps. Nixon and Killingbeck 'placed themselves behind the Counsel attending the Court of Chancery, [Killingbeck] standing before Nixon.' Nixon had 'his hat under his arm, and the packet . . . in the crown of it, and a vial (with the powder in it) in his other hand.' After a few moments, 'Nixon gave the sign to [Killingbeck] to move off.' Everything seemed to be going smoothly.

Samuel Killingbeck needed no encouragement to make himself scarce. He 'made off directly to the alehouse and called for a pint of beer, drank once of it and paid for it.' Then he settled down to wait for the others. But when Spittell and Nixon didn't appear quickly, he started to worry. What if the bomb hadn't gone off? He had heard no explosion. Maybe he had mistaken the signal. Maybe Nixon had lost his nerve. He had seen how quickly the gunpowder exploded the evening before. Something must have gone wrong. Abandoning his drink, Killingbeck hurried out into the street. But there, to his relief, he saw Spittell coming towards him. Back in the pub, Spittell told him 'that Westminster Hall was all in an uproar, people tumbling over one another and the Constables busy with their staves; [and] while he was saying this came in Nixon, who said that when he . . . got to the place where the Grand Jury usually sit he heard it (the packet) give a great bounce.' The only disappointment was that the plan for two other explosions had to be abandoned. 'In the disorder and confusion [Spittell] saw in the

Hall he took the two packets out of his pocket and dropt them in the crowd.'

Back in Westminster Hall, business was slowly getting back to normal. The smoke soon cleared; gradually everyone realised this wasn't a second Gunpowder Plot. 'At first,' the Duke of Newcastle reported, 'the business a little stopped in the respective courts; but they soon proceeded, till the ... seditious and treasonable paper was brought into the King's Bench by some of the officers of the court, who had picked up several of them in Westminster Hall.' Hardwicke, the Lord Chancellor, immediately sent a message to Middlesex Quarter Sessions, which was then sitting, to issue a warrant against the libellous paper and its author. A Jacobite demonstration so close to the heart of government was a serious matter, even if it was more *coup de théâtre* than *coup d'état*. Newcastle, Hardwicke and Walpole moved fast. The King was away in Hanover, but the Queen and Council issued a proclamation and reward the same weekend.

Sir Robert Walpole, for one, had no doubt who was to blame for the outrage. Nor did he doubt that sooner or later he would track them down. 'Since my coming to town,' he wrote to his brother a fortnight later, 'I have been endeavouring to trace out the authors and managers of that vile transaction, and there is no reason to doubt that the whole was projected and executed by a set of low Jacobites ... Of this I have had an account from the same fellow that brought me these and many such sort of intelligencies.'[6] Walpole's spy network was in good shape. In the end it didn't take long to pick up Nixon, Spittell and Killingbeck. Fringe members of the gang – printers and associates – soon cracked. It wasn't long before Samuel Killingbeck was giving the authorities chapter and verse.

Robert Nixon, arrested after a tip-off on 14 August, was the only one who put up anything of a fight. The Duke of Newcastle interviewed him personally, but Nixon denied knowing anything about either the libel or the bomb. Then the Duke tried another tack. The clergyman had been arrested on his way back from church. 'Being asked whether they prayed for the King in that congregation, [Nixon] said, "Yes, always."' The question was which King? 'Being asked whether they pray'd for King George, he said, they never named names.'[7] It was forty-seven years since James Stuart fled his throne, and twenty-one since the 1715 rebellion, but the Jacobites still hadn't given up.

Jacobitism was the fly in the ointment of Hanoverian stability; it was Britain's loose cannon, its unfinished business. Nearly half a century after the Glorious Revolution, the Old Pretender still waited in Paris with his ridiculous court and his bogus ceremonial; whenever a French king wanted to annoy the English, he still had only to start talking about invasions and restorations. Back in England, the wounds of the Glorious Revolution had still not healed over.

All the same, Jacobitism had changed in the past few decades. The passage of half a century was bound to change something. Even in 1715, restoration had been a real possibility. There had been a real Stuart army in Britain, with real support from Jacobite aristocrats, and from at least part of the people. The replacement of the unknown fifty-five-year-old German who sat on the throne with the late Queen's half-brother seemed perfectly plausible.

By 1736, it didn't seem so any more, or only to people like Robert Nixon and Samuel Killingbeck. After twenty years of Hanoverian stability, the Stuarts had receded several steps into the realm of myth. A French-speaking king didn't seem any more desirable than a German-speaking one. And although he had ditched much of the baggage of absolutism, James Stuart had stubbornly refused to turn away from Rome. The world had moved on. The opposition had found other ground on which to fight its battles.

Jacobitism had become something more diffuse; the king across the water was wreathed in mist. The mist was partly made up of romantic memories and partly of dreams for a better future. Nine years later, in 1745, when the mist briefly evaporated and a real Jacobite army was marching through England behind a real Stuart prince, the main emotion among English Jacobites was one of alarm. The Pretender didn't realise it himself, but after twenty-one years Jacobitism in England had turned into something quite different from a campaign to restore him.

Instead, it had become a general form of protest against those in power. As long as there was Jacobitism, there was an alternative to the Hanoverians. Jacobitism became a way of withholding support. That way, the King of England and his ministers, like everyone else, had to live with uncertainty. It had metamorphosed into a general spirit of subversion. Disgruntled Tory squires toasted the 'King over the Water' to express their disenchantment with London, the times and Walpole's ministry. Jacobite songs like 'The King Shall Enjoy His Own Again' became a way to cheek anyone in authority.[8] Smugglers adopted Jacobite oaths and slogans. Wesley, attending an execution at Tyburn, saw that two of the condemned men had white cockades in their hats. In the great age of popular satire, it was easy to find ways of annoying the establishment without going so far as to overthrow it. The accession of James II on 11 June could be marked by a sprig of rue and thyme; the Pretender's birthday, four days later, by a white cockade.

And if the aim was to give those in authority sleepless nights, Jacobitism certainly had its effect. Sir Robert Walpole, for one, could never convince himself that his position was secure. 'I am not ashamed,' he told the House of Commons in 1738, 'to say I am in fear of the Pretender.' And there was still enough of real substance in Jacobitism to keep the fear alive. In 1734 there were disturbances in Suffolk Street on the anniversary of Charles I's execution. The divisions of the Civil War and the Glorious

Revolution were still there, and so were French armies, Jacobite cells, and Jacobite plots.

It wasn't just Robert Nixon's packet of phosphorus that alarmed Walpole, or his blurry paper attacking government legislation. It was what lay ahead. The Gin Act was due to come in on Michaelmas Day – 29 September – and already that looked like a flashpoint. 'There are great endeavours,' he wrote to his brother, 'to inflame the people, and to raise great tumults upon Michaelmas Day, when the Gin Act takes place ... These lower sorts of Jacobites appear at this time more busy than they have for a great while. They are very industrious, and taking advantage of everything that offers, to raise tumult and disorder among the people.'

Tumult and disorder followed the Westminster bomb by no more than a fortnight. In the event, the alarm was given by the Deputy Lieutenants of Tower Hamlets. They were barricaded inside the Angel and Crown tavern in Spitalfields, on Tuesday 27 July, and calling desperately for reinforcements. Outside, the East End had erupted in violence.[9]

It was feeling against the Irish that triggered it. London was full of Irish workers. They flooded into the capital in search of jobs on building sites or out in the fields and, like all immigrants before and after them, they were accused of stealing English jobs. Within hours of the trouble starting, Walpole had informers mingling with the crowd, and sending back regular reports from public houses. 'Some of [the crowd] told me,' Joseph Bell scribbled hastily to his master, 'there was such numbers of Irish who underwork them, they could not live and that there was an Irish man in the neighbourhood who employed numbers of them & they was determined to demolish him and drive the rest away.' It turned out that the contractor for Shoreditch Church 'had paid off his English labourers and imployed Irish because they worked cheaper.'[10] The same thing was happening in the weaving industry. Out in the countryside, there were disturbances against low-waged Irish harvest-workers.

But if the Irish problem had started it, there was plenty more discontent simmering under the surface. As he mingled with the crowd, Joseph Bell heard hints which would realise all Sir Robert Walpole's worst fears. 'In other parts of the crowd,' he wrote to the Prime Minister, 'they told me their meeting was to prevent the putting down Ginn.'

On the first night of the riots, Irish public houses were attacked. A squad of fifty soldiers under Major White, officer on duty at the Tower, found itself up against a crowd he estimated at 4,000. On Thursday, a boy called Thomas Larkin was shot dead in Brick Lane. The next night was even worse. Richard Burton, a brewer's assistant, 'saw the mob coming down Bell Yard, with sticks and lighted links. One of them made a sort of speech directing the rest to go to Church Lane, to the *Gentleman and Porter*.' The crowd was organised by now. These were no longer spontaneous demonstrations. Quite a few of the leaders had papers with lists of Irish pubs on them. 'One of them was called *Captain Tom the Barber*, and was in a striped banjan. I would have taken notice of him,' Richard Burton told the Old Bailey later, 'but he turned away and would not let me see his face.' The authorities were having to take ever stronger measures to deal with the situation. Clifford William Phillips, a Tower Hamlets magistrate, was woken by neighbours about ten o'clock, despatched a message to the Tower for help, and then set off towards the riot. 'The street was very light,' he recalled afterwards, 'and I could see (at a distance) the mob beating against the shutters with their clubs and hear the glass fly ... I heard the hollowing at my house, and the cry in the street was *Down with the Irish, Down with the Irish*.' As Richard Burton remembered, it was only the appearance of magistrate and soldiers that prevented worse violence. 'Justice Phillips coming down, and the captain with his soldiers, they took some of [the crowd], and the rest made off immediately, and were gone as suddenly, as if a hole had been ready dug in the bottom of the street, and they had all dropped into it at once.'[11]

In the end that was the worst night of violence. By the weekend the authorities had flexed their muscles. Irish workmen had been laid off and the trouble was over. But the July riots showed what a powder-keg London had become. Some of Walpole's informers insisted the trouble was all to do with Irish labour, but others couldn't get deeper fears out of their minds. 'It is very difficult to judge whence this riot arose,' reported the Tower Hamlets magistrates. 'Some say the Irish ... were the causes, but I am afraid there must be something else at the bottom, either Mother Gin or something worse. Captain Littler of the Guards said he heard the words High Church among them.' 'High Church' had been one of the slogans of the Sacheverell riots which broke out against the Whig ministry in 1710. For Walpole, it was a sure sign of Jacobite involvement. Meanwhile, a witness at the rioters' trial, Peter Cappe, told how he had seen a group of watermen on the Thursday night swearing 'they would lose their lives before they would suffer one stone to be laid on [Westminster] Bridge.' Another of Walpole's correspondents reported 'great discontents and murmurings all through this mobbish part of town. The Ginn Act and the Smuggling Act sticks hard in the stomachs of the meaner sort of people and the Bridge Act greatly exasperates the watermen insomuch that they make no scruple of declaring publiquely that they will joyn in any mischief that can be set on foot.'[12]

As he read through the reports, Sir Robert Walpole found plenty to alarm him. There was the mysterious figure of 'Captain Tom the Barber' and the lists of Irish houses. This was no grassroots disturbance. Another report claimed that among 'the greater and more ignorant part of [the] mobb' there were 'many intriguing persons of better sort amongst them in disguise particularly several who are strongly suspected to be popish Priests.'[13] 'Although the complaint of the Irish was the first motive,' Walpole wrote to his brother, 'the Jacobites are blending with all other discontents, endeavouring to stir up the distillers and gin retailers, and to avail themselves of the spirit and fury of the people.'[14]

As if he wanted to add to Sir Robert's woes, the King had gone off on one of his summer trips to Hanover. An agent who managed to infiltrate a Jacobite cell reported that 'the conversation turned chiefly upon the advantages that their party will receive by His Majesty's frequent visits to Hanover.'[15] Then a Jacobite arms cache was found.[16] Further signs of trouble came when a distiller in High Holborn, Francis Griffiths, received an anonymous letter:

> Sir, Strike and free yourselves and country. Rise in arms against the dog that governs this unfortunate land and fight for your right King. [Resist], and your properties and you will much oblige your Country and me youre King of right.
> Take Place
> J. St.[17]

There may have been distillers in London who were fool enough to think James Stuart wrote personal notes exhorting them to rebellion, but Francis Griffiths wasn't one of them. He contacted an agent called John Ibbut and passed it on to the authorities.

By now, the chances of bringing in prohibition without trouble seemed remote. 'By the seditious ballads and discontent that appears about the Gin Act,' a Tower Hamlets magistrate wrote to Walpole, 'it looks to me as if it would be very difficult to carry it thoroughly into execution, of which the Jacobites will not be wanting to take advantage and set us in a flame if they can.' From another of the Prime Minister's regular correspondents came an even more chilling warning. 'It is the common talk of the tippling ale houses and little gin shops,' he wrote, 'that Sir Robert Walpole and the Master of the Rolls will not outlive Michaelmas.'[18]

Sir Robert Walpole was rattled. A fortnight before Michaelmas, Joseph Jekyll told Thomas Wilson 'that Sir Robt. Walpole was afraid to use rigorous methods against the Rioters.'[19] The Prime Minister, the 'Great Man', 'Bluff Bob', had been in office for fifteen years; he had the support of the King; he was undisputed master of Parliament. But now he was rattled. It wasn't just disgruntled distillers or Captain Tom the Barber. Storm clouds were gathering. All the different strands of opposition to his ministry were starting to come together.

It all went back to the Excise Crisis in 1733. Then Walpole had been forced to abandon a prized scheme to extend Excise duties and cut the Land Tax. Crowds had pursued him from the Commons with the slogan of 'no slavery, no Excise, no wooden shoes.' He had been caricatured as the 'Excise Monster', riding on a barrel and trampling Magna Carta. At a key moment in the crisis, the King's support had wavered, and the scheme had been lost.

For ten years before that he had hardly encountered strong opposition. But Excise had struck a chord on all sides. Excise was seen as foreign, an instrument of tyranny – hence the jibe about wooden shoes. It was an assault on English liberties. 'The Excise man,' as one writer grumbled a few years later, 'is our constant companion from the crown of our head to the sole of our foot. If we clean our hair, he examines the powder, even the washing the ladies' linen does not escape inspection. He walks abroad in our shoes, at our tables he seasons our meat . . . Is it daylight? He peeps in at our windows. Is it night? He shines in our candles. Have we sweets or sours, light or darkness, the custom house officers or Excise men are our constant attendants.'[20]

The City of London, until then carefully managed by Walpole, had rebelled. The Lord Mayor, John Barber, had promoted an anti-Excise resolution from the Court of Common Council. The City MPs, John Barnard and Micaiah Perry, had led the parliamentary opposition, and in the ensuing elections the ministry had lost control of London. The Excise Crisis had drawn in all London's diverse oppositional elements: its merchants, its Jacobites, its satirists, its anti-government newspapers. The Tories and the 'Country' Whigs had united. Popular protest had thrown fuel on the flames. The King had wavered. It had been enough to shake Walpole's ministry to its foundations.

There had been a lull in the opposition after the Excise Crisis. Bolingbroke had returned to France; Pulteney declared himself weary of the whole business. But three years later the Gin Act, another Excise measure, looked likely to drag Walpole back into the same turbulent waters. Micaiah Perry, for one, was a long-term supporter of the distillers. And by now Sir Robert had other problems to struggle with as well. He had lost the bishops. The Mortmain Bill in the last session of Parliament – another of the Acts which Robert Nixon had exploded – had provoked a rift with 'Walpole's Pope', Edmund Gibson, Bishop of London. At court, there was trouble brewing with the marriage of Frederick, Prince of Wales. Relations between the King and his son were famously bad. By summer 1736 Frederick was starting to provide a focus for the opposition. Meanwhile in Parliament there was fresh blood coming in to challenge the ministry. 'Cobham's Cubs', William Pitt and George Lyttelton, had entered the House the year before. Guided by Viscount Cobham and Lord Chesterfield, a leading Excise rebel, these 'boy patriots' would provide a fresh nucleus of opposition to Walpole's ministry.

If Walpole was expecting political trouble out of prohibition, he didn't have long to wait. It came, not surprisingly, from the

*Craftsman*, the magazine sponsored by Henry Bolingbroke, the Tory leader, and William Pulteney to foster 'Country' ideals, and a 'Country' coalition between Tories and opposition Whigs. The editor, 'Caleb D'Anvers', was sharp and funny, and he knew exactly how to get on the ministry's nerves. Madam Geneva soon caught his eye as a way to stir up political mayhem.

Madam Geneva, the paper noticed, had crossed the political floor. Once, she had been King William's darling. But now 'the ministerial advocates have made themselves very merry with the approaching fate of poor Mother Gin, whom they are pleased to represent as . . . a Jacobite.' With a month to go before Michaelmas, Caleb D'Anvers raised the temperature with a scrap of dialogue which supposedly took place 'on the borders of Scotland . . . between Mr Hearty, Innkeeper, and Mr Gage, Exciseman.' Readers were left in no doubt of the point. Prohibition gave power to the Excise men. The Gin Act was the Excise scheme revisited, another attempt on English liberties. Along the way the *Craftsman* paused to ridicule Parliament's record on the gin issue: 'The last Parliament upon mature deliberation made a law against Gin; and finding themselves mistaken upon maturer deliberation, repealed it. The present Parliament upon the maturest deliberation, finding the last Parliament mistaken in repealing that act, have obliged us with the present; and who knows . . . but they may likewise find themselves mistaken, upon still more mature deliberation, and repeal even this law?'[21]

Satirists generally had a field day that summer. Someone published the *Life of Mother Gin*, containing 'a true and faithful relation of her conduct and politicks, in all the various and important occurrences of state that she was engaged in during her time; her transactions with several eminent patriots and great Ministers.' The *Life* followed the twists and turns of Madam Geneva's career from the Glorious Revolution through all the party conflicts of Queen Anne's reign. By 1736 Madam Geneva was confirmed as a Jacobite, and her biographer could see how important she had become to the opposition. Gin gave the Tories and patriot Whigs a populist issue from which they could draw public support. They 'knew . . . that if they lost her, they must, by a necessary consequence, lose what they called the voice of the people, which was entirely under her influence and direction; and from which they had received very considerable advantage.' The irony of all that was not lost on the writer. 'Mother Gin,' he noted, 'who formerly was a zealous asserter of the divine right of Kings, became now convinced of the divine right of the people.' The Tories had discovered populism.

It wasn't all newspaper articles and tracts. There was poetry too. 'Ye link and shoe boys, clubb a tear,' wrote Timothy Scrubb of Rag Fair in *Desolation: or, the Fall of Gin*,

> Ye basket-women join;
> Grubb-street, pour forth a stream of brine,
> Ye porters hang your heads and pine;
> All, all are damn'd to rot-gut beer.

Discussed in the newspapers, serenaded in the streets, Madam Geneva became the 'It girl' of summer 1736. But there was even better to come. If it had been the early twenty-first century, she would have wanted her face on television. In London, in 1736, Madam Geneva started a career on the stage.

London theatres in the 1730s were packed and noisy. Riots were commonplace. The plays – particularly the short 'afterpieces' put on after the main show – were topical and fast-moving. Political satire was always in the air.

Most riotous and daring of all the London theatres – also the smallest and shabbiest – was the 'Little Theatre' on the Haymarket.

Fifty yards up from Pall Mall, it was on the east side, cocking a snook at Vanbrugh's grand Italian Opera House across the way. The booking office was a snuff shop next to the entrance. In 1736, the Little Theatre happened to have been taken over by a new manager. In the past he had written for the official theatres but in 1736 he was out of favour, anti-government, and looking for trouble. He was famous as librettist of the 1734 hit, *The Roast Beef of Old England*, and in 1736 would have the smash of the season with *Pasquin*. Styling himself 'the Great Mogul', he was the *enfant terrible* of London theatre, Henry Fielding.

It might well have been Fielding, writing as 'a Moderate Man', who penned the *Craftsman*'s first attack on the Gin Act.[22] He was certainly close to the opposition. He was patronised by Chesterfield, Bedford and others, and was an old school-friend of 'Cobham's Cubs', George Lyttelton and William Pitt. On 28 April, Fielding premièred a new afterpiece at the Little Theatre, *Tumble-Down Dic, or Phaeton in the Suds*, which had a rake singing a ballad in favour of Madam Geneva and, in the evening's *coup de théâtre*, the Genius of Gin rising out of a tub brandishing a wand which held the magical power of transformation.

Then, as another afterpiece, Fielding put on a 'heroic comi-tragical farce' entitled *The Deposing and Death of Queen Gin, with the ruin of the Duke of Rum, Marquee de Nantz, and the Lord Sugarcane &c.* (the author, 'Jack Juniper', styled himself 'a distiller's assistant'). The Duke of Rum described how the people reacted to news of Queen Gin's banishment:

Rum:  By different ways their discontent appears:
      Some murmur, some lament, some loudly roar . . .
      This day in pomp she takes her leave of all:
      Already has she made the tour of Smithfield,
      Rag-Fair, Whitechapel, and Clare Market: Now

To broad St Giles's she directs her steps.

In a heart-breaking climax, with a mob of 'ragged men and women' outside shouting, 'Liberty, property, and Gin for ever,' courtiers urged the deposed Queen Gin to fly abroad, but her strength failed.

Gin:    Oh! what is this that runs so cold about me?
        A dram! a dram! – a large one or I die.
        Tis vain! [drinks hastily]
        O, O Farewell! [dies]

Mob:    What, dead drunk, or dead in earnest?

To the authorities, in summer 1736, none of that seemed particularly funny. Exactly a year later Walpole would pass the Stage Licensing Act to curb the excesses of unlicensed houses like the Little Theatre. Reformers had been gunning for playhouses for years. But the Prime Minister's real reason, according to at least one writer, was the 'extraordinary liberties that had been taken with great characters upon the stage.'[23]

As for magazines like the *Craftsman*, 'Nothing,' raged the official *Daily Gazetteer*, 'was ever more notoriously designed to rouse up the minds of the people to rebellion ... It is an evident exhortation to the multitude to rise and tear to pieces all the great ... the *Craftsman* ... is now full of glee, hoping for confusion, sedition and rebellion.'[24]

Sedition and rebellion were on Sir Robert Walpole's mind as well. On 6 August he wrote a letter to his brother worrying 'what may happen on Michaelmas-day.' Informers were sending through copies of anti-prohibition ballads they picked up on the streets. And then, with two weeks to go before Michaelmas, Edinburgh suddenly erupted in flames. Rioters had lynched a Captain Porteous for firing on the crowd at a smuggler's execution. It didn't help the Prime Minister's nerves when an informer reported that 'within eight or nine months . . . past, there have been considerable quantities of arms, exceeding ten thousand at least, landed on the northern coast [of Scotland] & some small ports in the Western Islands, & have been distributed among the common people, who are generally now trained in new arms.' He knew exactly where the next flashpoint would come. 'If upon the commencement of the Ginn Act there are any tumults in London they are to follow that example.'[25]

Government nerves were strung taut. All the signs of trouble were there. And it was then, just five days before Michaelmas, that the Gin Plot suddenly came to light.

The code-word was to be 'Sir Robert and Sir Joseph', the names of the two men blamed for prohibition. The information came from a public house-keeper, William Alexander, of King's Street, St James's. He had received a letter telling him 'that he should have a quantity of ginn . . . sent to his house on Monday night, in order to distribute among the populace on Tuesday night.' Free gin would put the people in the mood for trouble. And then the signal for the uprising would be given. 'When he heard the word Sir Robert & Sir Joseph, [he was] to joyn with an Huzza.' There was a vague promise of support from outside London, including a hint of rebel units in the army. 'There will be people of distinction that will surprise [you],' the letter ended. 'The Red-Coats are marching to London, but they will be the enemies to the Russetts, you need not fear.'

In the end, four of the letters were picked up by Walpole's agents. Excise officers reported that similar communications had been sent out to distillers all over town. Some carried ominous headings like 'September. Critical Month,' or '1736. Dreadful

Year.' All proclaimed that 'the body of the distillers, farmers &c., aggrieved by the late pernicious and enslaving Bill on spirituous liquors have agreed to show they are not blind to the design in hand of bringing on a general Excise.' When Michaelmas came, Madam Geneva was to be the Jacobites' secret weapon. Enraged by prohibition, the mob would erupt in riot, the army would mutiny, and the Hanoverian régime would collapse. The trigger for the whole revolt would be free gin:

> The dealers in distill'd liquors to keep open shop on Tuesday next, being the eve of the day on which the act is to take place and give gratis what quantities of Gin, or other liquors, shall be call'd for by the populace ... then christen the streets with the remainder, & conclude with bonfires ... All retailers whose circumstances will not permit them to contribute to the festival shall have quantities of liquor sent in before the time ... Invite as many neighbours as you can conveniently, & be under no apprehension of the Riot Act, but whenever you hear the words Sir Robert & Sir Joseph joyne in the huzza.[26]

Walpole, for one, wasn't going to leave anything to chance. As Michaelmas approached, orders were issued and troops posted. The redcoats were, indeed, coming to town. With five days to go, London awaited the Gin Act in a mixed state of fear and suppressed excitement. One thing was for certain. Madam Geneva would go out in a blaze of glory. Along Fleet Street new streetlamps had been erected. They were lit up for the first time on 25 September. On the same day, Sir Robert himself ostentatiously left London for Houghton, accompanied by servants and cooks. Joseph Jekyll was on his estate at Bell Bar. Sir Robert and Sir Joseph might have been the signal for Jacobite uprising, but neither man would be in town to hear it given.

They weren't the only ones to keep out of the way. Everyone could see that the chief promoters of prohibition would be the first targets of the mob. Thomas Wilson suddenly discovered urgent business in Stoke Newington.[27]

# CHAPTER TEN

## THE DEATH OF
## MADAM GENEVA

Nothing happened. The world didn't come to an end and the state wasn't overthrown. England didn't erupt in flames.

A journeyman tailor called Genns 'died intoxicated with Geneva at the Crown in Wapping,' as the *Daily Journal* reported, 'and several lay in the streets dead drunk, with their taking leave of that liquor.' A few were arrested and committed, 'some to prison and some to hard labour, for publickly and riotously publishing *No Gin, No King*.'[1] Walpole and Jekyll weren't the only absentees from town; the King was still in Hanover. Meanwhile, the *London Magazine* recorded some demonstrations of grief outside London as well: 'Several people at Norwich, Bristol and other places . . . made themselves very merry on the death of Madam Gin, and some of both sexes got soundly drunk at her funeral, for which the mob made a form of procession but committed no outrages.'[2]

There was no Jacobite uprising, and no landing of French troops. The only soldiers in London were there on Walpole's orders. 'Yesterday morning,' reported the *Daily Post*, 'a double guard [was] mounted at Kensington; at noon the guard at St James's, the Horse Guards and Whitehall were reinforced, and last night about 300 life-guards and horse-grenadier guards paraded in Covent Garden, in order to suppress any tumult that might happen to arise at the going down of Gin.' It was quite a show of strength. The Westminster horse militia were posted in the suburbs of Westminster. Another detachment of horse grenadiers was held at the ready in Hyde Park. Care had also been taken to station guards at likely targets of protest. At three in the afternoon, the day before Michaelmas, 'an officer and a company of foot soldiers came to the Rolls in Chancery Lane, to protect his honour the Master of the Rolls, and the records in the chapel there; in case any persons should offer to attack the house &c. on account of the suppressing of Gin.'[3] Some people wondered about that gesture. Walpole usually had an ulterior motive of some sort. Lord Hervey reckoned the guards were there, 'rather, I believe, to mark out who was the author of this Act than in favour to the Master of the Rolls (for he hated him heartily).'[4]

On 1 October the *Daily Journal* was still reporting that 'every thing remains very quiet, and no disturbance has happened about the Cities of London and Westminster.' Scribbling a postscript on a letter to his brother the same day, Robert Walpole added 'that last night is likewise past over in perfect quiet, although the patrols in the street were taken off.'[5] Five days later, the papers could officially write Michaelmas off as a damp squib. There had 'been no manner of disturbance,' one reported, 'Mother Gin having died very quietly.'[6]

That didn't mean there was no mourning. Up in the City, according to the *Grub Street Journal*, punch-houses 'put their punch bowls, irons on which they were erected, and signs, in mourning, being painted black &c.'[7] Excise men had already picked up a rumour 'that Mother Gin is to be buried in great pomp on Thursday night.'[8] The funeral took place in Swallow Street, just off Piccadilly. 'Mother Gin lay in state yesterday at a distiller's shop . . . near St James's Church,' wrote the *Daily Post*. But not even in death would Madam Geneva be allowed to rest in peace. 'To prevent the ill-consequences from such a funeral,' the paper went on, 'a neighbouring Justice took the undertaker, his men, and all the mourners into custody.'[9]

For some of her followers, the prospect of life without Madam Geneva was simply too terrible to bear. Even before Michaelmas arrived, 'one William Alexander, who liv'd near the Bull's Head in Nightingale Lane, a bricklayer, a profess'd votary to Gin, being too deeply affected at the approaching fate of his idol, and resolv'd not to see that unhappy day, took a rope, went upstairs, shut himself in, and hang'd himself up to a staple drove into a beam in his room.' He wasn't the only one. 'A man who kept a brandy, rum and wine cellar, over against Cree-church in Leadenhall Street, cut his throat with a razor; and notwithstanding an able surgeon in that neighbourhood came to his assistance, he died.'[10]

For others, all the weeping and wailing was getting out of hand. Printed on a black-bordered page and embellished with skulls and crossbones, *An Elegy on the Much Lamented Death of the most Excellent, the most Truly-Beloved, and Universally-admired Lady, Madam Gineva* heaped scorn both on hand-wringing distillers and their weeping customers. 'Unhappy Briton!' it scoffed, 'more enslaved than Turk, forc'd to be sober and compelled to work!'

As for the distillers and vendors, most were just interested in keeping their businesses going until the last possible minute. Two hundred of them turned up at the Excise Office on Michaelmas Day to ask if they could open their doors or not. Some pushed their luck too far. The day after the Act came into force the *London Evening Post* reported that 'a man in Bride Lane sold upwards of fifty gallons of Geneva on Thursday, which brought such a number of people together, that the neighbours were obliged to send for an officer, who took him into custody, and he was afterwards committed to prison.'[11] Not everyone was deterred. 'Several shops,' added the *Daily Journal* next day, 'continued yesterday to sell drams in Southwark, Wapping &c. and kept open their shops till late.'

For the ministry, the immediate danger was passed. But Walpole certainly wasn't going to drop his guard. 'The murmuring and complaints of the common people, for want of Ginn,' he wrote to his brother, 'and the great sufferings and loss of the dealers in spirituous liquors in general, have created such uneasiness, that they well deserve a great deal of attention and consideration. And I am not without my apprehensions, that a non-observance of the law in some may create great trouble.'[12]

It wasn't just riots and mobs he had to worry about. He had to put up with the Little Theatre as well. The Tuesday after the Act came in, they advertised *The Fall of Bob* – meaning Robert Walpole – *or The Oracle of Gin*, *A Tragedy* by Timothy Scrubb of Rag Fair. It described a town where 'distillers' shops . . . are hush'd as death, their floors and counters clean,' and 'shrieks of desponding matrons wound the air.' Walpole was now cast as a Nero who had destroyed London for his own gain, and firebrand leaders rose up to preach rebellion to the mob:

> Reflect, my friends, Gin is the noble cause
> For which your swords should hew away the laws,
> Wipe out the senate, drench in blood the nation,
> And spread o'er the state wild desolation.

All the same, no one was being drenched in blood quite yet. Maybe one reason was that no one expected prohibition to last. It wasn't just William Pulteney who thought 'the whole scheme' of the Bill would have to be changed in the very next session of Parliament. Rumours that it would be repealed had started before the ink was even dry on the Act. ''Tis not questioned,' thought the *Daily Journal* back on 4 May, 'but that all proper relief, consistent with the general interest of his Majesty's subjects, will be given in the future sessions of Parliament.' During the summer, Walpole had even done his best to keep the rumour going. One of his agents had suggested it as a way of heading off trouble. 'Even the court writers have not endeavoured so much to justify the act,' the *Craftsman* scoffed, 'as to soothe the people with hopes that . . . it will . . . be repealed.'[13]

With the next session of Parliament in mind, the pamphlet writers even started gearing up for another campaign. The first tract appeared just four days into prohibition. It urged a still head duty of five shillings a gallon as the only sensible long term solution. Others lobbied for punch to be excluded from the Gin Act. The distiller's old friend, Thomas Robe JP, returned to the fray with a suggestion that would give members of the Company of Distillers free retail licences, while others had to pay £5 for them. That, unfortunately, was to be Eboranos' last contribution to the debate. He 'had published his proposals without consulting the Company,'[14] and when he asked for payment, they turned him down flat. The Company was on its uppers. Having broken with the distillers, Robe would go on to fall out spectacularly with his brothers on the bench. After a spat which ended up with Robe trying to sabotage the work of Quarter Sessions, Lord Chancellor Hardwicke finally removed him from the Commission of Peace.

Distillers and spirit sellers may have started looking ahead to the next session of Parliament, but in the meantime they still had a whole winter to get through. None of them chose the obvious solution. Michaelmas may have been greeted by Jacobite plots, suicides, and funerals for Madam Geneva, but there was no flood of applications for the £50 retail licences. Some people reckoned there were 10,000 gin-sellers in London, but only two of them sold spirits legally in winter 1736. J. Ashley, of the London Punch House on Ludgate Hill, had already published a smug advert in the *Grub Street Journal* to reassure the public 'that at Michaelmas next I shall take out a licence, and in all things strictly conform to the law.'[15] Down the road at the London Bridge Punch House, Amos Wenman also offered 'punch made by licence.' And those two, as the *Craftsman* put it, 'are the only persons in England or Wales, that can make punch, or vend spirituous liquors, in less quantities than two gallons, without incurring the penalty of the Act, which is £100 for every offence.'[16]

There were legal alternatives. Some punch-houses tried to brew up a spiritless hooch to keep their customers satisfied. At Gordon's Punch House, opposite the New Exchange in the Strand, customers were served 'with a most excellent liquor called sangree, [Mr Gordon] having for that purpose bought the finest full-flavour'd Madeira wine; [which] by a particular preparation in the sherbett, equals, if not excels, the so much approved liquor, punch.' As for the common people, 'Tho [they] . . . are deprived of Gin,' reported the *London Daily Post*, 'there are various drams invented and sold at gin-shops, in lieu thereof; as sangree, tow-row, cyder boiled with Jamaica pepper &c.'[17]

Everyone was on the look-out for loopholes in the law. The 1729 Gin Act had exempted apothecaries who brewed up spirits as medicine. There was a widespread belief, seven years later, that medicines had been let off the hook again. 'A certain person near St James's Market,' reported *Read's Weekly Journal* on 9 October, 'continues selling drams, being colour'd with red, having a large label tied to the bottle, on which is wrote, "Take two or three spoonfuls of this four or five times a day, or as often as the fit takes you."' Unfortunately, apothecaries were supposed to take out spirits licences like everybody else, and were liable for prosecution if they didn't. When one apothecary's case came to court, a month or so later, learned counsel joked 'that it . . . had been a more sickly time lately than usual, seeing the apothecaries &c. had more people frequented their shops for the cholick and gripe water than ever were known.' To that, the apothecary standing in the dock replied 'that the late Act of Parliament had given many people the gripes . . . which occasioned a great laughter in court.'[18]

Another scam took advantage of the way the Act was drafted. It wasn't illegal, after all, to sell gin, only to sell it in quantities less than two gallons. There was an obvious way round that, and the *London Daily Post* helpfully talked Londoners through it on 5 October: 'Mr A comes to me, to you, or to any other great dealer that can supply two gallons, and says, Mr B, I have a great call for spirituous liquors . . . Mr B replies, I can serve you, sir . . . Mr A answers, Do you sell for money or upon credit? Mr B replies . . . a little money would not be amiss. But, says Mr A, I have not at present warehouse room to stow two gallons. O, sir, says Mr B, pray don't let that be any hindrance to the bargain; my warehouse, shop and even dwelling house, is at the service of so good a customer.' It looked promising. Buy two gallons on credit, take away a little at a time and pay a little at a time. One group of distillers even went so far as to seek legal advice. But by mid-November, the two-gallon scam had been firmly squashed. The distillers were 'given to understand from the Board of Excise by their Surveyors, that such a practice is within the said statute.'[19]

That still left people with the option of buying two gallons legally and taking it away all in one go. But they found two gallons of gin an awful lot to get rid of. An Irishman bought two gallons to split with his workmates, 'but on his asking them to pay for their drams, they sent him to the further end of the field to one of their companions, under the notion that he was their master and would satisfy him, who, instead of giving him the money, fell foul of him and took away the remainder of his gin, with which they all got drunk and fell asleep.' Four farmers in Earls Court bought two gallons with the idea of making it last, but temptation proved too great. The four 'drank to such excess, that . . . two [of them] died soon after; and the other two have with great difficulty been recovered.'[20]

Meanwhile, the authorities were getting on with the business of enforcement. One week into prohibition, Excise men submitted their first lists of violations, and twenty prosecutions were ordered. The first gin-sellers in the dock were hardly the vicious drug-pushers that reformers had campaigned against. On the first day, cases were brought against Mr Kirkpatrick, a prominent apothecary, and Mr John Thomas, a distiller and chemist. These were estab-lished businessmen, and they were prepared to stake their livings on the result. Both defendants employed legal counsel. But expensive lawyers and two and a half hours of argument were not enough to save them. Both men were found guilty and charged the £100 fine for retailing spirits without a licence. Everyone had known the penalties of the Gin Act were harsh. For Kirkpatrick, they proved too much. A week later, Excise men were seen raiding his shop in Turnmill Street, and his worldly possessions were wheeled away on a cart.

Apothecaries were sitting ducks for the Excise men. Everyone knew them; they weren't going to fade away into the slums when trouble arrived. If they couldn't afford the huge fine, they probably had goods enough to cover it. To make matters even easier, the apothecaries had been feuding with distillers for decades, and a steady stream of information came flooding into the Excise Office. There was no secret where it came from. 'Several distillers,' it was reported in mid-October, 'made severe complaints against certain apothecaries within the liberty of Westminster, for selling liquors by retail, as chymical prescriptions, which upon proof were found to be Geneva.'[21]

As they surveyed the scene in late October, reformers found every reason to feel pleased with themselves. Michaelmas had come and gone without incident. They felt optimistic; they even started to claim victory. 'The good effects of the Gin Act,' reported the *Gentleman's Magazine* on Sunday 31 October, 'have appeared in the sobriety and regular conduct of the soldiery and common people; so that there have not been half the number of courts-martial, or quarrels brought to the justices as before; and some observed, that the bakers and sellers of old clothes, had a brisker trade since Michaelmas.' Freed from the tyranny of Madam Geneva, the poor had money in their pockets again. 'Since the suppression of Gin,' the *London Daily Post* reported, 'beef &c. has sold much better at the several markets about town than before; the lower class of people, being deprived of that liquor, have now got stomachs.'22

If some of these stories seemed to bear out Thomas Wilson's predictions about life after gin with uncanny accuracy, that was hardly surprising. A good few of them were planted by Thomas Wilson himself. He recorded in his diary for 12 October that he 'put into the papers a paragraph that whereas there used to be [military] Court Meetings twice a week for the punishment of vices and consequences of drinking gin, there had not been one since the Act took place and there is a visible alteration in the behaviour of the lower kind of people, as I am informed from the constables and watch men.' The *Daily Journal* ran the story the very next day.

But if the reformers thought they had won an easy victory, they were fooling themselves. Instead of celebrating, they would have been better off looking out for warning signs.

There were plenty of them. Gin-sellers were supposed to have shut up shop on 29 September. But a month later, all the newspapers were still reporting that 'great numbers of idle and disorderly people ... do daily carry [spirituous liquors] in barrows, baskets, and in bottles about the streets, in contempt of the ... Act.' It was easy enough to clamp down on apothecaries' shops, but apothecaries had never caused any trouble in the first place. The problem was the dram/shops and chandlers' shops, the market stalls and basket/ women. And nothing there seemed to have changed. 'The following drams,' reported the papers in the last week of October, 'are sold at several brandy/shops in High Holborn, St Giles's, Thieving Lane, Tothill Street, Rosemary Lane, Whitechapel, Shoreditch, the Mint, Kent Street &c. viz, *Sangree, Tow Row, Cuckold's Comfort, Parliament Gin, Make Shift, the Last Shift, the Ladies Delight, the Baulk, King Theodore or Corsica, Cholick and Gripe Water*s, and several others, to evade the late Act of Parliament.'[23]

The Gin Act had given magistrates the sweeping powers against gin/sellers which they had been clamouring for since 1721. Now it was time to use them. They could fine a street/hawker £10 or sentence him to two months' hard labour. On 18 October, 'one Samuel Scott, a ... sailor, was committed to Bridewell ... being convicted for selling Gin last Saturday night in St Paul's churchyard.'[24] Samuel Scott was 'the first man committed [for street/hawking] in this City on the [Gin] Act,' but he wasn't the last. To the magistrates' consternation, it made no difference. By the end of October, alarm bells were ringing loud and clear. Something odd was going on. Parliament had passed a major piece of legislation to stamp out a major social problem, but the gin/sellers hadn't packed up their bags and departed. They were still out there in the streets. 'Gin is still sold in several markets about town,' the *London Daily Post* reported, 'especially about four and five of the clock in the morning, by women and others, out of small bottles, which they conceal under their clothes until asked for.'[25]

It was time for firmer action. And the right man was in place to set it in motion. Sir John Gonson was Chair of Quarter Sessions for Westminster. 'Yesterday,' reported the *London Daily Post* on 26 October, 'a great number of His Majesty's Justices of the Peace (Sir John Gonson . . . being one) met at Col. De Veil's house in Leicester Fields.' The aim of the meeting was to agree 'the most effectual methods to put in execution that clause in the Act of Parliament made against selling spirituous liquors upon bulks, stalls, or in the streets by idle vagabonds.' The authorities had decided to raise the stakes.

It was significant that the meeting took place at the house of Colonel Thomas De Veil. They were a mixed bag, the Middlesex magistrates. There were the zealots, like Sir John Gonson, who liked the committees and the speeches. There were the trading justices, and the justices who never lifted a finger, and the justices who wrote tracts in favour of gin. Thomas De Veil was something else again. He was the nearest thing to a professional law-man that London had in 1736. If the Gin Act was running into trouble, the burden of enforcing it was going to fall on him.

Thomas De Veil was no traditional gentleman magistrate. He 'passed thro' many scenes of life,' as his biographer afterwards put it, 'and raised himself by his personal merit, from carrying a brown musket, to make a very considerable person in the world.'[26] His qualities were 'courage, indefatigable diligence, and a certain boldness in address, [which] will carry a man through most of those troubles, that are incident to setting out in the world, with few friends, and a very small fortune.' In other words, he was a chancer and self-made man, a creature of the Age of Risk. De Veil's father, a Huguenot, was librarian at Lambeth Palace. De Veil started an apprenticeship, but his master went out of business. At seventeen, with no more money in the family, Thomas De Veil had ended up a private in the army.

He never lost his chip on the shoulder about that. Throughout his life, 'people took the liberty of aspersing him, as if he had been a foreigner by birth, and meanly descended, neither of which were true.' Thomas De Veil hadn't stayed a private soldier for long. He caught the eye of his officers, made contacts, and won a commission in the dragoons. When peace came and he found himself in London on half-pay, he opened an office in Scotland Yard as a political lobbyist. In 1729 old army friends got him onto the Commission of Peace for Middlesex and Westminster. The immigrant's son, the private soldier, was on his way up.

The post he was aiming for was 'court justice'. It wasn't quite an official job. It suited the ministry to have a magistrate in Middlesex whom they could trust, and to whom they could turn for advice on law and order, or help when the Westminster election turned nasty. 'To this,' De Veil's biographer explained, 'he was moved by many motives; first, it gratified his ambition. He loved to be about great men, and to have an interest in them . . . In the next place he knew it would give him credit and power, for which he had also a very strong appetite.'

In 1735 Thomas De Veil got lucky, broke up a gang of thieves, survived an assassination attempt, and found himself 'recommended to the notice and protection of the ministry, who thought it very requisite to distinguish a justice capable of acting in such a manner.' His office, first in Leicester Fields, then Thrift Street* in Soho, became a permanent court of summary justice. Even before the Gin Act, De Veil worked a twenty-four-hour day, seven days a week. The harder he worked, the more business came his way and the more money he made. Enemies called him a trading justice; De Veil reckoned himself a professional. 'Though he did much of [the trading justices'] kind of business,' as his biographer put it, '[he] did it in another manner; so that

* Now known as Frith Street. Leicester Fields is now called Leicester Square.

though his office was profitable, yet it was not liable to any scandal.'

That wasn't quite true. There may not have been scandals about money, but money wasn't Thomas De Veil's weakness. 'His greatest foible,' his shamefaced biographer admitted, 'was a most irregular passion for the fair sex.' And when it came to women he was quite prepared to abuse his office. If whores were brought in, Thomas De Veil made sure to get their address, whether their house had a back door, and when was a good time to visit them. He was adept 'in distinguishing ladies of a certain character.' 'You see, madam,' he would say as he led women out of his study after a 'private examination', 'that I am capable of being particularly diligent and expeditious, in doing a lady's business.'

The Gin Act had at last given magistrates like Thomas De Veil the powers they needed to clean up the streets. It was up to Excise men to take care of unlicensed shops and distillers, and to charge them with the £100 fine for selling spirits without a licence. Magistrates were there to tackle the hawkers and barrow-boys, the pedlars and stallholders who infested the alleys of Middlesex. Getting to grips with the problem, De Veil found the Gin Act gave him one immediate advantage. It offered rewards for anyone informing on gin-sellers. Buy a dram, squeal on the person who sold it to you, and the court would award you half of their £10 fine. That fine was De Veil's first sanction against gin-sellers, but £10 turned out to be beyond the means of most of them. A poor woman could work hard all year and barely earn £10. Commit trespass and assault and you were rarely fined more than a few shillings. So with most of them, Thomas De Veil fell back on the alternative. He sent them to the House of Correction.

Bridewell, the original House of Correction, was down by the Fleet River, but by now there were Houses of Correction all over England, and they were all called Bridewells. Middlesex had two, in Clerkenwell and Tothill Fields, and there was another one in Southwark. They weren't quite prisons. Back in the sixteenth century, when they were introduced, Bridewells had been meant as part of the welfare system; they were the stick to balance the carrot of parish relief, the short, sharp shock for whores, beggars and the idle poor. Duly corrected, beggars would come out as honest labourers, and whores as dutiful wives and daughters. The reality, by the start of the eighteenth century, was rather different. Uffenbach, visiting a Bridewell, was shocked by the women locked up there, who 'were very bold and we had to give them a few shillings for brandy.'[27] Ned Ward was even less impressed. He and his friend watched a woman being whipped with the doors kept open so that the court could see. Outside, his friend asked 'whether you think this sort of correction is a proper method to reform women? . . . Why, truly, said I . . . I only conceive it makes many whores, but that it can in no measure reclaim 'em.'[28]

With punitive fines in one hand, and Bridewell in the other, the magistrates meant business. From Thomas De Veil's house in Leicester Fields they sent strict instruction out to their constables. The magistrates themselves agreed 'to meet at the several vestries once or twice a week, to receive informations against all such offenders, and to punish 'em with the utmost severity.'[29] Thomas De Veil's office soon filled up with hawkers and barrow-boys, and market-women with gin bottles 'concealed under their clothes.'

The result was shocking. The enforcement drive didn't make any difference at all. All the magistrates achieved was to fill up the Houses of Correction. Two weeks later, the *London Daily Post* reported that 'gin is still sold about streets every morning about six and seven o'clock, by women and shoe-blackers.' The paper found it, 'very surprizing, considering what numbers are now in gaol, for retailing that liquor.' Another morning, they described how 'last night, and for several nights past, gin was publickly sold by women and ordinary fellows, on the bulks on Ludgate Hill, and about Fleet Ditch; and there are running shabby fellows, that still sell it about the streets.'[30] Other vendors had simply moved out of town. 'The skirts of the town are pester'd with great numbers of ... walking distillers,' reported the *Daily Post* on 19 November, 'insomuch that no less than six of them were taken up yesterday on Southwark side ... for retailing the same in the fields.'

Two months into prohibition, a horrible realisation began to dawn on the authorities. They had feared uprising, riot and overthrow of the state, but something far worse was happening. They were being ignored.

Sir Robert Walpole was the only one who had seen it coming. He had never been a reformer; he had never had any illusions about the Gin Act. A month before Michaelmas he had predicted to his brother that 'the lower sort of brandy-shops, whose poverty secures them from the penalties of the law, [will] continue to sell in defiance of the law, and in hopes that no body will think worth their while to prosecute them for what they cannot possibly recover.'[31]

It was in the last week of October that the authorities realised events were running out of their control. Thomas Wilson dined with the Lord Mayor that Sunday and found him worried. 'He says that ... his management ... has kept things pretty quiet, but that it will not be so long. That people are generally uneasy and dissatisfied ... both Scotland and England are ripe for a Rebellion.' It didn't help that the King was still abroad. 'The citizens of London cry out their trade is ruined by his Majesty's going and long stay,' Lord Egmont noted in his diary the same week. 'The mob, dissatisfied with putting down their beloved gin, exclaim publicly, No gin, no King, and many of them have taken it into their heads that the late King is still alive; others that the present will never return. Some of better fashion say (whatever face the Queen puts on it) that whenever a packet arrives from Hanover she falls into hysterick fits.' The Queen had already been mobbed in the street. Driving back to Kensington Palace, 'the mob got round her coach and cried, "No gin, no King."' Caroline did the best she could. 'She put forth her head,' Lord Egmont recorded, 'and told them that if they had patience till the next Session they should have again both their gin and their King.'

Even the Master of the Rolls couldn't help commenting to his protégé on 'the great and general uneasiness that the people are under.' For Thomas Wilson himself the public mood seemed one of unfocused anger. 'The Nation . . . [are] ripe for a change without knowing what scheme would make them easier and more free,' he wrote nervously in his diary that week. 'Angry with the Prime Minister and yet no other better offered to succeed him.'[32] But he, for one, had no intention of taking his share of the blame. Thomas Wilson never was cut out for martyrdom. Madam Geneva had served her purpose; he had made his reputation. He dined with the Lord Mayor and visited all the senior bishops of the Church of England. The Queen knew his name. The Master of the Rolls was lobbying for a place for him. Now prohibition was starting to get too dangerous. In the same week that the magistrates met, the champion of reform 'wrote to Dr Hales excusing myself from meddling any further in supporting the Gin Bill.' His reason was 'the hazard I am [in] of my life or being abused by a Mob.'[33]

Maybe the 'mob' were starting to enjoy the sight of a law sinking without trace. London's constant undercurrent of subversion and disrespect had bubbled up to the surface. There was even a new anti-hero to admire that autumn. 'Yesterday morning,' reported the *Daily Journal* a week before Michaelmas, 'about nine o'clock, a gentleman with his lady and son, in a coach and six, were attacked by two highwaymen well-mounted . . . on Barnes Common, and robbed of their watches and money to the value of about £40.' The paper couldn't be sure, but the highwaymen were 'supposed to be

Turpin and his companion.'[34] Dick Turpin, an Essex farmer's son, was on the path which would take him to the gallows and a place in popular mythology.

Madam Geneva had been blamed for crime and social break-down, for uppity tradesmen, dishonest servants and the decline of the nation. Outlawing her was supposed to return the country to a better, more wholesome age. But, on 2 December, it was reported in the press that 'the Commissioners of Excise ... have clearly discovered the late act to be ineffectual; and notwithstanding the high penalties inflicted on the retailers by the said act, it is daily sold in garrets, workshops &c.'[35] Two months into prohibition, it was all going horribly wrong.

## CHAPTER ELEVEN

# BOOTLEG

**B**efore prohibition there were gin stalls; afterwards there were basket-women with bottles under their skirts and 'running shabby fellows.' Before prohibition there were distillers' shops and apothecaries; afterwards, there was Captain Dudley Bradstreet.

Dudley Bradstreet was an adventurer, a soldier and a con-man. His autobiography read like a work of fiction, and probably was one. His life was as random as any eighteenth-century novel. In the '45 Rebellion he would be a spy in the Young Pretender's camp. He was the one – he claimed – who persuaded Bonnie Prince Charlie to turn back at Derby. The irony was how like Colonel Thomas De Veil he was. Captain Dudley Bradstreet was another ambitious chancer with an immigrant background, another military man with 'a bold address' but no cash. If things had turned out differently, Dudley Bradstreet could have been the one sitting in a magistrate's office, sending bootleggers off to Bridewell.

But he wasn't. In 1736, Dudley Bradstreet was in London, in debt and at a loose end, and when prohibition came he saw an opportunity. 'The mob being very noisy and clamorous for want of their beloved liquor,' he wrote in his memoirs, 'which few or none . . . dared to sell, it soon occurred to me to venture upon that trade.'[1] He wasted no time about it: 'I got an acquaintance,' he recalled, 'to take a house in Blue Anchor Alley.' He bought the sign of a cat and nailed it to the window. 'I then caused a leaden pipe, the small end out about an inch, to be placed under the paw of the cat.' The other end of the pipe, inside the house, had a funnel on it. Dudley Bradstreet asked around for the best gin in London, and spent the last £13 he had at Langdale's distillery in Holborn. Then he was ready.

He had the word put about 'that gin would be sold by the cat at my window next day.' Business was slow to start with, but when the first customer arrived it was worth the three-hour wait. 'I heard the chink of money, and a comfortable voice say, "Puss, give me twopennyworth of gin."' Two pennies appeared through the cat's mouth. Dudley Bradstreet raised his bottle and poured two penn'orth of gin carefully into the funnel. By the end of the day he had made six shillings.

That was only the start. Soon Dudley Bradstreet was turning over £3–4 a day. Parliament could pass whatever laws it liked against Madam Geneva, but Londoners hadn't lost their taste for her company. 'The street now became quite impassable,' Bradstreet went on, 'by the numbers who came out of curiosity to see the enchanted cat, for so Puss was called. This concourse of idle people had such an effect, that my neighbours went to their several landlords and declared, their houses were not tenantable unless they got the cat-man removed; they asked who the cat-man was, but received no other information than that he was the greatest nuisance they ever saw or heard of.'

Imitators were soon copying Dudley Bradstreet's idea. The cat caught on. 'In the parish of St Giles-in-the-Fields,' reported

*Read's Weekly Journal*, 'and other parts of the town ... the buyer comes into the entry and cries *Puss*, and is immediately answered by a voice from within, *Mew*. A drawer is then thrust out, into which the buyer puts his money, which when drawn back, is soon after thrust out again, with the quantity of gin required.'[2] All over town, gin-sellers were finding ways to keep the gin flowing. Londoners weren't going to give up their favourite dram when the gentlemen who had banned it were still knocking back the port and smuggled French brandy. It was that discrimination between poor and rich that Lonsdale blamed for the Gin Act's failure when he addressed the House of Lords in the debate on its repeal. 'It was this invidious distinction,' he declared, 'that set the mob so much against the execution of that law.' If anything, prohibition 'made them more fond of dram-drinking than ever; because they then began to look upon it as an insult upon the rich.'[3]

Insulting the rich was, after all, one of London's favourite pastimes. Watermen abused their betters as a matter of professional pride. 'A man in court dress,' Casanova moaned, 'cannot walk in the streets of London without being pelted with mud by the mob.' Another foreign visitor was shocked to see that 'the people in general testify but little respect for their superiors ... Even the Majesty of the throne is often not sufficiently respected.'[4] Uffenbach described an election at Tothill Fields where one noble candidate was opposed by 'a common townsman and brewer called Cross.' When the nobles appeared, 'we were amazed to hear the vile remarks and insults that the others hurled at them, and the mob even made so bold as to pursue them with filth and stones.'[5]

There was a devilish kind of humour flowing beneath early eighteenth-century London. Lord Hervey reported how during one of George II's extended trips to Hanover, 'on St James's Gate this advertisement was pasted: "Lost or strayed out of this house, a man who has left a wife and six children on the parish."'[6] A *Brief*

*Description of London* in 1776 tried to put its finger on 'that sort of pleasantry in conversation, which is . . . peculiar to [Londoners]. It . . . gives its sharpest edge to ridicule. Their comedies abound with it, and it never fails to influence the gesture and the tone of voice in a way that cannot easily be explained, but is irresistibly engaging.'[7] It was subversive, and it was satirical. A group of coffee-house drunks hired a hackney coach, dressed coachman and postilion in street scavenger's clothes, and rode it round the Hyde Park ring, in among all the fashionable equipages. In March 1742 a satirical 'procession of the scald miserable masons' tagged onto the real freemason's parade, lampooning their ceremonial with 'fellows on jack asses . . . cow horns on their heads, [and] a kettle-drummer on a jack-ass with two butter firkins for kettle-drums.'[8] The undercurrent of subversion was there in London's flirtations with Jacobitism as well, and in its popular heroes. When Jack Sheppard broke out of Newgate for the last time, he spent fifteen days being fêted around London and drinking in the gin-shops of Clare Market before they caught him again. Highwaymen posed as latter-day Robin Hoods. Thomas Easter, told by a victim that he looked surprisingly honest, replied, 'So I am, because I rob the rich to give to the poor.'[9]

Maybe the urge to tweak aristocratic noses came from an idea about English liberties. Their rulers, after all, were forever telling Englishmen that they were raised above all other nations by being free. 'I that am born free,' a pressed sailor told James Oglethorpe in 1728, 'are not I and the greatest Duke in England equally free born?'[10] 'This nation is passionately fond of liberty'[11] was Montesquieu's comment. It was hard to understand of a nation where real political power was still gripped by a small élite. Disraeli would later raise his eyebrows at the way 'a people without power or education had been induced to believe themselves the freest and most enlightened nation in the world.'[12] But Disraeli was writing at a time when the vote seemed the only measure of political freedom. For most Londoners in the early eighteenth century, the vote wasn't even on the cards. Instead, they found other ways of demonstrating their freedom from authority. They hurled verbal abuse; they satirised and they ridiculed. They turned law-breakers into heroes.

And they drank gin. When gin was banned, subversion almost became too easy. To cock a snook at the ruling classes in winter 1736, all you had to do was buy a dram. If Parliament was going to outlaw Madam Geneva, that would only make Londoners love her more than ever. By disobeying the law, Londoners could take control of it. The 'mob', as Henry Fielding would lament in 1751 – by then he had changed sides and joined the reformers – 'have not as yet claimed that right which was insisted on by the people or mob in old Rome, of giving a negative voice in the enacting laws, [but] they have clearly exercised this power in controlling their execution. Of this it is easy to give many instances, particularly in the case of the Gin Act some years ago.'[13]

Londoners took to prohibition like ducks to water. A subversive counter-culture grew up around illegal gin, a culture of passwords and Puss and Mew houses. And as with any banned drugs, counter-culture names for it proliferated. Londoners didn't just drink Geneva anymore. They drank Max, Partiality, Blue Ruin, and Flashes of Lightning. They drank White Satin, Bob Makeshift and South Sea Mountain. They got topsey-frizey on My Lady's Eye-water, the Baulk, the Last Shift, Old Tom. They ended up in the straw on Cock-my-Cap, Kill-Grief, Comfort, and Poverty.

Maybe the fancy names made the drams taste better. The taste of rebellion might have been the only thing which made them palatable at all. Thomas Wilson once claimed that gin was made 'not so much ... from malt, as rotten fruit, urine, lime, human ordure, and any other filthiness from whence a fermentation may be raised, and by throwing in cochylus indice, and other hot poisonous drugs.'[14] For once Thomas Wilson was hardly exaggerating. He didn't need to. The truth about 1730s gin was already bad enough. When a market-woman pulled a brown bottle out from under her skirts, the name was usually the only fancy thing about it.

A hundred years before, distillers had published careful recipes for how to make compound waters. But times had changed since then. For a start, the old, slow way of purifying raw spirit by repeated distillations was out. Bay salt and quick lime – anything alkaline – would do the same trick faster. 'Calcined and well purified animal bones' didn't cost anything at all. When the flavours went in, things went from bad to worse. Even twenty years later, the distiller Ambrose Cooper reckoned that more gin was flavoured with turpentine than with juniper berries. 'It is surprising,' he added, 'that people should accustom themselves to drinking it for pleasure.'[15]

It wasn't all that surprising. Londoners had spent four years drinking Parliamentary Brandy. But the old way of flavouring spirits by slow distillation was too expensive for bootleggers, and it took too long. It was simpler to add neat flavourings to the raw spirits and give them a quick stir. 'The only still used in all the . . . houses in London,' according to one report at the end of the century, was 'a glass or brass pestle and mortar.' That way anyone could brew up gin themselves on the kitchen table at home. One guide for publicans published a recipe. To 120 gallons of raw spirit, twenty under proof, it added a splash of turpentine (for taste), half an ounce of sulphuric acid (for kick), the same of bitter almonds (for bite), a gallon each of lime and rose water (for the bouquet), plus eight ounces of alum boiled up in water and a pint of wine spirits.[16] That was a fancy drink. In St Giles's, they didn't bother with the rose water. It was a moot point, anyway, whether any of the drinkers much cared what their gin tasted like.

'The delicacy of flavour,' as a 'bystander' put it, 'is not courted by the vulgar. What they chiefly regard is its being a dram.'[17] Maybe it was no surprise that bottle labels made their appearance in April 1738, when a Hungary-water producer advertised that 'to prevent counterfeits, the Black Boy and Comb is pasted on all bottles.'[18] There was no shortage of counterfeits in St Giles's.

There wasn't even any guarantee of how strong the dram was. It depended on how much the gin-seller watered it down. Ambrose Cooper called proof gin 'Royal Gin', while most everyday Geneva was diluted by a third, but Ambrose Cooper wasn't a bootlegger. It was academic anyway, because the first workable hydrometer, Clarke's, had only appeared ten years before, and it was a long way from perfect. Excise men relied on old tests like dipping a cloth in the spirit and then setting fire to it, but most of those could be faked. The physician Peter Shaw defined proof spirit as fifty per cent alcohol by volume. In his hands, the compounder Thomas Cooke reckoned, it took '1 to 6 to reduce [spirits] to the strength gin and compounds in London are constantly sold to the retailer at'[19] (known as phial proof). That made 1730s gin about the same strength as modern London Dry. But compounders had plenty of tricks for faking strength as well as taste. 'Pepper, ginger, and other fiery ingredients are put into the still,' explained a later reformer, 'which makes the spirit hot to the palate, and burning to the stomach, though mixed with water, and under proof.'[20] Distillers called it 'the doctor'. They started with powdered quick lime, then mixed in varying proportions of almond oil and sulphuric acid.[21] The final ingredient, cocculus indicus, was a poison, and a strong one, but that didn't stop them from putting it into the stills. Constables counted up gin-shops, and Excise men busily recorded the gallons distilled. But when it came to the numbers of Londoners who were killed, maimed or blinded by bootleg spirits, no one was keeping a tally.

\*    \*    \*

It didn't seem to put them off. Three months into prohibition, the gin was still flowing. And if reformers and politicians spent Christmas looking for signs of popular subversion, they didn't have long to wait. On 17 January 1737, the *London Evening Post* reported a disturbing incident.

It happened in Hanover Square, in the heart of the polite new West End. 'Yesterday,' the paper reported, 'one Pullin, a chairman,\* was carry'd in effigy about the several streets, squares &c. in the parish of St George, Hanover Square, for informing against a victualler in Princess Street for retailing spirituous liquors.' Londoners never did like informers. The Societies for Reformation of Manners had discovered that. 'After the procession was over he was fixed on a chair pole in Hanover Square, with a halter about his neck, and then a load of faggots placed round him, in which manner he was burnt in the sight of a vast concourse of people.'

For the authorities, the only good news was that the crowd's attack on Pullin had been symbolic. The real violence would come later. But it was enough to cause them panic. They had legislated against gin, and they were being ignored. Thomas De Veil was up all night collecting fines and sending gin-sellers to Bridewell, but it didn't make any difference.

The new session of Parliament opened just two weeks later. On the first day the King declared to the assembled Lords and Commons that 'it must be matter of the utmost surprise and concern to every true lover of his country, to see the many contrivances and attempts carried on ... in different parts of the nation, tumultuously to resist and obstruct the execution of the laws and to violate the peace of the kingdom. These disturbers of the public repose ... in their late outrages, have either directly

\* He carried one end of a sedan chair.

opposed, or at least endeavoured to render ineffectual some acts of the whole legislature.' The government was thinking of the riots of the year before: the summer riots in London, the disturbances in Edinburgh, the scare over a Jacobite rising. It didn't help that for the past four months they had had to sit by and watch a major piece of legislation being ignored.

Distillers had spent nine months waiting for the new session to start. There was no shortage of voices calling for the Gin Act to be scrapped. The *London Magazine* launched a long attack on informers. The *Grub Street Journal* proposed scrapping prohibition and replacing it with increased duties and better licensing controls. No one doubted that the Gin Act had gone too far. '[If] rigorous methods are chosen at the same time that moderate methods ... offer themselves,' the *Grub Street Journal* argued, 'people can never be brought to think that such methods were ... designed for the public good.'[22]

But moderation was the last thing on the government's mind as the 1737 session opened. It was thinking only of riot and rebellion. 'His Majesty,' the King went on, 'thinks it affords a melancholy prospect to consider to what height these audacious practices may rise, if not timely suppressed.' Suppression was the key note. In their loyal reply, the Commons could find no words harsh enough for those involved 'in tumultuously resisting and obstructing the execution of the laws.'

Not everyone saw things the same way. 'I am as great an enemy to riots as any man,' declared Carteret, one of the opposition leaders. 'I am sorry to see them so frequent as they are; but I shall never be for sacrificing the liberties of the people, in order to prevent them engaging in any riotous proceedings.' Any clamp-down would only drag the nation further from its freedoms. 'The people seldom or never assemble in any riotous or tumultuous manner unless when they are oppressed,' Carteret warned, 'or at least imagine they are

A city spinning out of control: Hogarth's 'South Sea Scheme', 1721

Zealot: Sir John Gonson enters to make his arrest in Hogarth's 'Harlot's Progress', 1732

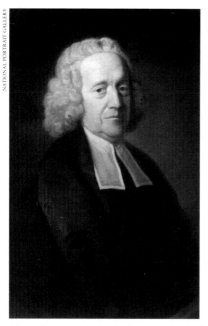

The reformers (clockwise from top left): Dr Stephen Hales, General James Oglethorpe, Isaac Maddox, Bishop of Worcester, and Sir Joseph Jekyll, Master of the Rolls

The House of Commons, 1749

Westminster Hall.
The Jacobite bomb was placed on
the steps between the Courts of King's
Bench and Chancery, at the far end

In the firing line: Sir Thomas De Veil, Westminster magistrate

Hogarth's 'Night', 1738

'No Saint, no Spartan, no reformer':
Sir Robert Walpole

Thomas Wilson: no Saint,
but an ardent reformer

Henry Fielding (seated, left) in his Bow Street court room:
'a poor, emaciated, worn-out rake'

'Beer Street', 1751

'Gin Lane', 1751

The future: industrial distilling, 1754

Excise man at work, 1752

Gin Palace:
Cruikshank illustrates Dickens

oppressed . . . You may shoot them, you may hang them, but, till the oppression is removed or alleviated, they will never be quiet.'[23]

But when ministers contemplated Pullin's effigy blazing in Hanover Square, they didn't see free Englishmen with their liberties under threat; all they saw was a mob carrying sticks. For them, there was no point speculating what went on in the minds of the lower orders. As Lord Chancellor Hardwicke loftily put it, 'as none but persons of the lowest rank has been concerned in any . . . riot . . . it is below the dignity of parliament to enquire particularly into them.'[24] For the ministry, the debate was nothing to do with civil liberties. It was about respect. And the apparent failure of the Gin Act was all part of the same picture. 'There is scarce a law made,' William Hay, MP for Seaford, noted in his diary that year, 'but the people . . . immediately prepare to resist it . . . so that it is now become a question whether this nation is for the future to be governed by a mob or the legislature.'[25] By early 1737, prohibition wasn't about gin any more. It was about authority.

For Sir Robert Walpole, in particular, it was about authority: his own. If he had been rattled the summer before, he was still more so now. The rift between the Prince of Wales and his father was widening, and the opposition were doing all they could to woo the Prince their way. It was only a few months before he would set up his own court in Leicester Fields with opposition leaders thronging the anterooms. Walpole could see Tories and dissident Whigs uniting under the banner of liberty, the City of London sticking up for distillers, mob rule in the streets. The sooner the lid was slammed down on popular protest, the better.

There was no more talk of repeal. Instead of pulling back, Parliament waded further into the mire. Instead of a new Gin Act, they passed an enforcement measure. The key clauses were buried in an Act to reduce taxes on British fruit wines, or 'sweets'. As usual, Sir Robert was killing several birds with one stone. By dropping the duty on sweets, he hoped to increase consumption, make a revenue windfall, and cheer up the West Indian sugar merchants, who had lost their market for rum. There was a theory, in case any reformers were listening, that sweets might 'be made to answer all the good ends of spirituous liquors, without being attended with any of the fatal consequences.' With elderflower wine in the shops, Madam Geneva might just be out of a job.

But the Sweets Act had a sting in its tail. Its final clauses turned their attention to gin-sellers. Until now, they had been sent down for hard labour if they couldn't pay the £10 fine. The Sweets Act decreed that before they were discharged from Bridewell they should be 'whipped bloody'. Until now, informers had only received their reward if their victims paid the £10 fine, not if they went to Bridewell. But now a reward was guaranteed for anyone giving information under the Gin Act. Parliament was determined to see prohibition through.

It was April by the time the Sweets Act went through. On 27 April a farrier, Briat, talked half a pint of Geneva out of a distiller called Mound. Briat's story was that he needed the spirits to treat a sick horse. When he took the gin to the Excise Office instead, and informed against the distiller for selling it to him, 'the mob rose upon him at Stocks Market, and increased to such a number by that time he got to Whitechapel Bars, pelting him with stones, brickbats &c. that with much difficulty he was brought back in a coach to the Excise Office, at the hazard of his life.'[26] If the authorities thought that informers were going to save the Gin Act, they had made a terrible mistake.

Back in January, gin-drinkers had made effigies of informers before burning them. From now on, the attacks were for real. An informer was ducked in the Thames at the end of July and almost lost an eye; he was rescued by a passing waterman. On 20 August, a husband and wife informed on a woman for selling gin, but were cornered by a crowd in Honey Lane Market. 'The man [escaped],' reported the *London Evening Post*, 'but the wife they seized upon, and pelted her with all manner of filth, and rolled her in the kennel. Then they forced her to the Swan and Two Necks in Lad Lane, in order to pump her; but the people of the inn shut the gates against them.' The crowd had to take her all round the City in their search for a pump. In the end they dragged her into Guildhall yard, where 'they pumped her for a long while.' The informer only escaped by crawling into the porch, 'where a gentleman belonging to Guildhall Hall took her in and saved her from the fury of the mob, who it is thought would else have killed her.'

No one had tried to help the woman as they dragged her from pump to pump. The *London Evening Post* thought it 'remarkable that she begged for mercy and protection of the shopkeepers &c. all the way they dragged her and pelted her; but nobody showed her any compassion.' Londoners had never cared much for informers.

Some among the authorities weren't all that keen on them either. For the *London Magazine*, campaigning for repeal at the start of the parliamentary session, reliance on informers was the fundamental flaw in prohibition. 'I hope it will be granted,' it wrote in January (about the time Londoners were burning Pullin's effigy in Hanover Square) 'that treachery in every degree is wicked . . . It ought . . . to be the care of every people, but especially a free people, to prevent as much as possible the character of a treacherous informer from ever becoming tolerable among them.'[27] Societies depended on mutual trust. 'A general spirit of treachery among the people,' the magazine warned, 'is one of the main supports of arbitrary power.'

The trouble for the authorities was that they had no alternative. Enforcing the Gin Act was always an uphill struggle. There was no police department. There were no special agents to get in behind the counter and pull Dudley Bradstreet out by the ears. The justice system depended on private individuals. If you caught a robber in your house, you were expected to prosecute him yourself. Law enforcement depended on citizens, and when the citizens wouldn't co-operate, the authorities ran dangerously short of options. It was no good relying on constables when it came to gin. Almost half the Middlesex constables were gin-sellers themselves. 'As every other trade makes interest to be excused having this office,' magistrates had complained in their 1736 report, '[victuallers and dealers in spirituous liquors] are the only ones who covet it.' Victuallers and dealers in spirituous liquors were hardly going to be enthusiasts for enforcing prohibition.

So there was no other option but to rely on informers. At least, with a £5 reward on offer, there was no shortage of informers coming forward. Five pounds was a year's rent for a poor family, six weeks' wages even for a skilled craftsman. By summer 1737, the Gin Act hadn't yet had any effect on gin-drinking in London, but it had, at least, had one result. In the words of Thomas De Veil's biographer, it had 'let loose a crew of dangerous and desperate people who turn'd informers merely for bread.'

Informers worked in organised gangs. The same names turned up time and again in reports of convictions. Samuel and Marjory Brookes, along with their friend Elizabeth Jenkins, were responsible for numerous prosecutions around Spitalfields. Another regular team of informers, Margaret Dawson and Mary Fountons, only came to grief when they were caught out blackmailing their victim as well as turning him in to the authorities. Under the Gin Act, magistrates were supposed to convict a hawker 'on the oath of one or more credible witness,' but in practice no one was too fussy about how credible the witnesses were. It was a hard enough job as it was, trying to enforce prohibition in a city addicted to gin.

But after almost a year the risks of depending on informers were starting to show. Even in the first months of prohibition, there had been alarming signs of informers' evidence falling apart in court. In January the Commissioners of Excise had put out an order that officers should check informers' names, '& that when any sample of any goods or liquors are taken by any officer intended to be produced at the hearing of an information, that he keep the same in his own custody until the information is heard.'[28] Informers couldn't be trusted not to tamper with evidence.

And now a new danger had emerged. If informers were set on by mobs, they would no longer dare to come forward. The flow of information would dry up. The 'dangerous and desperate crew' would crawl back into the woodwork. On 20 August, the same day the woman informer was dragged under the Guildhall pump, the Commissioners of Excise wrote to the Treasury to tell them what was going on. 'Several mobs,' the Commissioners warned, 'have of late assembled themselves in a riotous manner and have greatly insulted and abused divers persons concerned in detecting the retailers of spirituous liquors ... some of whom have been in great danger of losing their lives.' The fear was that 'outrages of this kind ... must necessarily deter all persons whatsoever from giving the like informations for the future.'[29]

Nor was it only informers. 'The Constables and Officers belonging to this Revenue,' the Commissioners went on, 'when imployed in suppressing the like illegal practices, have been assaulted in the same outrageous manner, and some of them very much wounded.' If there was anything Londoners hated more than an informer, it was an Excise man. Within days of the Gin Act coming in, the *Daily Journal* had reported that a Southwark Excise man 'going through St Olave's Street ... without meddling with anybody, some people who were drinking gin in an open shop thereabouts knew him, and thinking he was watching the house, or intended to go in, came upon him, and beat him in so barbarous a manner, that he is now under the surgeon's hands.'[30] Three more Excise men had been beaten up on their rounds in June.

The message, that August, was that the whole apparatus of enforcement was under threat. Informers were being attacked and Excise men abused. Maybe it was to boost morale that the Excise Office released figures for the numbers of unlicensed gin-shops they had managed to prosecute since the Gin Act came in. There were 587 of them, all liable for the £100 fine.[31] The trouble was that even the enforcement measures against gin-shops and distillers were running into difficulties. The Commissioners of Excise only made themselves unpopular by targeting respectable citizens like Dr Sayer Rudd, a Unitarian minister and physician with a diploma from the University of Rheims, convicted for selling half a pint of colic water to a patient in November 1736. His £100 penalty was, as the *Daily Post* sarcastically put it, 'a fine sum for an Exciseman's breakfast.'[32] The Excise Office had started out by refusing all requests for the huge fines to be reduced ('Their honours,' the *Daily Post* reported, 'stick close to the letter of the act').[33] But most owners of spirit-shops found it impossible to pay up. Five hundred and eighty-seven may have been liable for the fine, but all too few had managed to pay it. Now the Commissioners were forced into a U-turn. Summoning those who had already been charged, 'after admonishing them . . . and desiring them to take care for the future, they were pleased to mitigate their fines, some to £20 and others to £30 . . . The remaining part of their . . . sums were returned to them.'[34] They would soon just about give up trying to get the £100 penalty out of unlicensed gin-shops. Most shopkeepers and distillers were taken along to the magistrates instead, and fined £10 as if they were street-hawkers.

In response to the Excise Commissioners' worries about attacks on informers, the Treasury offered a reward to help catch those 'guilty of insulting persons concerned in detecting the retailers of spirituous liquors.'[35] If they thought that would be enough to safeguard the informers, they were about to be disappointed. On Tuesday 20 October, an informer was cornered by a crowd outside a cook's shop in Aldersgate Street. 'They laid hold of him and dragged him through all the channels along Aldersgate Street,' the *London Evening Post* reported, 'beat him with sticks, kicked him about in a terrible manner, dragged him to a dunghill in Bishop's Court, St Martin's, and there buried him for some time with ashes and cinders.' The man's wife and a friend came to the rescue and were beaten up themselves. A tradesman who tried to help had to escape into his own shop. Thomas De Veil committed the owner of the cook's shop to Bridewell, but for the informer it was too late. He died of his injuries a few days later. Opposing the Gin Act was no longer just a matter of cheeking the authorities. The scale of protest was escalating.

An informer in Bristol was tarred and feathered. A few days after the attack in Aldersgate Street, two informers tricked the landlady of the Black Horse in Grosvenor Mews into selling them a quartern of gin. They were caught on their way out. 'The coachmen in the Mews being informed of the affair, seized them and dragged them through the channels into Bond Street, where one of them was run over by a chariot and bruised in a desperate manner. The other was carried to the stable yard in Hanover Street, where they ducked him several times, after which he was conducted by the Beadle to the end of Swallow Street, and attacked again by the mob, who used him so roughly that 'tis thought his life is in danger.'[36]

It was all starting to get out of hand. A woman had been rescued on her way to Southwark Bridewell in September. On 2 November, when constables came for a gin-seller in the Strand, 'she cried out *informers*, on which the mob rose, and the fellows who had laid the information ran away.' Not all of them made it.

One fell into the hands of the crowd. They dragged him along the street before beating him up, 'and then making water in a pot . . . poured it down his throat; in short, they used him so ill, that tis said he cannot live.'[37]

He couldn't. 'This is the second person that has been murdered this week,' the *Daily Post* commented, 'for informing against people for selling of gin.'[38] There was even a riot at the funeral of the informer who had been killed in Aldersgate Street. 'A prodigious mob attended [the coffin],' reported the *London Evening Post,* 'pelting it all the way it went, [and] would not suffer the burial service to be performed.'[39]

And for all this trouble, it soon became clear that Madam Geneva was far from buried herself. When Excise figures were published in November, it turned out 'that there never was so much spirituous liquors distilled in any three months as in August, September and October last, so that consequently,' as the *London Evening Post* commented drily, 'the people must drink more of it than ever, altho' there are daily so many people sent to Bridewell for selling it.'[40]

For all Thomas De Veil's efforts, for all the riots and rescues and prosecutions and convictions, prohibition was having no effect. The authorities had got themselves into a no-win situation. The harder they tried to enforce the Gin Act, the more public anger they provoked. There had been a near-riot outside Thomas De Veil's house late in October; a month later there was another. An informer had been beaten up and tried to take refuge there, 'almost ready to expire, being [so] terribly beat, cut and bruis'd, and all over mire, that it was impossible to guess he was a man but by his walking, he being (as it seemed) one entire lump of dirt.'[41] That night, Thomas De Veil had to read the Riot Act. A third informer was killed in Dean Street on 19 November. There was another riot outside

St Mary-le-Strand which ended with shopkeepers boarding up their windows.

As 1737 drew to a close, few could see the silver lining in fifteen months of prohibition. The Bridewells were crammed with gin-sellers – 350 of them at a time, according to one statistic. Even Sir Joseph Jekyll, the Gin Act's sponsor, had to contemplate failure. He confided to Thomas Wilson that 'there is no putting an end to the pernicious custom of drinking gin etc. without laying such a duty upon the still-head as will prevent its being retailed unless at an excessive price.'[42]

But it was too late for the authorities to turn back. Giving up the Gin Act would have meant giving in to the mob. Even though he knew it couldn't succeed, Sir Joseph's instinct was still to force his legislation through. Instead of backing down gracefully, he had Thomas Wilson approach the Excise Office to discuss further enforcement measures. Nor was he the only one still thinking in terms of enforcement. 'Sir R.W. and the Parliament,' as Thomas Wilson noted in his diary, 'would willingly come into any scheme to suppress it.'

That didn't stop rumours circulating as the year drew to a close. On Christmas Eve the *London Evening Post* reported that 'in the next session of Parliament, we hear, there will be an alteration in the Gin Act.' 'We hear that no less than seven schemes are prepared for laying a duty on malt spirits,' it added a few weeks later. A month after that, the paper thought 'a duty will be laid on [spirits] at the still-head, in order to prevent the excessive drinking of it, and to put a stop to the many notorious riots upon informers.'[43]

Informers were at the root of the problem. In the last months of 1737 a stream of stories was published to illustrate their methods. There were even signs that magistrates were getting sick of them. In late November, Thomas De Veil committed an informer for trying to extort a guinea from a gin-seller in Gray's Inn Lane. A

Southwark woman was bound over by Sir John Lade for bribing someone to bring false information against a distiller.

The *Craftsman* launched its own attack on 3 December. 'The most shocking circumstance of the Roman bondage under their emperors,' it warned, 'was the encouragement given to informers and accusers, who . . . carried their villainous practices to such an height, that all offices of friendship, conversation and society were in a manner extinguished.'[44] The death of Madam Geneva had been meant to save society. Instead, prohibition was tearing society apart. Respectable apothecaries were branded as convicts; men and women informed on their neighbours; a whole industry had been driven underground. No one would pay a £100 fine if they could bribe their way out of it for a fraction of the amount.

In the first week of January 1738 another informer was killed. This time it was a woman. The newspapers reported that 'the populace used her with such severity, by beating, kicking, and cramming dirt into her mouth, that we hear she is since dead of her wounds. Even her own sex exposed her to great indecencies.'[45]

But the troubles of the authorities were only just beginning. So far they had only seen murder, perjury and spectacular disregard for the law. Three weeks later they had a full-scale riot on their hands.

# CHAPTER TWELVE

## CLAMP-DOWN

It started on a Friday afternoon in late January. Two informers, Elizabeth Beezley and Martha Sawyer, trapped a gin-seller called Elizabeth Voucher, and brought her to Thomas De Veil's new house in Thrift Street. But before Elizabeth Voucher had even been committed, a troublemaker, 'one Edward Arnold . . . went to the informer's habitation, threatening to kill the said Beezley, and to have the house she lived in pulled down.'[1] Someone brought news of this to De Veil, who immediately committed Arnold to Newgate. It was the wrong thing to do. Arnold had friends. He 'brought such a mob with him to the Justice's house, that in a very little time there were about 1,000 people assembled before his door.'

There had been near-riots over informers before, but this was the real thing. Even allowing for press exaggeration, the scene in narrow Thrift Street must have been frightening. The crowd filled the street, climbing up on the projecting house signs, swarming over street-traders' stalls. They were baying for blood, 'threatening destruction to the said Justice; and that the informers, who were then in the house, should never come out of it alive.' Inside Thomas De Veil's house, the two informers crouched upstairs, listening in terror to the noise outside the shutters.

Thomas De Veil did the only thing he could do. He read the Riot Act.

It was the magistrate's trump card. When a magistrate read the Riot Act, any crowd of more than twelve was supposed to disperse within an hour. But that night the Riot Act didn't work. 'Instead of dispersing the mob, [it] increased it greatly,' the *London Evening Post* reported, '[the] riotous assembly remaining before the Justice's house above three hours after he had read [it].' Maybe that was why the authorities would become so worried about this latest escalation in the gin protests. The Riot Act was their cure-all, their nuclear option. They had uttered the magic words, but the genie of popular protest hadn't gone back into the bottle. The Riot Act had lost its magic.

Peering through the shutters, Thomas De Veil spotted a ringleader. No one ever accused De Veil of ducking a fight. 'Observing among the rest a profligate fellow, who was the great encourager of this tumultuous assembly, (one Roger Allen) and who encouraged them to pull down the Justice's house and kill the informers, [he] had him seized.' But it took the army to disperse the crowd and escort the two informers to safety. Roger Allen was committed to Newgate under the Riot Act. He was 'the first of that kind to be tried, since the Gin Act took place.'

The authorities had every reason to be worried. It wasn't only the failure of the Riot Act. Attacks on informers were getting more frequent. Within a week of an informer being murdered in Chelsea, two other women had been attacked, one in Brewer Street and one in Bond Street. When an informer hid from an angry crowd in a house in Phoenix Street, the crowd pulled the house down. There were more rescues as well. A few days before the riot in Thrift

Street, a waterman's wife had been convicted for selling gin near Christ Church Spitalfields, and sent to Bridewell, 'but the mob having notice thereof rescued her just as the constable was delivering her into the keeper's hands.'[2] It happened again in Southwark a fortnight later.

It couldn't go on. A law was being disregarded. Rioting had broken out; informers had been killed; convicted criminals had been rescued and set free. It was time for the clamp-down to begin.

On 8 March 1738 the King issued a proclamation. It demanded measures 'for putting in Execution the ... Act against retailing of Spirituous Liquors, and for protecting the Officers of Justice, and all others ... to assist the Magistrates therein.' It called for 'suppressing all Combinations and Confedaracies [which] encourage Disobedience to the said Law; and for punishing all Attempts ... to insult and abuse those who give Informations.' But the Gin Act was only half of its concern. It was also a proclamation 'for putting in Execution the Act of Parliament made against Riots.' The ministry was as worried about the failure of the Riot Act as the failure of the Gin Act. Now, more than ever, prohibition was about authority. Alongside the clamp-down on gin, there would be a general push on law and order. Fifty-two would be hanged at Tyburn that year.

If they were going to win the battle, the magistrates needed more than proclamations, and Parliament was ready to give it to them. It was Sir Joseph Jekyll himself who, in the last week of March, brought in the 'Act for enforcing the execution [of the Gin Act]'.

It was a last-ditch measure. The Bill, the *London Evening Post* had no doubt, 'will put an end to *Puss and Mew*, and all other tricks and artifices to evade the law, and entirely prevent the retailing of [gin].'[3] It was a Bill against bootleggers. It attacked clandestine gin-sellers who 'are not seen, but are hid behind some wainscot, curtain, partition, or are otherwise concealed.' It was an Act against Dudley Bradstreet. Prohibition was leaking like a sieve, and desperately the Enforcement Act tried to plug the holes. It defended JPs against malicious prosecution. It sorted out licensing in tenements with multiple sub-lets. Rescuers and people who assaulted informers would be transported. Constables who 'refused or neglected to be aiding or assisting in the execution of the ... Acts' would be liable to a £20 fine.

The magistrates had new teeth and a Royal Proclamation to back them up. Now they were ready for the clamp-down. One by one, the various divisions of London justices gathered to agree their strategy. The Tower Hamlets magistrates, chaired by Sir John Gonson, decided on daily sittings to prosecute gin-sellers. In Westminster the magistrates gathered at the Court of King's Bench in Westminster Hall. They found themselves sitting alongside the steps where Robert Nixon's bomb had exploded. They resolved on a general meeting to instruct constables, and a standing magistrates' court to meet three days a week.[4] The Commissioners of Excise would be requested to give support. A clerk was appointed.

Thomas De Veil was among them. For him, of course, it all meant more work and more trouble. He was getting used to that by now. When fellow freemason William Hogarth published *Night, March 25, 1738* (the date was in the week of the magistrates' meetings) it showed someone emptying a chamber pot on Thomas De Veil's head. In February, De Veil had been rewarded with a sinecure in the Customs Office, but there must have been times when he wondered whether it was all worth it. A story in the papers the year before had had everyone laughing up their sleeves. A barrow-boy who was taking a quartern of gin to De Veil's house to inform on a gin-seller met some friends on the way and 'could not keep the secret, but told [them] of his design, and let them see the liquor.' One of his friends diverted his attention while the others drank the gin, then 'piss'd about the same quantity in the bottle.'

Unsuspecting, the boy took the bottle of urine to De Veil, 'and told him he was come to inform against a person who had just sold him a quartern.' Thomas de Veil 'ordered a glass to be brought, and some of the liquor to be poured into it, which he tasted.'[5] For magistrates, as well as for everyone else, the Gin Act could leave a nasty taste in the mouth.

Higher up the political ladder, events were being monitored closely by the Duke of Newcastle, who had overall responsibility for affairs in Middlesex. He asked magistrates for monthly reports, with statistics. Tacked onto the end of each report he wanted remarks on how the constables were performing. The problem of the constables hadn't gone away. The Westminster magistrates had agreed unanimously that one of their biggest problems was 'the numbers of persons serving the office of High Constable, Constables & Headborough, who are dealers in liquor.' But for once the authorities were prepared to put their own house in order. In May, the papers reported that 'for the future no victualler, distiller, coffee-man, or any other person whatsoever dealing in spirituous liquors, will be permitted to serve the offices of constable or headborough.'[6] It spelled the end for the gin-selling constables who had sabotaged the magistrates' surveys and dragged their feet over enforcement. A constable called Percival, landlord of the Blacksmith's Arms at Chelsea, had boasted that all through prohibition he had gone on selling gin at his pub undisturbed. Now his wife was hauled up for a £10 fine.[7]

If it was any comfort to him, the constables weren't the only ones being purged. The Enforcement Act stopped distillers from acting as JPs in any matter to do with gin. In May, all magistrates would be banned from taking fees on Gin Act prosecutions. And in August the Lord Chancellor would make a clean sweep of the Middlesex Bench, striking out no fewer than seventy-five trading justices, timeservers and lame ducks. 'Informers now may find th' employment bad,' crowed the *Gentleman's Magazine*, breaking into verse. 'And Justice may from Justices be had.'

That remained to be seen. For the Westminster magistrates, the clamp-down began with a pep-talk in Westminster Hall. Their chairman, Nathaniel Blackerby, was the son-in-law of the architect Nicholas Hawksmoor, recently deceased. He exhorted Westminster's magistrates to 'resolution, courage and perseverance.'[8] Just like the MPs in Parliament next door, Blackerby could see what would happen if the attacks on informers went on. 'If . . . persons who lay the informations before the justices are . . . to be knocked on the head . . . how are our laws ever to be carried into execution? . . . If there be no information, in consequence . . . laws made by the wisdom of Parliament . . . will all prove a dead letter.' As the magistrates filed out of the hall, none of them stopped to ponder the significance of the date. It was April Fools' Day, 1738.

The first special session was held two days later. It wasn't a particularly auspicious start. A woman called Martha Walker was committed to Bridewell. Two other precepts were sent out, but neither gin-seller could be found. The magistrates didn't give up, though. By the end of the month eighteen cases had been heard by the special sessions, and another thirty-three by Thomas De Veil in Thrift Street. Two gin-sellers had been discharged, eighteen paid the £10 fine, thirty were committed to Bridewell, and one escaped. Forty-two magistrates had taken part in the hearings (including James Oglethorpe, making a token appearance before he went back to Georgia). The constables had 'behav'd very well.' They were using new short staves, to make them less conspicuous when they were shepherding informers. As another way of avoiding attacks, the magistrates had also agreed to pay for informers to be picked up in hackney coaches.

It hadn't all been smooth going. A woman called Judith Walmsley went down for contempt of court after 'threatening the informers that she would wait their coming out.' But by the end of the month there was 'great unanimity among the Justices,' Nathaniel Blackerby reported to the Duke of Newcastle, 'who . . . can and will carry on this service with that duty and zeal as becomes them.'⁹

But duty and zeal weren't going to be enough. The clamp-down was about to run into trouble almost before it had started. Six weeks in, on 10 May, Roger Allen's case came up for trial.

The authorities probably thought the timing would work their way. The Enforcement Act received Royal Assent the same week. Maybe they thought that hanging Roger Allen would make a good example. Even so, there were some in the ministry who had twinges of doubt. The solicitor of the Treasury, Nicholas Paxton, was one of them, and he had a reputation for common sense. The way Paxton saw it, 'as the Ginn-Act was in the judgment of most people, a very severe law, it would look like doubling the severity of it, to make it become the subject of a capital prosecution, and therefore he was against it.'¹⁰ In the end it was Thomas De Veil himself who insisted Roger Allen's trial should go ahead. Maybe the Gin Act was starting to get to Thomas De Veil. Maybe he couldn't forget that quartern of urine. Maybe he just had it in for Roger Allen. The month after the riot he had sent down Allen's wife, Mary, for house-breaking.

To the authorities, after all, it seemed an open-and-shut case. You couldn't stage more of a riot than the trouble Roger Allen had fomented outside Thomas De Veil's house. He had ignored the Riot Act, threatened informers, and tried to assault a magistrate. A crowd of a thousand had watched him do it, and so had the court justice, peering out through the shutters. If there was anyone in London they could throw the book at, it was Roger Allen. To the authorities, it didn't seem as if anything could possibly go wrong.

Except that someone, somewhere, stumped up the cash for a defence lawyer. The lawyer could see exactly what Roger Allen's trial was about. He could see what the Gin Act was about; he could see what Londoners thought of prohibition, and Thomas De Veil, and informers, and what they were likely to think of Roger Allen. His first move was an objection 'to all Esquires being on the Jury.'[11] Most people saw the Gin Act as an attack by the rich on the poor. Roger Allen was going to be tried by a jury of the poor.

The defence didn't waste time querying the details of the case against Roger Allen. In a six-hour trial, as Thomas De Veil's biographer put it, 'the facts were incontestably proved.' They took a different tack instead. Roger Allen pleaded insanity. His old master swore 'he was so weak and silly he could be of no service to him in his trade, nor would he ever learn it.' Allen's mother 'depos[ed] he was *an idiot*, and *a silly weak fellow*.' The jury couldn't deny what had happened in Thrift Street, but they weren't being asked to. The defence had given them room for manoeuvre. After an hour's deliberation, Roger Allen was acquitted of all charges.

Public reaction was ecstatic. 'Westminster Hall was so full one might have walked on the people's heads,' reported the *London Evening Post*, 'and the mob on hearing of his being acquitted, were so insolent as to huzza for a considerable time, whilst the court was sitting. In the Hall Yard a set of butchers waited for the issue, and finding the fellow was acquitted, they rung him home with a peal upon their marrow-bones and cleavers.' That was the traditional fanfare of Londoners' disrespect. As for the hero of the moment, now legally classified insane, the crowd chaired him out of the hall and set him up on a wall in Old Palace Yard. Roger Allen decided to make a speech. He was feeling pleased with himself. He should have been on his way to Tyburn; instead, he was the hero of the hour. 'Gentlemen,' he said, 'I thank you very kindly for this honour, but the great liberty of mobbing a justice now and then (and my own life) had been certainly lost, if I had not had wit enough to prove myself a fool.'[12]

For the authorities, it was a devastating blow. They were supposed to be living in the Age of Oligarchy. They were defending the Riot Act, their main weapon of social control, and a recent law which was the subject of a vigorous enforcement drive. No one in London disputed what Roger Allen had done. And despite all that, they had failed to bring in a verdict against him. It was a blow to Thomas De Veil's prestige, and a blow for the clamp-down on the Gin Act. The Westminster magistrates tried to pick up the pieces a few days after the trial. Even before Allen's acquittal, two constables had had to abandon an arrest when some passers-by started shouting, '"Informers, Mob them,"' and 'followed the constables all the way to the Old Palace Yard calling out "Mob them, Mob them" several times.'[13] Now, the High Constable told the bench, 'on Allen's being acquitted the constables were afraid to go out with precepts as they had done, lest the populace, encouraged by his acquittal, should rise on them. And . . . the Excise Officer who [attends] the Justices . . . inform'd the bench that the witnesses were so terrified on Allen's acquittal that he could not prevail on many of them to appear as usual.' No gin-sellers were sent to Bridewell that day.

The authorities were in a hole, but all they did was keep digging. The next day, 1,000 copies of the Riot Act appeared on church doors all over Westminster.

It didn't make any difference. In late May the Riot Act was read again outside the special sessions of Middlesex Tower Division. A bad fortnight in late August saw three assaults on informers and constables. An informer in Swallow Street was stabbed. At the funeral of Pinchin, another informer, the body 'was attended to the grave by a great concourse of people, many of whom play'd on salt boxes, some on jews harps, and others diverted the company with marrow-bones and cleavers.'[14] Afterwards they made a fire and burned Pinchin in effigy.

There were other symptoms of protest as well. Some spirit-sellers insisted on going to Bridewell rather than pay the fine. When Mary Simpson of St George's Southwark was convicted, she couldn't pay the fine, 'but was so well·beloved in the neighbourhood, that the money was raised to save her from going to gaol.' Martha Walker, the first person to be convicted in Westminster special sessions, was the wife of a well·known publican in Henrietta Street, Covent Garden. The day after the magistrates sent her to Bridewell, 'a hundred of her neighbours went, some in coaches and others on foot and redeemed her, and brought her home . . . in triumph to her own house.'[15]

Even for those with no neighbours to save them, the Bridewells were losing their power to terrify. A magistrate speaker in Parlia· ment commented how he had 'within 12 days, sent above 40 of the poor creatures . . . to prisons of correction; but they did not seem to value that punishment, since they were always sure of being free in a short time, and of gaining their bread in the same way after they were free.'[16] And sometimes it seemed as if however many gin·sellers the magistrates locked up, there was always another one standing on the street corner. 'There have been about 100 committed by His Lordship,' reported the *London Evening Post* of proceedings in the City, 'and scarce a day passes without some informations of that nature, so that it may truly be called a *Hydra*.'[17] The Board of Excise had 'so great a number of informations depending . . . that their honours have determined to sit eight hours every day next week in order to finish their examinations.'[18] All they did was fill up the jails. Surrey Assizes reported, that summer, that its prisons were 'very sickly on account of the great number of prisoners there for selling spirituous liquors.'[19]

At the end of July, statistics were published for the numbers of prosecutions made since the clamp·down began. 'We hear that claims have been already made . . . for near 4,000 persons sent to the several Bridewells,' reported the *London Daily Post*. Three thousand gin-sellers were said to have paid the £10 fine. Added to nearly 5,000 convicted by the Excise Commissioners, the rumour in mid-summer was that in London alone, 'there has been about 12,000 persons in all convicted on this Act.'[20]

Someone was massaging the figures. The magistrates hadn't sent down anything like 4,000 people, and the Duke of Newcastle knew it – he was reading their monthly reports. The authorities were failing to control the gin problem, so they had resorted to spin.

Some fell for it. 'The populace are behaving now in a more quiet and peaceable manner,' commented *Read's Weekly Journal*, 'since they are prevented getting at that intoxicating liquor; nor are the streets infested with street robbers and drunken people as before, the publick selling it in brandy shops being pretty well over, few venturing now to sell to strangers, but to those only whom they think they can confide in.'[21] The trouble was the authorities ended up fooling themselves. Even the magistrates started to sound upbeat about the clamp-down. In June, Nathaniel Blackerby reported to Newcastle 'that there has been no rioting or mobbing during this month's service ... The practice of selling spirituous liquors is chiefly restrain'd to private places, very few selling now in open shops.' The next month there was a swoop on 'houses and places where spirituous liquors are sold by persons concealing themselves by the name of Puss and Mew.' Philip Cholmondly, High Constable of Holborn, reported that he 'dispersed great numbers of idle disorderly persons whom he had found so assembled, and had caused seven Puss and Mew houses to be shut up.'[22] With a few successes like that under their belts, the magistrates started to claim victory. Westminster saw fewer than half the number of gin-sellers in October as in former months. In his report, Nathaniel Blackerby proudly asked 'whether from hence it may not justly be inferr'd that the zeal and diligence of the Justices in Westminster for the publick service in these prosecutions has not had in some measure the desir'd effect in checking the publick selling of spirituous liquors.'[23]

He was whistling in the wind. Spirit production had dipped when prohibition came in, but by 1738 production was up 28 per cent on the previous year. Someone, somewhere, was still drinking gin. If fewer gin-sellers were ending up in court, it wasn't because Londoners had taken to elderflower wine. There had to be another explanation.

Some people thought Madam Geneva had gone into the country to lie low. Back in May the *Daily Post* had remarked how 'the retailers of spirituous liquors multiply . . . in the towns and villages near London, as Stockwell, Mewington, Dulwich, etc.'[24] Five years later, Bishop Secker would claim that during prohibition, the distillers 'sent [gin] where they could in the country,' with the result that 'the disease' of gin-drinking was driven 'from the heart into the extremities.'[25]

Others thought Madam Geneva had just gone underground, into the tortuous slums of St Giles's where neither constables nor magistrates could find much trace of her. 'Those crowds,' one commentator thought, 'which were daily and nightly seen drinking and enflaming themselves, carousing and debauching in petty gin-shops . . . are now to be found in just the same abominable pickle in cellars, garrets, back-houses, and hutts, where they are kept without suffering them to go out into the street, in order to screen them, whilst in that filthy condition, from public view.'[26]

The explanation may have been even simpler. The magistrates were getting tired. They were amateurs, after all. No one was paying them. When the clamp-down started in April, fifteen magistrates had attended each session. The average hearing attracted nine. By October that average was down to four. After October, when sixty-nine made the journey to Bridewell, commitments would run swiftly downhill. The early eighteenth·century justice system had simply worn itself out.

But in the end, maybe it was the informers who finally killed off the authorities' chances of enforcing the Gin Act. Faced with public anger and the threat of attack, informers started to change their tactics. They moved outside London, where their faces were less well·known. In mid·May, distillers in Bristol found themselves targeted by 'two women, strangers, who belong to a gang of informers now harbouring about this city and parts adjacent.' Informers were reported to have appeared at 'Highgate, and other places near London.' Bath was troubled by 'a vile fellow, who . . . inform[ed] against fifteen persons for retailing spirituous liquors.'[27]

At least those travelling informers were still working inside the law. Faced with the risk of a mugging – or worse – if they denounced gin·sellers openly, others came up with a different tactic. They started to blackmail them instead. In late April it was reported that the Lord Mayor 'committed several persons to gaol, for extorting money from people to stifle informations which they were going to lodge against them.'[28] The problem of crooked informers soon became too obvious for the authorities to ignore. In August, the Duke of Newcastle had to write to magistrates, exhorting them to prevent 'the great abuses and perjuries committed by informers against the supposed retailers of spirituous liquors.'[29]

It didn't work. In October, an advert appeared in the papers asking readers to send in stories of informer abuses. The results were compiled into a pamphlet and published. It made depressing reading. William Tyson and his wife ran the Red Cow in Hammersmith. They were charged under the Gin Act when Elizabeth Gardiner, an occasional customer of theirs, swore she had been sold a dram of gin by Mrs Tyson on 4 July 1737. A friend of Gardiner, Charles Darley, had been with her and backed up her story. But at the subsequent trial, under intense questioning from a suspicious magistrate, it had come out that both Gardiner and Darley belonged to a gang of informers. Gardiner had met them '[at] the Crown in one of the seven streets*, in the Parish of St Giles-in-the-Fields.' When Darley asked her if she knew anyone who sold liquors, she 'told them that she owed Mrs Tyson, at the Red-Cow in Hammersmith, half a crown. And the said Darley said *Have you had no liquor there lately, why do not you inform against her?*'[30]

Thomas Pepper ran a chandler's shop in St Botolph-without-Aldersgate. A regular informer call'd Mary Pocock claimed that on a Saturday night in May, about nine o'clock, 'I went to Mr Pepper's shop, as I usually did, and . . . call'd for a halfpenny brick,** and a ha'p'orth of new cheese. Mr Pepper serv'd me; nobody was in the shop but he, then I call'd for a quartern of gin; he serv'd me, and I paid him 3 halfpence for it.' Pocock, a self-confessed gin-addict ('I lost my husband and children by it'), filled her evidence with impressive detail: 'There was a candle in the shop; and on one side of the shop lies coals, and salt in the other. He brought the bottle from behind the counter, and went into a narrow passage, between the kitchen and the parlour, and there he serv'd me with his own hands.' But in Thomas Pepper she had picked on a determined man. Pepper had paid a £100 fine earlier in prohibition, but had stopped selling gin when the clamp-down began in April. One of the witnesses he called was his lodger, a Temple Bar watchman who testified 'that from the beginning of April, to this present day, there were no spirituous liquors in the house.' A carpenter who had been doing some work in the shop also backed up the story. Pepper's father dolefully gave evidence that 'he had not a drop

* Seven Dials.
** A loaf.

for ME. If I wanted it I was forced to go out and get it where I could.'[31]

*A Short History of the Gin Act*, appearing in October, supplied even more tales of informer skulduggery. 'Wretches not worth a groat,' its author complained, 'women with hardly a petticoat to cover their nakedness, and men as destitute and dissolute as ever crawled upon the earth, have been admitted to swear innocent people out of their bread.' There were some signs that informing was being taken over by organised crime. In August 'nine persons, men and women,' were overheard in a private room in a Hammersmith pub, 'plotting and contriving to lay false informations against divers people of that town.' In September, 'Sarah Clewly, an infamous person under confinement in Bridewell in Southwark for perjury, in falsely swearing an information against an innocent person for retailing spirituous liquors, was detected in offering a bad guinea to be changed, and being carried before a Justice, upon examination confessed she had been concerned among a gang of coiners, and discovered several accomplices.'[32]

Informers had alienated the public and dragged the whole enforcement effort into disrepute. But for the authorities, there was worse news to come. As autumn set in, an even darker rumour started going the rounds. The whole apparatus of prohibition was about to be undermined. The talk was of corruption deep inside the Excise Office.

Excise corruption wasn't new. There was always the danger of Excise men getting to know their patch too well. But prohibition introduced new temptations. In February 1737 John Lloyd, a surveyor in the 13th Division, lost his job for 'proposing a person to be prosecuted for offences which upon examination appeared to be vexatious, frivolous and groundless.'[33] In December the same year, when two gin-sellers were convicted

by Justice Engier at St Thomas's, one of the informers confessed they had been plotting the entrapment for a month. They
had been 'influenced by a superior Officer of Excise.' The same
'superior Officer of Excise' would get more publicity than he
wanted in January, when the *London Evening Post* reported that
he 'has been instrumental in convicting to the number of 96
persons ... whereby, at £5 penalty for each person, his share
will amount to £480.' That, as the paper commented acidly,
was 'a fine sum raised out of the ruin of several poor families.' The Officer would be dismissed in February for 'indirect
practices.'[34]

But even that scale of malpractice paled into insignificance
beside what the *Short History of the Gin Act* revealed in October
1738. 'The Act against spirituous liquors,' the author thundered,
'has produced a villain ... never, God be praised, heard of in
a Christian country before ... This man ha[s] a large banditti
which [is] kept in weekly pay, to swear against whomsoever he
pick[s] out for sacrifice; some [have] twelve, others, more expert in
perjury, [have] fourteen shillings a week ... we are told this fellow,
who is well known at a certain Office has been concerned ... in
not much less than 4,000 informations.'

A common thread ran through many of the stories which the
public had sent in about informers. In her confession, Elizabeth
Gardiner had testified that 'one Edward Parker told her, that she
should have a guinea for every one convicted, that paid the money,
and half a guinea for such as ... were sent to Bridewell.' When
Mary Pocock laid her accusation against Thomas Pepper 'she had
gone to the Lord Mayor with Edward Parker, an Excise Officer.'
The Officer's job 'was chiefly to testify to the character of those
before the justices, many of whom ... readily took his word.'
Up in front of the magistrates, the landlady of the White Lion
found that 'her innocence and defence were not worth a straw.

The informer had a *Parker* to stand up for his reputation, and the credibility of his testimony.'

Edward Parker didn't look like the worst villain in Christendom. Two years earlier he had been a low-ranking officer in Candles (3rd Division), covering Wire for an officer on secondment to Hair Powder. He was on £30 a year, and not even his bosses had heard of him. But when the Gin Act came in, the Commissioners of Excise needed extra officers on the streets, and Edward Parker was an obvious candidate. At Michaelmas 1736, he was moved over to 'be employed on the retailers of spirituous liquors.'[35]

Edward Parker could see there were opportunities in prohibition, but to start with he couldn't work out how to make them pay. In August 1737 he ran into trouble. He and his partner, Waters, went into the King's Bench prison one Friday, looking for anyone who would sell them gin. 'By some stratagem,' as *Read's Weekly Journal* reported, '[they] got a dram of gin of the poor tapster.' But they needed details as well, and that was where the sting went wrong. 'Not knowing [the tapster's] name, and endeavouring to find it out, they were discovered, upon which the prisoners ducked and pumped them to such a degree, that 'tis feared that one, if not both, will die of the bruises they got there.'[36]

Edward Parker didn't die. But when he was beaten up again, in November 1737, he started thinking. There was no point risking his own skin going into gin-shops. He was better off paying informers to do it for him. He might not able to pick up the whole £5 reward for himself, but he could still take the lion's share. The informers would be paid off. It didn't matter whether their victims had ever sold a dram of gin in their lives. Elizabeth Gardiner later revealed that she got her reward 'whether she had liquor or not.' Edward Parker's role would be to spot targets, arrange the informers, and then use his office to make sure magistrates accepted them as 'credible witnesses'.

Some of them didn't. Clifford William Phillips, the Tower Hamlets magistrate who had helped put down the East End riots in summer 1736, was well-regarded by almost everybody. Lord Chancellor Hardwicke was surprised, therefore, to receive a complaint against him in November 1737. It came from a group of Excise Officers led by Edward Parker. They claimed that Clifford William Phillips – who happened to be a distiller – had encouraged gin-sellers to break the Act. He had 'done his utmost to discourage all endeavours to bring the offenders to justice by abusing and threatening not only the Excise and Peace Officers, but also a gentleman in the Commission of the Peace.'[37] He had protected a gin-seller called Mary Bryan from prosecution. Most important of all, he had questioned the veracity of one of Parker's informers. In the subsequent row, Clifford William Phillips denied that he had ever pointed at Edward Parker and said 'that such scoundrels and rascals . . . made the Excise stink in every person's nostrils,' although later events would prove him right. This time Edward Parker had bitten off more than he could chew – there were any number of people ready to testify to Phillips' good name. But he had demonstrated exactly how far he was prepared to go.

And it wasn't long before he found another way to get round the problem of suspicious magistrates. In April 1738, when Westminster magistrates announced their special thrice-weekly sessions to clamp down on gin-selling, they requested that an Excise man should be in regular attendance 'to enquire . . . into the characters of the persons who give evidence upon the informations.'[38] There were no prizes for guessing who got the job.

Edward Parker didn't mind testifying to the character of any informer; most of them were on his payroll. By then he was running a network which spread all over town. When the gin-sellers were dragged off to Bridewell, and the informer pocketed his reward, ninety per cent of it went to Edward Parker. His role in

Westminster special sessions was a licence to print money. Over the next eight months, 300 men and women were convicted by Westminster magistrates, and every one put £4 in Edward Parker's pocket.

It couldn't last – not with rumours swirling round Westminster and his name splashed all over tracts and pamphlets. The end came quickly. On 4 December Edward Parker didn't turn up for work. Nathaniel Blackerby adjourned the session but two days later there was still no sign of Parker. 'About the beginning of December,' Blackerby later reported, 'the . . . Justices [were] credibly informed that . . . Edward Parker, the usual Informer, and Joseph Porter, who . . . acted as Clerk at the . . . meetings . . . had made great and illegal advantages to themselves by these prosecutions.' They weren't just pocketing rewards from the informers. What sunk Edward Parker in the end was a different scam. While half of the gin-sellers' £10 went to the informer, the other half was supposed to be passed on to their parish to pay for poor relief. Edward Parker had been embezzling it. It was when magistrates asked to see accounts that he called in sick.

But he knew the game was up. This time he had pushed his luck too far. On 20 December the magistrates' new clerk recorded a terse minute that Edward Parker was dead. *Read's Weekly Journal* filled in the background. By then, 'there were several bills of indictments found against him . . . by the Grand Jury for the County of Middlesex, for subornation of perjury. He took the same much to heart . . . which was the occasion of his death.' His funeral had to be kept private 'for fear the mob should tear his corpse to pieces.' Edward Parker was said to have had more than 1,500 gin-sellers informed against. After the funeral, his executors 'laid their claim at the Excise Office, for £1,535 as due to the deceased for informations against persons selling of spirituous liquors contrary to law.'[39] It didn't do him any good. He barely left enough even to pay for the funeral.

The *London Evening Post* had the last word on the career of prohibition's Godfather. '"Tis said he died in a miserable condition,' it reported, 'as such rascals generally do.'[40]

By the end of 1738, the attempt to enforce the Gin Act was winding down. Informers had been running out of time even before Edward Parker's death. When Richard Dyer and Mary Norton, one of the most active informer teams, trapped a Clerkenwell woman on 16 December, the court refused to believe their evidence. As Dyer was leaving the court, the *London Evening Post* described how '[he] was taken [on] a warrant from the Lord Mayor, for an assault and suspicion of a robbery, and by him committed to Wood Street compter.' By the end of December, most of the papers agreed that 'the business of informing seems . . . to be pretty much at a stand.'[41]

Informers hadn't just run out of time. They had run out of cash as well. Asked a few years later for an account of the fines they had collected during prohibition, the Commissioners of Excise reported that they had taken in almost £9,000, but 'no part of these fines have been paid into the Exchequer, the whole having been expended in . . . rewards to informers.' Prohibition ran at a loss. On 21 December 1738, the *Gentleman's Magazine* reported that over 400 informers were still waiting for their rewards, 'the Commissioners . . . having no money in their hands.'[42] No one was going to risk death for an Excise IOU.

At the peak of the clamp-down Westminster magistrates had convicted fifty gin-sellers a month. In December they convicted eight. There would be no special sessions after January 1739. By July 1739 only one for the sixty-seven commitments to Tothill Field Bridewell would be for gin-selling.

It wasn't just the magistrates who were tired. The papers were tired of the Gin Act as well. When the clamp-down started they had reported every magistrates' session in detail, but the reports soon dwindled to regular round-ups. By December their attention had switched elsewhere.

There was plenty else for them to concentrate on. In August that year, twenty-five years of peace finally started to crumble, and from then on the papers could talk of nothing but remobilisation. Gin-drinkers and gin-sellers alike were pressed into the service. Informers were swept up as well. 'Last Thursday,' reported a gleeful *London Evening Post* on 5 August, 'a victualler in St James's Street, being informed against for selling spirituous liquors, and having paid the penalty, the informer went into a house in the neighbourhood to meet others of the profession to divide the spoil. The victualler by accident met with a press-gang, and telling them that several young fellows had hid themselves in that house for fear of being pressed, the Lieutenant immediately entered the house, and pressed them into his Majesty's service.'[43]

The enemy was Spain, and the excuse was a spate of attacks on British vessels by Spanish customs boats. There were rumours of outrages. As evidence of what he had suffered, a Captain Jenkins had brought back his severed ear in a jar.

The public were ecstatic about the war. *Read's Weekly Journal* found it 'impossible to express the joy which appeared among the generality of people on Thursday, upon the hopes of a war with the Spaniards, to revenge the robberies, murders and insults committed on the British subjects for years past.'[44] Only Sir Robert Walpole failed to join the general rejoicing. Just two months earlier he had lost his new wife – and long-term mistress – Maria Skerrett, after a miscarriage. The end of peace was yet another blow. 'It is your war,' he told Newcastle, 'and I wish you well of it.' It wasn't just that he longed for peace. The war was another sign of the opposition's strength. Sir Robert had been pushed into it by the same coalition which had first come together over Excise, and then to attack the Gin Act. Independent Whigs proclaimed themselves 'patriots' and combined with the Tories. In October, with the support of Sir John Barnard and Micaiah Perry, 153 merchants from the City of London added their weight with a petition against Spanish privateers. The Prime Minister's political confidence would never quite recover. The next year, in a torrid Westminster by-election, ministerial candidates would be ousted in favour of the war's first hero, Admiral Vernon, and the ministry would resort to shutting down the poll. The government candidate for Lord Mayor, Sir George Champion, would be voted down by the Court of Common Hall. Walpole's power was waning.

For Hardwicke, in spring 1737, it had been beneath the dignity of Parliament to speculate about the motives of rioters. That confidence hadn't lasted long. Only two years later, the Duke of Newcastle would warn the same Lord Chancellor that 'if we go on despising what people think and say, we shall not have it long in our power to direct what measures will be taken.'[45]

There was only one consolation for Sir Robert Walpole. The war was a smokescreen behind which the Gin Act could quietly be forgotten. At the end of August Sir Joseph Jekyll had died, aged seventy. In the next session there would be no one left in Parliament to keep the Gin Act alive. Prohibition in England could end not with a bang but a whimper. It would be another five years before it was formally repealed, but long before then any attempt at enforcing it had been quietly dropped. As Thomas De Veil's biographer delicately put it, 'it was at last found necessary to soften the severity of [the Gin Act], by becoming relax in the execution of it.' The 'boldest experiment . . . ever made in a free country' had failed.

*    *    *

Prohibition would be remembered most of all for its absurdities. It had set out to save society from crime and insubordination, but achieved the very opposite. The Gin Act had turned law-abiding citizens into criminals. Shopkeepers who had never seen themselves as law-breakers had been carted off to Bridewell and whipped. The law had alienated a whole sector of public opinion. Even those honest citizens who had done their best to stay legal ended up walking away in disgust. In March 1738, Amos Wenman, one of the few who actually took out a £50 licence, was convicted by the Excise Office on a technicality. John Ashley, the only other original licence-holder, was caught out the same way. If you could take out a licence and still be convicted, what was the point in obeying the law? In late July, the few legal licence-holders walked away from the Gin Act. They wrote to the Commissioners of Excise, petitioning 'that they may surrender up their licences, the same being attended with great incumbrances and ill conveniences as not to be surmounted.'[46]

The drink trade had been taken out of the mainstream and handed over to organised crime. 'The business has been transferred,' explained the *Short History of the Gin Act*, 'from those who have legal settlements, pay all taxes, do all offices, to those who have no settlement at all ... wretches, who leave no persuasives untried to tempt and prevail upon people into all the abandoned excesses this law was passed to prevent.' Reformers had thought they could stamp out crime by outlawing Madam Geneva; they had achieved the very opposite.

Then there was the absurdity of the parish money. Half of each fine was supposed to go to the gin-seller's parish, to pay for poor relief. It was a tidy sum; a year into prohibition, St Anne's Soho was getting almost fifteen per cent of its income from gin fines. But one of the results of the Gin Act, as one writer pointed out, was to 'expose ... numbers of unhappy people, who before the selling of spirituous liquors ... became a crime, had got a livelihood thereby, to be distressed, beggared, and sent to prison.' Distressed and beggared, gin-sellers had to turn to the parish for relief. The gin fines simply went round in circles. In summer 1738, parishes even began to short-circuit the system. 'Some churchwardens,' magistrates were told, 'instead of applying ... convictions money to the use of the poor of their parish, have returned the same back to the party or parties so convicted on pretence of their being poor.'[47]

The Gin Act discriminated between rich and poor. It drove a wedge deep into society. The *London Magazine* had warned what would happen right from the start. 'The social virtue and liberty of the people,' it declared, 'must always depend upon a mutual confidence between the rich and the poor, between those in authority and those under authority ... When a law is made for restraining the poor only, from being guilty of ... a particular sort of drunkenness, which is equally heinous in the rich, what can the poor think of such a law?' There was only one thing they could think. They had no choice but to opt out altogether. 'It will introduce among them,' the paper warned, 'a total neglect for the public good and a regard for their own private interest only.'[48]

But it was the crimes of informers which would stick in the memory the longest. 'We have, sir,' concluded one critic in the 1738 parliamentary debates, 'seen very little reformation in the manners and very little alteration in the constitutions of the common people since the law against retailing of spirituous liquors took place; but we have heard of many instances where the magistrates enforcing 'em has produced the most flagrant perjury, and brought many persons to utter ruin.'[49]

Whatever else the Gin Act achieved, it certainly didn't end the problem of gin. Spirit production had briefly dipped when prohibition first came in, but from then on it soared ever higher. No one pretended that Madam Geneva had gone away. 'The walking dram-sellers,' wrote the author of *A Short History of the Gin Act* in October 1738, 'the itinerant vendors of liquors ... infest not only every street, but almost every door ... to say nothing of what is transacted upon the water; all the foot-paths, lanes and highways around the town are filled with them; and no less than seventy, eighty or a hundred of these have been counted at an execution, at a fair, and at several other places of like resort.' His conclusion was simple. ''Tis notoriously known,' he finished, 'the excessive drinking of spirituous liquors ... is little or nothing abated among the meaner sort of people.'

In the end there were only two real beneficiaries of the Gin Act. One was Thomas Wilson. The ambitious young cleric had met Sir Joseph Jekyll through the reform campaign, and it was Jekyll, in the end, who got him the job he wanted. In May 1737, Wilson heard 'that Dr Watson of St Stephen's Walbrook was very ill.' He 'ventured to ask the Master of the Rolls to beg that living of my Lord Chancellor for me;'[50] Jekyll agreed. The only problem was that Dr Watson took a whole six months to die. On 13 September, 'a message from town that Dr Watson was supposed to be dead carried me in some hurry to London,' Wilson reported; but he added crossly: 'found that he had been very ill, but not dead.' Thomas Wilson spent most of the time camped out in the Master of the Rolls' apartments. Dr Watson didn't finally expire until the last day of November. Then Wilson 'waited upon the Master of the Rolls who sent immediately to the Lord Chancellor, which gave me good hopes I shall succeed.' It was almost the last entry in his diary. In spring 1738, as worried magistrates struggled to cope with the consequences of the Gin Act, he was installed in the lucrative living of St Stephen's.

The only other winner was Madam Geneva herself. She never

did leave London during prohibition. There were plenty of places for her to hide — in back-alleys and poor men's rooms, in tumbledown workshops and attics, in the hubbub of markets, or four flights up a Rag Fair tenement. She must have regarded the antics of MPs and magistrates with a faint amusement as they totted up the gin-sellers they had sent to Bridewell. She knew the only statistic which really mattered . . .

In the seven years the Gin Act was in force, spirit production rose by more than a third.

# CHAPTER THIRTEEN

---

# WOMEN

There is only one picture of Madam Geneva.

She is disguised as one of her devotees, sitting on some broken steps somewhere in St Giles's. Around her is the chaos and despair of all slums everywhere: tumbledown buildings and pawnbrokers' shops, crowds on the streets, beggars in the gutter. But Madam Geneva is too drunk to notice any of it. She is in a world of her own. Her fingers fumble for some snuff. She's even forgotten about the child on her lap. It takes a moment to realise what's going on: the child is falling off the steps onto the paving below. Not even maternal instinct has survived the ravages of gin.

Nor has shame. Madam Geneva's blouse hangs open. Sometimes she has to take to the streets to pay for her habit; her legs are covered with the sores of syphilis. She might have been a beauty once, but now her hair is filthy and dishevelled, her lips slack, her cheeks sunken. No one could gaze on that goggling, unfocused face with any feeling of tenderness.

There are other people on the steps as well, although the woman is too drunk to take any notice of them. Just behind her right shoulder a carpenter is pawning the tools of his trade to buy gin. Below her, a ballad-seller has passed out. There are men in the background, too, but when Hogarth drew *Gin Lane*, in 1751, he was in no doubt who had to be its centrepiece. It had to be Madam Geneva herself. It had to be a woman.

Or what had once been a woman. What William Hogarth drew was the perversion of woman, the symbol of everything a woman ought not to be. She was the degeneration of mother into child-killer, beauty into something filthy, wife into shameless whore. A contemporary gloss on the print minced no words. 'If a woman accustoms herself to dram-drinking,' it warned, 'she . . . becomes the most miserable as well as the most contemptible creature on earth.' Looks went first but honour followed. 'For so sure as she habituates herself to drinking, so sure it is she will never be satisfied without it, whatever means she uses to procure a supply . . . thro' mere necessity [she] becomes a street-walker, and at last an abandon'd prostitute.' As for her children, it was they who paid the heaviest price of all. 'So indulgent are these tender mothers,' the writer went on, 'that to stop their little gaping mouths, they will pour down a spoonful of their own delightful cordial. What numbers of little creatures, who, had they grown up to maturity, might have proved useful members of society, are lost, murder'd, I may truly say, by these inhuman wretches, their mothers!'[1]

Hogarth didn't draw just any woman; he drew Judith Defour. The woman on the steps in Gin Lane wasn't a figure of pity but one to inspire fear and loathing. She wasn't only destroying herself, she was spreading her foul disease among London's men. She was turning the world's greatest city into an object of disgust. She was robbing the nation of the workers who ought one day to enrich it, the soldiers and sailors who should protect its shores.

Madam Geneva, Mother Gin; from the moment she appeared on the streets, Londoners always recognised their new patron as a woman. A hundred years later she would be Mother's Ruin. Her followers were women as well. They were the *London Spy*'s 'tattered assembly of fat motherly flat-caps . . . with every one her nipperkin of warm ale and brandy.' Another satirist gave them names: Dorothy Addle-Brains and Sarah Suckwell, Jenny Pisspot and Rebecca Rag-Manners.

Beer was always a man's drink. For a start, it needed John Bull's stout frame to down a gallon of warm, sour liquid. But it was more than that. Beer was drunk in the alehouse, a male enclave whose windows were steamed up with the fug of male tradition. Women weren't shut out, but when they crossed the threshold of an alehouse, they knew they were entering a man's world. By contrast, gin was drunk in places where women went. 'Almost at every herb-stall,' wrote a 1751 commentator, '[women] will find a private room backwards, where they may take their glass in secret very comfortably.'[2] It was sold on street corners, in the chandlers' shops where women bought their everyday groceries. With the arrival of Madam Geneva, women suddenly had access to a drug which wasn't loaded with male tradition, one which was easy for them to take, and which was available in the places they frequented.

Besides, women didn't just drink gin; they sold it as well. When the 1738 clamp-down on gin began, three-quarters of the gin-sellers hauled up before the magistrates' special sessions were women. A hundred years earlier, the bawdy alewife had been a stock character of comedy – as she had been for centuries. But ale-selling in the early eighteenth century was being taken over by large brewers and well-established victuallers. Tied houses, owned by big brewers, were appearing. Women were being squeezed out. Instead, the old alewife had turned into the market-woman with a gin bottle hidden in her petticoats. For many poor women and widows, selling gin was the only way they could scrape a living off the London streets.

And so, sipping gin in shops or dispensing it from barrows, women became the public face of the Gin Craze. When reformers had attacked drinking in the past, women had been victims. For Thomas Dekker, back in 1603, ale-drinkers left 'their wives . . . starving at home and their ragged children begging abroad.'[3] With the arrival of spirits all that changed. Women became villains instead. If more women than men were swept into Bridewell during the 1738 clamp-down, it wasn't only because most gin-sellers were women, or that women were easier targets than men for the informers. For magistrates, the gin-swilling, gin-selling woman was far more of a threat than her male counterpart. It was frightening enough to watch poor men abandon their roles as labourers and soldiers. Even worse was the thought of what a drunken woman might do when Madam Geneva dissolved her shame and loosened her morals. Knocking back drams outside the pawnbroker's shop, a woman discarded all the standards of behaviour which society had set out for her: her obedience, her humility, even her chastity.

Her chastity most of all. Sex had always been top of the reformers' agenda. 'It has been a common thing,' the Royal Proclamation lamented in 1738, 'to see men and women lie under . . . bulks, even in the daytime, so drunk, as not to be capable of standing . . . Women have been seen exposing their sex in such a condition, that 'twas an offence to every modest eye.' Every gin-shop, Thomas Secker added a few years later, 'had a back shop or cellar, strewed every morning with fresh straw, where those that got drunk were thrown, men and women promiscuously together: here they might commit what wickedness they pleased.' It was drunken women, of course, who cursed the town with the sexual health scourge of the early eighteenth century: syphilis. In the minds of reformers, sex, vice and retribution were inextricably linked.

Reformers' fears were inspired by transformations: the servant metamorphosed into master, the poor man into gentleman. The idea that women might abandon their natural station was the most frightening of all. But suddenly women were reeling drunkenly out of chandlers' shops, and selling drams on street corners. Frightened reformers could see women embracing all too many of the age's changes. They turned up in Exchange Alley to speculate on the markets. Thirty-five of the eighty-eight investors in the South Sea Company's second money subscription were women (speculation, after all, was one of the few ways women could make money; like gin, it was new; there were no traditional barriers to keep them out). When Hogarth drew his Lottery print in 1724, it was the figures of women who presided, and women – one dressed unnaturally in men's clothing – who pulled the tickets from the wheels.

It was all part of a pattern. Reformers were scared of the changes of the age, and the most frightening possibility of all was a change in women. They wasted no time in slamming shut the lid of Pandora's box. Increasingly, women were to be confined to a smaller, safer world. As the eighteenth century progressed, fewer and fewer women went to work. And a vapourish, delicate creature was born, obsessed with her virtue, pious, unadventurous and chaste. Moll Flanders was consigned to the unruly past. The future belonged to Pamela.

In all of their campaigns, it wasn't only poor women that reformers were concerned about – the market-women and servants, or the bedraggled prostitute on the steps in St Giles's. They were also worried about virtue closer to home.

Daniel Defoe started it. 'I was infinitely satisfied with my wife,' wrote his Colonel Jack, 'who was, indeed, the best-humoured woman in the world, and a most accomplished beautiful creature – indeed, perfectly well bred, and had not one ill quality about her.'[4] That was until Colonel Jack's wife fell ill. But the medicine she took, like most eighteenth-century medicines, contained spirits. Addiction to prescribed drugs had arrived. 'During her illness and weakness,' the Colonel went on, 'her nurse pressed her, whenever she found herself faint ... to take this cordial, and that dram, till it became necessary to keep her alive, and gradually increased to a habit, so that it was no longer her physic but her food ... She came at last to a dreadful height, that ... she would be drunk in her dressing-room before eleven o'clock in the morning ... In short, my beautiful, good-humoured, modest, well-bred wife, grew a beast, a slave to strong liquor, and would be drunk at her own table, nay, in her own closet by herself, till she lost her beauty, her shape, her manners, and at last her virtue.' Eighteen months later she was dead.

If drinking among the poor was the main target of the Gin Panic, drinking among middle-class women came a close second. 'Wherever the tea-kettle is, there must the dram-bottle be,' warned the *Tavern Scuffle* in 1726. 'One succeeds the other as naturally as the night does the day; when a woman once takes to drinking, I give her over for lost, she then neglects husband, children, family, and all for her darling liquor.' Thomas Wilson would follow the same line in *Distilled Spirituous Liquors the Bane of the Nation*. He turned to middle-class women in his second edition, not without qualms. 'My mind is wounded but to think of imputing any share of this depravity to them,' he fluttered. 'The subject [is] too delicate to be insisted upon.' Not that that stopped Thomas Wilson. 'I must, however, just observe, that it is always attended with the most terrible consequences, to their posterity, as well as to themselves. That most excellent part of the human species, whose principal glory is their affection to their innocent infants, would do well to reflect upon the shockingness of a fault, which entails misery upon their harmless progeny as long as they live.'

Thomas Wilson gave examples, and they weren't poor women. One was 'a lady of good fortune, whose family and husband a friend of mine intimately knows.' She 'began with Barbados waters.'* But when her husband locked the drinks cupboard, 'she sunk into a taste for the lowest English spirits she could procure.' This lady had only one child, 'and [she] was determined, by a well-intended tenderness, to suckle this herself.' The result was a warning to all mothers. 'The poison it had sucked in before and after its birth, from its unhappy mother, was so prevalent, that all the art of physic, all the care of its nurse, could not recover the mischief, and clothe its little half-dried bones, with aught but a shrivelled sallow skin. It has now the look of an old withered baby, its skin loose and wrinkled . . . [It] lives, if we may say lives, by the help of art, a miserable memento of its mother's unnatural habit.' The mother, as Thomas Wilson sorrowfully told his readers, was now dying of consumption.

The middle-class wife drinking at home had joined the gallery of reformers' villains. In January 1737 the *Grub Street Journal* even suggested a ban on selling spirits to women.[5] Later that year, the *Universal Spectator* ran an exposé of dram-drinking in women. 'When I behold the woman . . . who still is the delight of my heart,' wailed one wretched witness, 'degraded into the most infamous habit of drinking; when I view those eyes that were wont to sparkle with inviting lustre, with awkward goggling betray an unmeaning look; when I see deadness in her features, folly in her behaviour, her tongue faltering, her breath tainted, her health impaired, my concern, like her debasement, is inexpressible.'[6]

By 1751, when the Gin Panic next flared up, the stereotype of the middle-class female dram-drinker was everywhere. 'The wives of genteel mechanicks,' noted one author, describing a day in the life of London, 'under pretence of going to prayers in their

* Rum.

apartments, take a nap and a dram, after which they chew lemon peel to prevent being smelt.'[7] 'How does she behave in her family?' asked another tract on these secret tipplers. 'The poor children are kicked and tumbl'd about like so many footballs ... She gets rid on them as soon as she can, by packing them away to school with a bit of bread and butter in their hands.'[8]

In 1750 Eliza Haywood even produced *A Present for Women Addicted to Drinking, adapted to all the different stations in life, from a Lady of Quality to a Common Servant.* 'The prodigious progress made by this vice of female drinking within these few years,' she protested, 'is so incontestibly notorious, that the propriety and usefulness of the treatise cannot be disputed.' Eliza Haywood knew exactly whom she was trying to save. Her examples included 'a young woman of quality ... a gentleman's daughter ... a young gentlewoman of small fortune ... daughter of a middling tradesman ... the wife of a clergyman ... the dreadful effects of this vice in a married Lady of Quality.' For each, she provide advice and a terrible example. The gentleman's daughter would be tyrannised by servants who discover her habit. The 'married Lady of Quality' ('Lady Lucy') 'was the daughter of a very great man, and the sister of a greater, but her vices made her odious, and at the same time, ridiculous. She sought at last to take shelter in what had brought her misfortunes upon her; she drank to drive away thought; she did it effectually, she drank herself to death.'

Eliza Haywood was more sensitive than most reformers. She worried about how to draw drinkers' attention to her tract. It was easy enough with servants, harder with genteel boozers; still, 'a method may be found of dropping it in a closet, or a toilet.' She offered advice on how to kick the habit, which was more than the Societies for Reformation of Manners had ever done. Eliza Haywood 'knew a gentleman that cured his sister by furnishing her with romances.' For other 'sipping misses' she suggested 'painting, japanning, colouring of prints, or whatever else will fix the attention, and take off that inclination for indolence which made way for the other vice.'

With a role-model like Pamela and a life of japanning and colouring in prints, any sane woman would take to the bottle sooner or later. Middle-class women were on the way towards a vicious spiral. Debilitating role-models created debilitating habits. Laudanum, Mother's Ruin and the teapot full of sherry were only just around the corner.

The woman drinker was a threat. She was a threat to society, to her family, and to herself. She was a threat to her husband and children. Fallen onto the streets and infected with syphilis, she was a threat to other women, for the whore infected the rakish husband, who carried the poison back to his family. The middle-class woman who drank endangered her own servants by encouraging them to take up the habit themselves. In turn, gossiping in the chandler's shop, the servant ruined her mistress by spreading the secrets of the household around the neighbourhood. Reformers weren't short of reasons to castigate Madam Geneva and the women who followed her. Religion, morality, patriotism and regard for society all recoiled in horror from that slack-lipped, goggling figure on the steps in St Giles's.

But as if that wasn't enough, the doctors were ready to weigh in as well. It wasn't just immoral for women to drink spirits. It was unhealthy and dangerous as well.

The theory of humours still dominated medicine. It held that everything was made up of earth, water, fire and air, and had a corresponding mixture of qualities, dry or wet, hot or cold. And that explained human nature as well. People were choleric (hot and dry), sanguine (hot and moist), phlegmatic (moist and cold), or melancholic (cold and dry). Fevers and ailments were imbalances of the natural elements. They were cured by diet. And all foods, in detailed and complex ways, were combinations of qualities. Pepper was hot in the third degree and dry in the fourth. Fruit was cold, moist and bad for you.

Spirits were fiery, hot and dry. That explained why people in northern climates turned to spirit-drinking. '[People] cannot live without it,' one tract pointed out, 'through the intemperance of the air, viz. coldness and moisture in these northern countries ... Our bodies would become like bogs, or pools, if we did not drain them ... by the frequent use of hot spirits and cordial drams.'9 For women, though, spirits were dangerous. Heat and dryness were male attributes. Their disposition – anger – was the most masculine of qualities, the most unladylike. Women were generically cold and moist; spirits were anathema to their natures.

Hence Stephen Hales' advice against drinking spirits during pregnancy. Wet nurses were usually told to eat light herb soups and salads, wet and cold foods – the opposite of fiery spirits. It was no surprise to eighteenth-century campaigners that the child of a gin-drinker should have 'half-dried bones ... [a skin] all shrivelled and black;' nor that such a baby should came out 'half burnt and shrivelled into the world.'

And that, too, was the risk which awaited gin-drinkers themselves. Terrible stories began to circulate in the years of the Gin Craze. If women drinkers didn't kill themselves by gin itself, by syphilis or by exposure, a still more dreadful fate awaited them. Death by fire.

Grace Pitt was 'about fifty', the wife of an Ipswich fishmonger. She had always been fond of a dram, and enjoyed her pipe as well. Every night she would go downstairs and have a last pipe before she went to bed. On the morning of 10 April 1744, her daughter, who slept with her, woke up to find her mother's side of the bed empty. She called, but there was no answer. So she 'put on her

clothes,' it was later reported, 'and [went] down into the kitchen.'
A terrible sight met her eyes. Her mother was 'stretched out on the
right side, with her head near the grate; the body extended on the
hearth, with the legs on the floor.' But it took her a moment to realise
that the thing on the hearth was indeed her mother. Grace Pitt's
body seemed to have been consumed by fire. It had 'the appearance
of a log of wood, consumed by a fire without apparent flame . . .
The trunk was in some measure incinerated, and resembled a heap
of coals covered with white ashes. The head, the arms, the legs,
and the thighs had also participated in the burning.'[10] All that was
noted in painstaking detail by Pierre Aimé Lair, who collected
examples of 'the combustion of the human body, produced by the
long immoderate use of spirituous liquors.'

The first case of spontaneous combustion had been reported in
England in the *Gentleman's Magazine* in June 1731. It was taken
seriously enough for the Royal Society to debate the phenomenon
in 1745. Both for them and for Pierre Aimé Lair, there were
obvious links between the various cases. All the victims were
women. All of them were old – the theory of humours dictated
that everyone dried up as they aged. And, most important of all,
'the persons who experienced the effects of this combustion, had for
a long time made an immoderate use of spirituous liquors.' Grace
Pitt had been celebrating because another daughter had just come
back from overseas.

Reformers hated women who drank because they threatened
social order. But maybe older memories and fears lingered in
the background. Crouched over her market barrow, the old
basket-woman with a bottle in her hand evoked the memory of
other old women who had dispensed magic potions. She, too,
transgressed social norms; she held the power of transformation
and her end was death by fire. In the same year it passed the
Gin Act, Parliament finally outlawed the burning of witches. But

it was easier to erase witches from the statute book than to pluck them from the popular imagination. Grace Pitt, charred to ash on her own hearth-stone, had met the fate of all her kind. Spontaneous combustion had become the threatened end for women who turned to spirits. They carried their own stake and flames within them.

# CHAPTER FOURTEEN

## REPEAL

Seven years into prohibition, in 1743, production of British spirits hit more than eight million gallons a year. Gin was supposed to have been outlawed, but every man, woman and child in London was drinking two pints of the stuff every week.

The Gin Act was a dead letter. In 1741–2, only two of the £50 licences were taken out. Even more depressing than that, Excise men managed to collect the twenty-shilling duty on just forty gallons of spirits. The special sessions of magistrates were long over. For Madam Geneva, it was business as usual. For politicians, it was time for a new approach.

There was one reason in particular why they needed a new approach in 1743. Sir Robert Walpole was gone, ousted the year before by the same combination of patriot Whigs and Tories, City opposition and excited public opinion which had driven him into the war he never wanted. And that war was now spreading. In summer 1742, England had been drawn into active support for Maria Theresa, the new ruler of Austria and Hungary. Hanoverian and English armies were committed on the Continent for the first time in thirty years. Now Carteret, Secretary of State and dominant figure in the new ministry, had to find a way of paying for them.

For reformers, the problem gin presented was how to stop people drinking it; for Londoners, how to get hold of a steady supply. For politicians, the difficulty with gin had always been how to make money out of it.

It should have been easy. Vast quantities of spirits were being distilled and drunk. There had never been any trouble in transforming beer into hard cash. But so far both government attempts to raise substantial revenue out of the Gin Craze had ended in disaster. The Gin Acts of 1729 and 1736 had both been ignored.

This time, when they turned their attention to Madam Geneva, the government was going to play safe. Way back in 1729, everyone had known that the obvious answer to controlling gin was through still-head duties and licensing controls. The 1743 Act, repealing and replacing prohibition, would bring in both, but at rates so low as to render them harmless. The volume of spirits being made was now so great that even a small duty could throw up healthy revenues. The 1743 Act would double the duty on low wines made from corn to twopence, and the duty on most spirits to sixpence. On the most recent figures Carteret had in front of him, those modest increases would produce an additional revenue of nearly £140,000 a year. Retail licences had been a dead letter under prohibition. With their cost reduced from £50 to £1 a year, there was every hope that London's thousands of gin-shops might at last turn out to be some benefit to the country.

For critics, it was hardly surprising that the 1743 Gin Act took a softly-softly approach. It was said to have been drafted by Kent, one of the great malt distillers. But for the ministry, the important thing was that, however toothless, it should actually work. The Acts of 1729 and 1736 had both promised to hike the price of a dram far beyond the pockets of most drinkers. They had been driven by reform. This time the target was more modest. It would be enough if distillers, gin-sellers and drinkers simply agreed to obey the law.

Carteret didn't just need money; he needed it fast. The government brought its measure to the House of Commons on 17 January 1743. It was pushed through, as one opponent complained in the House of Lords, 'with the utmost precipitation, and . . . almost without the formality of a debate.' By 10 February, ministers were already working out how to spend the revenue (the new duties would pay interest on a loan of £1.8m at three per cent). Four days after that, the new Gin Bill was passed on to the House of Lords. But there, on 22 February, the repeal of prohibition suddenly ran into opposition.

The House of Lords debate of 1743 was one of the big parliamentary set-pieces of the decade. It took place in the hall of the House of Lords, vaulted and lined with Flemish tapestries. Most of the leading politicians of ministry and opposition – and most were now sitting in the Lords – spoke out, and their debates were reported at length in the press. Parliamentary reporting was still banned, but the larger papers had found ways around the restriction. The *Gentleman's Magazine* published 'Debates in the Senate of Lilliput'. Their reporter, writing up the Lords' speeches from his notes, was Samuel Johnson. The *London Magazine* published a slightly different version of the debate (parliamentary correspondents of 1743 weren't always reporting what the speakers actually said, but what they ought to have said). A third version survives in the notes of the Bishop of Oxford. Thomas Secker, SPCK member, acquaintance of Thomas Wilson, and ardent foe of Madam Geneva, was present throughout, fuming at the thought of repeal, planning his own contribution, and taking notes.

The debate was about everything that drugs legislation has ever been about. It was about what happened when governments started to depend on revenue from things they were supposed to be discouraging. It was about whether politicians should swallow the unpalatable truth that a war on drugs had been lost, and accept pragmatism in place of principle. It was about what governments should do when a substantial part of the population has voted with its feet, and walked away from their legislation.

That wasn't all, though. It was also about the war. The gin debate followed immediately after a passionate battle over Carteret's proposal that English money should pay for Hanoverian troops in Flanders. As far as some of the opposition were concerned, the gin debate was simply more of the same. First they had been talking about whether England should be paying foreign troops at all; now they had moved on to where the money was going to come from.

And it was about politics. For years, the opposition had promised that when Walpole fell, the Augean stables of Westminster would be cleaned out. But Carteret had taken power alongside many of Walpole's old ministers, and William Pulteney had ascended to the Lords as Earl of Bath. Most of the patriot opposition – men like Bedford and Chesterfield, Lyttelton and Pitt – had stayed out in the cold, while the Exchequer had gone to Samuel Sandys, a nonentity follower of Pulteney. Meanwhile, those of Sir Robert's creatures who had lost their places seethed with bitterness. Much of what happened in the 1743 gin debate was about political betrayal.

Politics achieved some surprising metamorphoses. The summer before, Lord Hervey had lost the Privy Seal. Now, rising on Tuesday 22 February to oppose the second reading of the new Gin Bill, the effeminate little courtier – Pope called him 'Lord Fanny' – had suddenly been transformed into a passionate moral crusader. Gin-drinking was 'an abominable and pernicious vice.' It was a scandal to use vice as 'a fund for bringing money into the King's Exchequer.' That was the key to the argument for all opponents of repeal, whatever their motivation. The state was condoning vice. As soon as they depended on gin revenues, Lord Hervey warned, 'ministers will encourage the consumption, and will neglect to execute, or pervert any laws you can make for preventing or diminishing that consumption.'[1] Maybe there would be some temporary benefit from tougher licensing restrictions. 'The Justices of Peace may, perhaps, for the first year or two refuse granting a licence to a house known to be . . . a gin-shop . . . but they will soon have private directions, and a licence will be granted to everyone that desires it.'

So much for the text; Lord Hervey was just as interested in the subtext. During the winter he had published two pamphlets attacking Carteret's war policy in general and the payment of Hanoverian troops in particular. For him, as for many of the opposition, the gin debate was a chance to renew the attack. The new duties the government proposed were going to be mortgaged to a massive loan. But if the Bill failed to raise any revenue – like all previous Gin Acts – the government's only option would be to dig into reserves. The Bill, therefore, was 'a mask . . . for concealing a design to mortgage the Sinking Fund.' The question before the Lords was 'whether you will agree to mortgage the Sinking Fund for supporting Hanover troops.' It wasn't about gin at all.

Ministers would come close to admitting, later in the debate, that the war was their first priority. But for the moment they stuck to defending the new gin policy on its own merits. Opening in favour of the Bill, Lord Bathurst wasted no time in pointing out an obvious truth: prohibition had failed. What they were putting forward was a 'new experiment.' It was an experiment in pragmatism. 'We find by experience, we cannot absolutely prevent the retailing of such liquors; because if we prevent their being retailed in an open, fair way, they will be retailed in a clandestine smuggling manner. What then are we to do?' Common sense suggested that if prohibition wasn't feasible, restriction was the next best thing.

'[The] proper method . . . is to allow their being publicly retailed, but to lay such a duty upon the still-head and upon licences, as, without amounting to a prohibition, will make them come so dear to the consumer, that the poor will not be able to launch out into an excessive use of them.'

The most important thing was to bring the gin industry, producers and retailers, back within the pale of the law. Now that they had allowed it to go underground, the government could risk only marginal duties if they were to tempt it back. 'The duty proposed upon licences,' Bathurst asserted, 'is so moderate, that every ale-house and coffee-house in the kingdom will take out a licence.' The hope was that once they were back in, licensed and respectable operators would help drive out the criminals.

To the eyes of Thomas Secker, sitting among the bishops with his notebook, the ministry's argument seemed pitiful. Bathurst suggested that the price of a dram might rise by a third, and consumption drop by the same amount. He was being pragmatic, but zealots like Thomas Secker had never had any time for pragmatism. Secker was the one who kicked off the 1735 gin campaign by ordering a record to be made of all the gin-shops in his parish of St James's. He had joined the SPCK alongside Isaac Maddox. He was a friend of Sir John Gonson and Thomas Wilson. Somewhere in his speech, Bathurst had remarked that he 'never heard that a single moderate dram, even of the pernicious liquor called gin, was either a crime or a sin.' For Thomas Secker, that was exactly where the ministry was going wrong. Gin-drinking was more than a crime and a sin. It was worse. It was an evil. Gin was what the devil drank in hell.

Thomas Secker's speech was a catalogue of fallen women in back-room dram-shops, of murdered children and maddened men. If prohibition had driven Madam Geneva underground, rather than exiling her, then that, at least, was better than giving in the fight.

'Vice,' in his opinion, '[should] always be . . . confin[ed] . . . as much as possible to holes and corners.'

Not all of the opposition lost their cool quite so comprehensively as Thomas Secker did. The Earl of Chesterfield brought the debate back to high politics and high finance. 'We have already the Civil List Fund,' he quipped, 'the Sinking Fund, the Aggregate Fund, the South Sea Fund, and God knows how many others. What name we are to give to this new fund I know not, unless we are to call it the Drinking Fund.' He even gave the House a spoof introduction to the new Act ('Whereas his Majesty has occasion for a large sum of money for maintaining his Hanover troops and the British troops sent, for what purpose we know not, to Flanders; and whereas a very considerable new revenue may be raised, by permitting the people of England to poison themselves with a liquor called gin'). He wondered whether there were any other breaches of the Ten Commandments the government could raise revenue from.

And so the battle lines were drawn up. It was a struggle between pragmatism and principle — although pragmatism and principle masked cynicism on both sides. It was a war on two fronts, an open battle raging over gin, a struggle over money and foreign policy bubbling below the surface. Defending a pragmatic line on gin, Carteret couldn't see the point in a government clinging to an absolutist moral position which had failed. Prohibiting gin had, in the end, stopped the authorities influencing events. They'd ended up writing themselves out of the script. 'The people will indulge themselves in this wicked habit,' Carteret concluded, 'and since there is no preventing it, the government ought to avail themselves of it; but . . . in such a manner as by degrees to put a stop, at least to the excessive use of this pernicious liquor.' For Carteret, as for Bathurst, the priority was to bring the industry back within the law. The answer, for him, was 'to begin with laying a small duty upon the still head, and another small duty upon licences. By this means you will put an end to the clandestine retail; for spirituous liquors will be retailed openly and fairly at so many places, and at so cheap a rate, that the clandestine retailers will meet with no encouragement.'

With battle joined, the debate went on at some length. Several speakers raised and cursed the spirit of Bernard Mandeville. Mandeville's prophecy was coming true before their eyes; private vices were indeed being harvested for public benefits. Thomas Sherlock, bishop of Salisbury, called it 'the most unchristian Bill that ever was thought of by any government.' Against that, supporters of the government could point to the political damage of a government pursuing a hardline policy that the people ignored. 'What has been the consequence, my lords?' asked one. 'It has raised among the people such a contempt of law, order, and government, as has spread itself among all degrees of men, and in everything that relates to public affairs ... The very dregs of the people pretend to be better judges of the interest of the nation, and the nature of our constitution, than those of the best estates ... This I take to be in some measure owing to the impunity and success the populace have met with in transgressing the late act against spirituous liquors.'

There was agreement only on one point. Not even opponents of repeal pretended that prohibition had worked. Whatever their Lordships said, whatever Thomas Secker scribbled in his notebook, outside the doors of the House, 'punch and drams of all sorts, even common gin not excepted, are ... sold openly and avowedly at all public houses, and many private shops and bye-corners; and ... [are] sold as cheap as they were before the present law was enacted.'

Prohibition had failed; everyone knew it had failed. But the idea of giving in to vice simply stuck in the hardliners' throats. To men like Thomas Secker, it was just plain wrong that a government should give up fighting a social evil and watch the people set off on the road to perdition. One opponent, Lord Lonsdale, had even gone out into the parishes of Middlesex to look at the problem for himself. What he saw there caused his righteous indignation to flare up all over again. This was vice that no government could condone. 'To see men enfeebled and consumed, or rioting in all the most horrid sorts of wickedness; to see women naked and prostituted; to see children emaciated, starved, or choked; and all by the use of this pernicious liquor called gin, would surely make you reject [this Bill] with disdain . . . The physicians and nurses of our hospitals . . . will inform you, that a vast multitude of diseases and accidents proceed from gin-drinking; the overseers of the poor . . . will tell you, what numbers of poor objects are brought upon the parish . . . and if any of the gin-shop-keepers themselves are honest enough, they will tell you, that when poor creatures fall once into the habit of gin-drinking, they never leave it off as long as they have a rag to wear, or a leg to crawl on.'

But the opposition didn't have a chance, in the end. Underneath all the rage about vice, this was a money Bill. The Lords couldn't amend it without provoking a constitutional storm; they could only reject the 1743 Gin Act out of hand. By the last day, ministers had even come clean about their real priorities. Carteret admitted that he had already negotiated the three per cent loans, and couldn't be sure of getting so good a deal if there was any more delay. William Pulteney was 'against a delay . . . into this affair . . . because of the dangerous and ticklish situation we are in with regard to foreign affairs.' Without English finance – dependent on the new gin revenues – the Dutch might pull out of supporting Maria Theresa, and Austria might make terms with the French. The whole balance of power might change; suddenly Madam Geneva was at the centre of world events. 'As trifling as this motion may seem to some of your lordships,' Pulteney declared, 'yet upon the fate of it may depend the fate and the liberties of Europe.'

Thomas Secker didn't give a damn about Europe. He voted against the Bill and ten other bishops joined him, Isaac Maddox among them. There was even a formal protest. The hardliners could see that 1743 was a pivotal moment. With the repeal of prohibition and the passing of the new Gin Act, the authorities had accepted that the war on gin had failed. They had conceded that it was less damaging to accept gin-drinking than to let the relationship between governors and governed be undermined by scorn. They accepted that Madam Geneva was here to stay, whatever ills she brought with her. Their priority now was to decriminalise gin and bring the industry back within the law. They even accepted that an industry controlled by respectable and profitable businesses would provide its own form of control.

It was a pact with the devil. 1743 would be the peak of the eighteenth-century Gin Craze. From that year onwards, spirit production would decline for the next forty years. Not until the mid-1780s would it start to rise again, and by then the population of London was exploding as well. Not until 1840 would London – by then a city of well over a million – drink as much gin as it did in the year the Lords ended prohibition. But it was a turning-point of another kind as well, and the bishops knew it. Never again would a British Parliament set out to eradicate gin-drinking. Madam Geneva had been given the freedom of the city. She was never going to get back on the boat to Holland. She was here to stay.

Fall-out from repeal of the Gin Act was muted. Most reformers pinned the blame on the Chancellor, the hapless Samuel Sandys. 'Deep, deep in S—'s blundering head,' sneered the *London Evening Post*,

> The new Gin Project sunk;
> O happy project! sage, he cry'd,
> Let all the realm be drunk.[2]

Sir Charles Hanbury Williams circulated a satirical ballad which had Sandys visited by the ghost of Sir Joseph Jekyll, who warned him that:

> Riot and slaughter once again
> Shall their career begin
> And every parish suckling babe
> Again be nursed with Gin.[3]

There was a certain amount of apocalyptic prophecy. The opposition *Champion* threatened that hordes of ragged gin-drinkers would one day 'pour forth unexpectedly from their gloomy cells, as from the body of the Trojan Horse, with design to lay the city in flames, that they might share in the plunder.'[4] As always, the decline and fall of Britain would follow.

For their part, the Company of Distillers had been taken by surprise by the new Act. Their lobbying machine was rusty; they hadn't paid their parliamentary lobbyist for four years. They settled Mr Kenn's bill, but when he failed to warn them that distillers would be banned from taking out retail licences, they 'express'd their resentment at [his] neglect & came to a resolution that he be from henceforth dismissed from being soll[icito]r to the Company.'[5] Another man was appointed in his place, but the counter-attack had to wait for another day.

The authorities, meanwhile, set about putting the new spirits régime in place. The 1743 Gin Act had always been more business-like than previous Acts. In 1743, for the first time, the government had actually taken expert advice, sending a draft of the Bill to the Excise Office in January. Now they accompanied introduction of the Act with a clamp-down on illegal gin-sellers. When it came to issuing the new licences, Middlesex and Westminster magistrates were exhorted 'not to grant licences for selling . . . spirituous liquors to any but such as are strictly qualified according to law, and as are not known to be guilty of any disorderly practices, or likely to suffer them in their houses.'[6] The 1743 Act put magistrates in a stronger position to control the trade than before. It wasn't just that no respectable gin-seller had any excuse for avoiding the twenty-shilling licence. Licences would only be issued, now, 'to such as keep taverns, victualling houses, inns, coffee houses or alehouses.' The days of the chandler's shop with a bottle behind the counter, the gin-selling grocer and tippling market-woman were over. When magistrates met at St Martin-in-the-Fields to issue the first batch of licences, a lot of applicants were disappointed. 'When many applied for licences not within the said act,' the *London Evening Post* reported, 'they were absolutely refused, and put entirely out of hopes of obtaining any.'[7]

With memories of Edward Parker still fresh, the Excise Office, too, saw the importance of cleaning up their act. Even before the Bill had passed into law, news came through that they had 'appointed Mr Nurse, Surveyor in the Distillery, to be General Surveyor in those duties in the room of Mr Webb, who is removed.' That was just the start of a wider purge. 'It is said,' the *London Evening Post* reported a week later, 'there are orders for a general remove of all Excise Officers throughout the kingdom, on the Gin Act taking place.'[8]

Zealots had warned of catastrophe when prohibition ended, but no catastrophe came. Even Tobias Smollett, fervent campaigner against gin, couldn't help admitting, later, 'that it has not been attended with those dismal consequences which the Lords in the opposition foretold.'[9] And on the ministry's own terms, the Act worked. Their first priority had been to bring the gin industry back inside the law. In the days of prohibition only a handful of gin-sellers had ever taken out retail licences; the rest of London's 10,000-odd gin-sellers had been on the black market. But when the Commissioners of Excise made their first report, in January 1744, more than 1,000 London gin-sellers had already taken out the new licences. Many of the rest would not, in any case, have been eligible. Nationwide, more than 20,000 licences had been handed out. The new Act was delivering all the rewards ministers had hoped for. They had found out how to milk Madam Geneva for cash. The £90,000 they made from duties was more than enough to pay interest on their war loans.[10] By contrast, the Gin Act's old twenty shilling-a-gallon duty had brought in less than £40 a year.

And the pragmatic policy set out by Carteret (low duties, gradually increasing; strict licence controls) was pursued in the years that followed. With Excise advice, a second Act was put through the next year to plug loopholes and clarify terms. Two years later, in 1746, Henry Pelham's ministry would start to ratchet up the duties, adding a halfpenny on low wines made from corn, and another penny and a half on spirits. Events seemed to be unfolding just as Carteret had predicted. Spirit production had fallen almost nineteen per cent in 1744, and seemed to have stabilised. The licences were working. Ministers were happily counting their new source of revenue. Gin, it seemed, could be taken off the agenda. With Bonnie Prince Charlie in Scotland and war in Europe, there was plenty else to occupy public attention.

It was all too good to be true. Madam Geneva was not quite ready for a quiet retirement. Men like Thomas Secker and Isaac Maddox had never been interested in compromise. It wasn't enough to see gin-drinking reduced. They wanted every dram-shop shut down and the stills thrown on the scrap-heap. And they had said all along that you couldn't trust the government. Ministers might start off with good intentions, but sooner or later the sweet taste of gin revenues would sweep them off their feet. It was only a matter of time.

It took four years. Distillers had never been happy about losing the right to sell spirits from their own shops. They lobbied hard to get them back. When Bonnie Prince Charlie invaded, the Company of Distillers subscribed £100 to the Hanoverian army, just to demonstrate their loyalty.[11] In 1746 they petitioned Parliament at length, asking that 'all reputable distillers [be] indulged with a power of retailing their own commodities.' They thought they could help in 'suppressing the iniquitous part of the trade.' They didn't seem to be asking too much. They were willing 'to be confined in the strictest manner can be devised, from any private tippling, or other irregularities, or any disturbance of the publick peace.'[12]

They weren't the only ones working to chip away at the 1743 Gin Act. The powerful malt distillers were lobbying behind the scenes. Sugar planters sent in petitions; they wanted a boost for the rum trade. And any government in the last throes of a war is always tempted by extra revenue.

The government gave way to temptation. In April 1747 the Court of the Distillers' Company received unexpected news. They heard that 'a Bill is expected to be speedily brought into Parliament for empowering the distiller residing within the limits of the Bills of Mortality* to sell by retail to be drank in their shops.' London distillers could pay £5 for a licence, and once again they would be able to sell spirits over the counter. There was no shortage of them ready to take up the offer. Almost 600 distillers' licences were issued in the first year. It wasn't the only sign of a collapse of good intentions. Back in 1744, spirit licences had brought in revenue of about £22,000 over the whole country.[13] By 1749, that figure had

---

* i.e. in London.

shot up to £35,108. Originally, 1,000 retail licences had been granted in London; five years later, London magistrates handed out no fewer than 5,297 spirit licences within the Bills of Mortality.

For reformers, all that was bad enough. But worse was to come. The war was about to come to an end. In 1748, the Treaty of Aix-la-Chapelle brought peace to Europe. In London the result was far from peaceful. In 1748, the soldiers came home.

When soldiers came home, there was a crime wave; everyone knew that. 'The approach of peace,' the *Gentleman's Magazine* worried, 'amidst all the joy ... has raised ... terror in many private gentlemen ... [and] those in publick stations, who consider well the consequences of discharging so many men from their occupations in the army, the fleet and the yards ... As one half of these poor men will not be able to get employment ... necessity will compel them to seize by violence, what they can see no method to attain by honest labour.'[14]

The government certainly wasn't going to help ex-servicemen out. When the regiments were broken up and the fleet put in mothballs, they were on their own. It wasn't just trauma counselling they lacked; they didn't even get a demob suit. The only comfort thrown their way was the kind of help that suited eighteenth-century Parliaments – the sort that didn't cost anything. They were allowed to follow any trade, even if they hadn't served an apprenticeship. Digging deep into their classical educations, MPs came up with a colony for retired soldiers (in Nova Scotia). More imaginatively, there was a scheme to employ sailors in building a British herring fishery.

It was never going to be enough. There were 70,000 servicemen, and they didn't all want to go to the New World with the convicts, or catch herring. Not many of them could afford to set up in business, whether they were allowed to or not. Most, as the promoter of the fisheries project warned, would be 'reduced to the sad alternative, either of begging from door to door; or of plunging into crimes.'[15]

They plunged into crimes. 'The frequency of audacious street robberies repeated every night in this great Metropolis,' protested the *Whitehall Evening Post* in January 1749, 'call aloud on our magistrates to think of some redress ... There is no possibility of stirring from our habitations after dark, without the hazard of a fractured skull, or the danger of losing ... property.'[16] Hangings soared. More than half Tyburn's victims in 1749 would be demobbed soldiers. It didn't help the jittering nerves of wealthy Londoners that crime seemed to be directed most often at them. The banker Sir Thomas Hankey and his wife were mugged, as was the Earl of Leicester and the Countess of Albemarle. The Prime Minister's eldest daughter started hiding her earrings under the seat when she travelled by sedan chair. Horace Walpole was set upon twice. Returning from Holland House by moonlight, about ten o'clock, he recounted, 'I was attacked by two highwaymen in Hyde Park, and the pistol of one of them going off accidentally, razed the skin under my eye, left some marks of shot on my face, and stunned me ... If I had sat an inch nearer to the left side, [the ball] must have gone through my head.' Within weeks he would be mugged again in the Royal Mews. Not surprisingly, he wrote to Horace Mann, 'you will hear little news from England, but of robberies; the numbers of disbanded soldiers and sailors have all taken to the road, or rather the street; people are almost afraid of stirring after it is dark.' 'One is forced to travel, even at noon,' he would add in another letter in March 1752, 'as if one was going to battle.'[17]

Anecdotes and urban myths whipped up fear. Everyone knew someone who had been mugged. The newspapers didn't help. Hack journalists, as the author of a 1752 description of London complained, spent Sunday evening 'in bed, instead of at their prayers . . . inventing stories of rapes, robberies, and riots &c. to fill up the newspapers of the ensuing week.'[18]

London's neuroses were bubbling to the surface again. Crime produced panic, and a panicking city looked round for scapegoats. And in this febrile atmosphere, just as in 1721, the hand of God intervened. Thirty years before it had been the plague in Marseilles which threatened a sinful town with divine retribution. This time, God's thunderbolt struck closer to home.

It happened on 8 February 1750, as Thomas Wilson recorded in his diary. 'At 45 minutes after 12 the two cities of London and Westminster were alarmed with a violent shock of an earthquake . . . There was first a trembling and then a report like thunder and then a shake . . . Most people thought it was the blowing up of powder mills.' Another quake struck exactly a month later, after weeks of unseasonably hot weather. The second tremor was stronger; the coincidence of dates was too obvious to ignore. This time most Londoners knew they were damned.

Horace Walpole reported 'showers of sermons and exhortations.' 'The churches,' Smollett later remembered, 'were crowded with penitent sinners: the sons of riot and profligacy were overawed into sobriety and decorum. The streets no longer resounded with execrations, or the noise of brutal licentiousness; and the hand of charity was liberally opened.'[19] The final cataclysm was predicted for 8 April. When the Day of Judgement came, the streets out of town were crammed with carts and carriages as Londoners hurried to escape. 'In after ages,' Smollett recalled, 'it will hardly be believed, that on the evening of the eighth day of April, the open fields, that skirt the metropolis, were filled with incredible numbers of people assembled in chairs, in chaises, and coaches, as well as on foot, who waited in the most fearful suspense until morning.'

They all knew what they had done to deserve this doom.

Thomas Sherlock, now Bishop of London, had written his diocese a letter to tell them. 'You never read so imprudent, so absurd a piece,' complained the sceptical Horace Walpole. 'The earthquake which has done no hurt, in a country where no earthquakes ever did any, is sent, according to the Bishop, to punish bawdy books, gaming, drinking etc.'[20] It sold 10,000 copies in two days. For Thomas Sherlock there was no doubt that the city was being warned. 'It will be a blindness wilful and inexcusable,' he told Londoners, 'not to apply to ourselves this strong summons, from God, to repentance.'[21] Among the sins of the town, he stressed 'the lewdness and debauchery that prevail amongst the lowest people, which keeps them idle, poor and miserable, and renders them incapable of getting an honest livelihood for themselves and their families.'

London contained too many beggars, buggers, boozers and fornicators. The town was being called to account. Madam Geneva was back in the frame again.

## CHAPTER FIFTEEN

# GIN LANE

For the poor of St Giles's, of course, for apprentices and journeymen, whores and market-women, for landlords and porters and watermen and chandlers, she had never been away.

One writer who cast his eye over London in 1752 described a world where gin-drinking was part of everyday life. In the small hours he watched 'common whores telling their lamentable cases to watchmen on their stands, and treating them with Geneva and tobacco.' At three in the morning the gin-shops were still full. At six, as the town woke up, 'servant women in public houses, who have just got up, [run] about with their stockings about their legs, caps and petticoat half off, drinking of Gin, taking snuff . . . and playing with fellows who have been drinking, swearing, and playing at cards all the past night.' By seven there were 'poor devils of women, with empty bellies, naked backs, and heads intoxicated with Geneva, standing and gossiping with each other in the street.' All day long Londoners drank, and at the end of the day, they 'shut up their stalls, and joyfully retire[d] to the Geneva-shop.'[1]

Gin-drinking still produced its share of tragedies. 'At a Christening at Beddington in Surrey,' reported the *Gentleman's Magazine* in 1748, 'the nurse was so intoxicated that after she had undressed the child, instead of laying it in the cradle she put it behind a large fire, which burnt it to death in a few minutes. She was examined before a magistrate, and said she was quite stupid and senseless, so that she took the child for a log of wood.'

Alcohol abuse was endemic in prisons. Middlesex magistrates in 1741 investigated the shocking rate of deaths in custody and found that some prisoners spent their whole allowance on gin. 'There have been no less than thirty gin-shops at one time in the King's Bench,' a reformer reported some time later, 'and I have been credibly informed by very attentive observers, that upwards of . . . 120 gallons of gin, which they call by various names, as Vinegar, Gossip, Crank, Mexico, Sky-blue etc. [were] sold weekly.'[2]

Nor was it only poor men and women who drank. The bookseller James Lackington had painful memories of his alcoholic father in 1750. 'As soon as he found he was more at ease in his circumstances,' he remembered, 'he contracted a fatal habit of drinking, and of course his business was neglected; so that after several fruitless attempts of my grandfather to keep him in trade, he was . . . reduced to his old state of a journeyman shoemaker.'[3] Even forty years later Lackington couldn't hide his bitterness. 'To our mother we are indebted for everything,' he wrote. 'Neither myself, my brother or sisters are indebted to a father scarcely for anything that can endear his memory, or cause us to reflect on him with pleasure.'

It was still quite normal to drink at work. 'Twenty years ago,' Francis Place would recall, 'few tailor shops were without a bottle of gin: the men drank as they liked: one kept the score, and the publican came at certain times to replenish the gin bottle.'[4] And in the terrible conditions of the slums, gin was the only comforter. Holborn and St Giles's were still a world of migrant labourers, of the destitute and hopeless and sick. Holborn's High Constable described the filthy dosshouses of St Giles's, 'set apart for the reception of idle persons and vagabonds, who have their lodgings there for twopence a night ... In these beds, several of which are in the same room, men and women, often strangers to each other, lie promiscuously; the price of a double bed being no more than threepence, as an encouragement to them to lie together; but as these places are thus adapted to whoredom, so they are no less provided for drunkenness, gin being sold in them all at a penny a quartern.'[5]

This was where Madam Geneva had put down her deepest roots, in the tangled alleys off Holborn, in digs behind Smithfield market. It was the London which most Londoners avoided, the other side of the coin, the underworld hidden away behind the grand squares and glittering shop-fronts.

But in 1751, at the height of the crime panic, this world would be opened to the shocked gaze of Londoners by a new witness. He described an afternoon in Shoreditch where the constables raided two small houses and counted seventy people living in them. When the houses' inmates were told to turn out their pockets, they were found to have less than a shilling between them. He described a world where normal life seemed to have been suspended, where people lived in 'excessive misery ... oppressed with want, and sunk in every species of debauchery.'

The writer was the new senior magistrate in Westminster. His name was Henry Fielding.

Back in 1736, Henry Fielding had lampooned prohibition in shows at the Little Theatre in the Haymarket. But the Stage Licensing Act had followed a year later, and that had been the end of his career as a playwright. Fielding never saved a penny from his like *Pasquin*. By the late 1740s he was broke and ill, disappointed, nearing the end of his life. He had had a success with his novel *Joseph Andrews*, but the legal career he had resumed when the theatres closed down had never prospered. He was always in debt. In 1744 his adored wife, Charlotte, had died. Only old friends had pulled him through. At the Bedford Arms, just round the corner from Bow Street, he ran a card game with William Hogarth and his blind half-brother, John. In that company, Fielding could still be 'a very merry fellow indeed,'[6] the landlord remembered. But his health was failing. He was paying the price for a youth spent in the coffee-houses and theatres, too much drink and too much good food. 'Fielding continues to be visited for his sins,' reported the young poet Edward More after a visit in late 1749, 'so as to be wheeled about from room to room . . . His disorder is the gout and intemperance the cause.' Another visitor found him 'a poor, emaciated, wornout rake.'[7]

His friends came to the rescue. Henry Fielding had always been feared as a political writer and he had been a good servant to the opposition (there had been only one major falling-out, in 1741). When Carteret fell, in 1744, Fielding's friends and patrons, Lyttelton and Bedford, came into the government; the next year he established his loyalty with searing attacks on the Jacobite rebellion in *The True Patriot* and *The Jacobite's Journal*. In 1748 he finally received his reward. He was made a magistrate in Westminster.

It was Thomas De Veil's old role as 'court justice'. In 1740 De Veil had moved to a house on the west side of Bow Street. Another magistrate, Thomas Burdus, had moved in after De Veil's death in 1746, but two years later it was empty again. To the town, the sight of Henry Fielding installed as principal Westminster magistrate was the best joke of the year. It was hard to say which was better value: the clown of the Little Theatre transformed into pillar of the establishment, the scourge of ministerial corruption working as a trading justice, or the chair-bound old rake sorting out the vices of the town. The comedian and impressionist Samuel Foote, then doing shows at the Little Theatre, cast Fielding, forever unkempt, as 'a dirty fellow, in shabby black cloths, a flux'd tye-wig, and a quid of tobacco in his jaws.'[8] A satirical puppet show in Panton Street sent him up mercilessly. 'A heavier load of scandal hath been cast upon me,' Fielding sighed, 'than I believe ever fell to the share of any single man.' To the heartless wits of London, there was poetic justice in that. In his days as a hilarious young man about town, Henry Fielding had never pulled a punch on anyone.

Quite apart from all the ribbing he had to put up with, being a Westminster magistrate was no easier now than it had been in Thomas De Veil's day, particularly for a sick man in a wheelchair, particularly during a crime wave. 'I should think it a nobler and less nauseous employment,' wrote Fielding's cousin, Lady Mary Wortley Montagu, 'to be one of the staff officers that conduct nocturnal weddings.'[9] James Boswell would visit the Bow Street courtroom a decade later and find it crowded with 'whores and chairmen, and greasy blackguards of all denominations.'[10] There was never any let-up in the work. 'Upwards of fifty criminals were committed last week to prison by Justice Fielding,' reported the *Whitehall Evening Post* in January 1751, 'many of whom were for capital offences, and seven for street-robberies.'[11] Fielding's life would be threatened in January 1753 by a gang he had broken up. And all day long he was surrounded by the outcasts of the slums and the dregs of Newgate. In April 1750, defendants who had been held in the squalid prison brought 'jail fever' – typhus – to the courtroom at the City Quarter Sessions. The Lord Mayor would die, along with two judges, an alderman, and a number of court officials and lawyers. That was why most gentlemen refused to serve on the London bench.

But Henry Fielding's finances were in dire need of repair. The

Duke of Bedford told him 'that he could not say that acting as a principal justice of the peace in Westminster was on all accounts very desirable, but all the world knew it was a very lucrative office.'[12] Lucrative for some; Henry Fielding couldn't even bring himself to profit out of the post. After leaving England for the last time, he wrote that 'by refusing to take a shilling from a man who most undoubtedly would not have had another left, I had reduced an income of about £500 a year of the dirtiest money upon earth, to little more than £300; a considerable proportion of which remained with my clerk.'[13]

And his timing couldn't have been worse. Henry Fielding took his oaths as a Westminster magistrate in October 1748, and in May 1749 he was elected Chair of the Westminster Quarter Sessions. The soldiers were coming home. The crime wave was just gathering pace.

By 1750 it was in full flood; God was sending monthly earthquakes; the town was in panic. Henry Fielding wasn't only court justice by then; he was a celebrated novelist – *Tom Jones* had been published in winter 1749. It was hardly surprising that, maybe prompted by friends in the ministry, he should pick up his pen to address the troubles overwhelming London. His new tract, published in January 1751, was dedicated to the Lord Chancellor, and he called it *An Inquiry into the Causes of the Late Increase of Robbers*. From his vantage-point in Bow Street, Henry Fielding knew more about crime than most of the armchair pamphleteers who pontificated about law and order that year. He looked at crime and he looked at the causes of crime. His tract ranged widely over the Poor Laws, pardons, executions and every aspect of the criminal justice system.

And among the causes of the crime wave, Henry Fielding found one that deserved special attention. A whole section of the pamphlet was dedicated to drunkenness.

He didn't just mean booze in general. 'The drunkenness I here intend,' he wrote, 'is that acquired by the strongest intoxicating liquors, and particularly by that poison called gin.' Henry Fielding saw them dragged into his courtroom at Bow Street: brawlers picked up in doorways and down-and-outs who could hardly walk, prostitutes slurring insults at the bench. 'Wretches are often brought before me,' he related, 'charged with theft and robbery, whom I am forced to confine before they are in a condition to be examined; and when they have afterwards become sober, I have plainly perceived ... that the Gin alone was the cause of the transgression.'

Gin, Henry Fielding had 'great reason to think,' was 'the principal sustenance (if it may be so called) of more than a hundred thousand people in this metropolis. Many of these wretches there are who swallow pints of this poison within the twenty-four hours: the dreadful effects of which I have the misfortune every day to see, and to smell too.' Gin corroded all the bonds of normal life; it destroyed families; it ate into society. And Henry Fielding's vision of the future could hardly have been more stark. 'Should the drinking of this poison be continued in its present height during the next twenty years,' he warned, 'there will be by that time few of the common people left to drink it.'

Maybe Henry Fielding was breaking new ground in uncovering for Londoners the darker side of their town. But when it came to solutions, he fell back on all the old clichés of reform. Luxury was the root of all evil; the poor turned to gambling and drink because they were too well-off. Fielding targeted masquerades and gaming-houses, social climbing, conspicuous consumption. The former playwright even attacked the vice of theatres. His fears were the fears of Sir John Gonson. 'What must become of the infant who is conceived in Gin,' he asked, 'with the poisonous distillations of which it is nourished both in the womb and at the breast? Are these wretched infants . . . to become our future sailors, and our future grenadiers? . . . Doth not this polluted source, instead of producing servants for the husbandman or artificer, instead of providing recruits for the sea or the field, promise only to fill almshouses and hospitals, and to infect the streets with stench and diseases?' The rich were let off the hook ('I am not here to satirise the great, among who luxury is probably rather a moral than a political evil'). And when it came to solutions for the gin problem, there would be neither compromise nor pragmatism. Henry Fielding stood four-square with the zealots. Calling for a return to prohibition, he recommended Thomas Wilson's tract from 1736. 'Nor will anything less than absolute deletion serve on the present occasion,' he insisted. 'It is not making men pay £50 or £500 for a licence to poison; nor enlarging the quantity from two gallons to ten, which will extirpate so stubborn an evil.'

There were good reasons why Henry Fielding should take a hard line on gin and crime. It wasn't just the horrors he lived with as a magistrate. He was keeping hardline company as well. In 1744, the year after repeal of the Gin Act, Henry Fielding had moved into Old Boswell Court, where his neighbour was Thomas Lane, member of the Society for Promoting Christian Knowledge and author of the Middlesex magistrates' report of 1736. Lane was now Chair of Middlesex Sessions. When Henry Fielding became Chair in Westminster, in 1749, the two men had every opportunity to discuss the scourge of the London slums.

It might have been through his neighbour that Henry Fielding met another old enemy of Madam Geneva. On 13 December 1750, he had dinner with Thomas Wilson.

In his diary, Thomas Wilson recorded that the two men 'talked over the affair of vice and immorality.' The '3 great sources of our present enormities about this city,' they decided, were 'Gin, gaming and the infinite number of places of diversion which ruin the Middling Tradesman.' They talked over the problems of dealing with Madam Geneva. 'As for gin,' Thomas Wilson noted, 'the government will never, 'tis feared, prohibit it in earnest while it brings in so prodigious a revenue, upwards of £200,000 a year.' What they had to do was to link gin with the other problems of the time. And that was where the *Inquiry* came in. Fielding, Wilson noted excitedly, 'thinks he has brought [it] into a system, and when it is called for by our Great Men will be ready for them. In the meantime he will publish a little pamphlet to introduce it.'

The zealots were back in action again, and prohibition was back on the agenda. With Thomas Wilson taking an interest, the campaign would be as skilfully co-ordinated as ever. After that evening with Henry Fielding, Wilson 'wrote an account of the conversation to the Bishop of Worcester . . . who is going to print his excellent . . . sermon preached last year at St Bride's with an appendix relating to Gin etc.' ('Dr Hales,' he added, 'Myself, and Mr Tucker of Bristol to be assisting in this.') The Bishop of Worcester was Isaac Maddox, a member of the SPCK since 1736. It was Isaac Maddox who had reignited the gin campaign the year before with an Easter Day sermon in which he unburdened himself of all the frustration and anger he had felt since the afternoon in 1743 when he sat in the House of Lords and watched the ministry sign its pact with the devil. For Isaac Maddox, pragmatism had always been a betrayal of principle. 'To say, "What can be done? Alas, the people *will* have this liquid poison,"' he proclaimed in his sermon, 'is one of the most dreadful and most fatal declarations that can possibly be made . . . It is contrary to the fundamental principles upon which communities subsist.'[14]

Thomas Wilson had been in the congregation that day and thought it 'an admirable sermon.'[15] Just a fortnight after Fielding's *Inquiry* came out, its text was published as *The Expediency of Preventative Wisdom*, with a dedication in the form of a letter about spirits to the Lord Mayor. It was even arranged that a copy should be sent to every member of the Court of Common Council.[16] The strategy was to tie gin-drinking in with the crime wave. 'I appeal ... to your Lordship,' Isaac Maddox wrote, 'whether by far the greatest part of all the atrocious crimes that come in judgement before you ... be not committed by persons ... enraged by these inflammatory spirits; whether the criminals themselves ... do not bear in their countenance, and their whole manner and appearance, the plainest and most shocking proofs that their blood is enflamed by the habitual drinking of gin.'

To push the new campaign against gin still further, those twisted countenances were about to be brought vividly to life before the eyes of Londoners. Henry Fielding was a close friend of William Hogarth, and just a month after his own *Inquiry* was published, Hogarth joined the attack on gin. His contribution took the form of a pair of satirical prints. The first was called *Beer Street*, the second, *Gin Lane*.

*Gin Lane* was set in the heart of St Giles's. In the background was the spire of St George's, Bloomsbury. Hawksmoor's church may have symbolised London's elegance, but in its shadow was an urban hell. 'Nothing but idleness, poverty, misery and ruin are to be seen,' Hogarth recorded in his *Autobiographical Notes*. 'Distress even to madness and death, and not a house in tolerable condition but pawnbrokers and the gin-shop.' Behind the woman slumped on the steps, drunkards brawled and ruined buildings decayed; children made themselves senseless with the ubiquitous drug. Above a cellar door was engraved the familiar sign, 'Drunk for a penny, Dead drunk for twopence, Clean straw for nothing.' Housewives pawned their cooking pots for gin; workmen handed over the tools of their trade. A man gnawed on one end of a bone and a dog on the other. A cook carried a baby impaled on a stick. High up in a ruined house, a bankrupt hanged himself from a beam. Outside the shop of Kilman, the distiller, a mother tipped gin down her baby's throat. The only prosperous house in the alley belonged to the undertaker.

It wasn't High Art, and it wasn't photo-journalism. *Gin Lane* and its companion were polemic. Together they were a tract in pictures instead of words. 'Neither great correctness of drawing or fine engraving were at all necessary,' Hogarth wrote, 'but on the contrary would set the price of them out of the reach of those for whom they were chiefly intended.'[17] Hogarth had always had an interest in reform. Back in 1729 he had drawn James Oglethorpe's Prisons Committee investigating the horrors of the Fleet. There was a special interest there; Hogarth's own father had been in a debtors' prison. And he might have carried a personal grudge against Madam Geneva as well. His mother had died 'of a fright' in June 1735 after a fire started in a brandy-shop in Cecil Court.[18]

The point of *Gin Lane* wasn't just to shock. Like Henry Fielding in his *Inquiry*, like the reformers of the 1730s, Hogarth was attacking all the evils of the age. In his composition, he drew St George's church spire lowest in a trinity of symbols. Above it came the crown, represented by the statue of George I, and highest of all a pawnbroker's sign. In the new world of early eighteenth-century London, all proper values had been inverted. Religion was debased below the power of the court. Money – in the form of credit – ruled over everything. When he turned to *Beer Street*, the proper order of things was restored. In Beer Street, the crucifix on a church spire rose above a decorous royal standard flying for the King's birthday. Far, far below came a drooping pawnbroker's sign. In Beer Street, things were as they should be. '*Beer Street*,' as Hogarth recalled, 'was given as a contrast, w[h]ere the invigorating liquor is recommend[ed] in order [to] drive the other out of vogue. Here all is joyous and thriving[.] Industry and jollity go hand in hand[;] the pawnbroker in this happy place is the only house going to ruin.'[19] Buildings were going up, not down. A healthy blacksmith brandished a leg of lamb (in the first version, it had been a terrified Frenchman). In Beer Street, as William Hogarth drew it, the only thin man was the artist.

Hogarth's prints, Henry Fielding's tract and Isaac Maddox's sermon had all been timed to follow the start of the 1751 parliamentary session on 17 January. Other attacks followed. On 12 March the reformer Corbyn Morris published a detailed study of the London death rate. It focused on the enormous deficit between births and deaths in London – the city's population only remained stable because of the immigrants flooding in from outside. He blamed the deficit in particular on 'the enormous use of spirituous liquors.'[20]* The birth rate had been dropping (according to the Bills of Mortality) since the early 1720s – just when the authorities had taken notice of gin. Since then, 'as [gin] consumption hath been constantly increasing . . . the amount of the births hath likewise been continually diminishing.' As for the death rate, 'inquire from the several hospitals in this city,' Corbyn Morris suggested, 'whether any increase of patients, and of what sort, are daily brought under their care? They will all declare, increasing multitudes of dropsical and consumptive people arising from the effects of spirituous liquors.'

Meanwhile, another reformer, Josiah Tucker of Bristol, set about linking gin-drinking to the decline of the economy. Josiah Tucker had been sent Thomas Wilson's memo of his conversation with Henry Fielding, and his argument followed the line Wilson had taken fifteen years before in *Distilled Spirituous Liquors the Bane of the Nation*. His results were even more startling. Every year, Josiah Tucker concluded after pages of calculations, Madam Geneva cost

* Some modern analysts have tried to find an explanation in the influenza epidemics of 1728–9 and 1741–2, although even they struggle to explain the long population stagnation at a time of cheap food.

the economy three million, nine hundred and ninety-seven thousand, six hundred and nineteen pounds, and eleven pence halfpenny.[21] (The people of Bristol didn't thank him for this insight. In April that year, as the *Gentleman's Magazine* recorded, they 'patrolled the streets with several effigies, one of which was ... designed for the Rev Mr Tucker, rector of St Stephen, who had wrote ... a pamphlet on the pernicious use of spirituous liquors.' The effigies were later 'committed to the flames with all the marks of detestation and contempt.'[22])

It all added up to a powerful attack on Madam Geneva. The tracts of 1751 brought a new kind of professionalism to the reform camp. As Josiah Tucker put it, they went beyond 'pathetical description of the miseries and destructive consequences occasioned by spirituous liquors.' The leading magistrate in Westminster had blamed Madam Geneva for the crime wave. A detailed analysis of the death rate had pinned London's mortality on her. When trade was subjected to careful scrutiny, it appeared that gin was crippling the economy as well. And up in his pulpit, the Bishop of Worcester had described in graphic detail the damage gin-drinking was doing to the nation's moral balance sheet.

Once again, Madam Geneva was the talk of the town. 'The fatal and destructive effects of the excessive use of spirituous liquors, especially Gin,' noted a letter in the *London Magazine*, '[are] at present a general subject of conversation.'[23] Henry Fielding's *Inquiry* attracted widespread publicity, with long extracts published in the *Gentleman's Magazine* and *London Magazine*. The *Monthly Review* thought that if Fielding had 'been heretofore admired for his wit and humour, he now merits equal applause as a good magistrate, a useful and active member and a true friend to his country.' Newspapers headlined the more shocking statistics. Since 1725, 84,000 children had died as result of gin-drinking. Spirit revenues in the 1740s had been more than £100,000 a year higher than

in the previous decade. By now they were said to be running –
licences, low wines and all – at £676,125 a year. 'According to a
list delivered in of private gin-shops,' gasped the *Whitehall Evening
Post*, 'on the best calculation, they amount to upwards of 17,000
in the Bills of Mortality.'[24] The temperature was starting to rise.
'O my unhappy country!' wailed a 'Gentleman in the Country'.
'What ruin must come upon thee if thou dost not quickly wake
from the luxurious dream of pleasure, which locks up thy sense . . .
Who, without grief, can behold England . . . laid waste by gin,
and hastening fast to desolation and ruin?'[25] *Read's Weekly Journal*
drafted the first public health warning:

> LABEL FOR A GIN BOTTLE
> When famed Pandora to the clouds withdrew,
> From her dire box, unnumbered evils flew.
> No less a curse this vehicle contains: –
> Fire to the mind and poison to the veins.[26]

Meanwhile, the reformer's central strategy of linking gin to the crime
wave was paying off. 'There is not only no safety living in this
town,' Bishop Benson of Gloucester wrote in a letter, 'but scarcely
in the country now, robbery and murder are grown so frequent.
Our people are now become what they never before were, cruel
and inhuman. Those accursed spirituous liquors which, to the
shame of our government, are so easily to be had, and in such
quantities drunk, have changed the very nature of our people; and
they will, if continued to be drunk, destroy the very race of people
themselves.'[27]

Parliament had assembled on 17 January. Opening the session,
the King's Speech deplored the 'outrages and violences, which are
inconsistent with all good government, and endanger the lives and
properties of my subjects.' Crime was firmly on the agenda. And

gin had been tagged by reformers high on the list of its causes.
There would be no compromise this time; they wanted Madam
Geneva dead and buried. 'As to gin-drinking,' insisted a letter in
the *Gentleman's Magazine*, 'the whole distillery should be suppressed:
making gin a penny a pint dearer is doing nothing . . . It would be
better for this kingdom if no sort of spirits was ever hereafter to be
tasted in it.'[28]

No one expected a turbulent session in Parliament. There was
no war on. The opposition seemed moribund. Carteret was gone
and Walpole's protégé, Henry Pelham, had a firm grip on power.
Once he was done with crime, George II seemed barely able to
keep his eyes open in his opening address. 'I have nothing further
to recommend to you in particular,' he yawned. 'Let me exhort you,
in general, to make the best use of the present state of tranquillity,
for improving the trade and commerce of my Kingdom.'

Maybe it was the 'state of tranquillity' that gave the Parliament
of 1751 its opportunity. It was thirteen years, after all, since
Parliament had been free from the burdens of war or its aftermath.
Before that, Robert Walpole had controlled its business, and Robert
Walpole was, by his own admission, 'no reformer'. 1751 was the
first year in decades when Parliament had had a clear run at
domestic issues. It was the first time in years that entrenched
divisions of party had largely dissolved. And the crime wave
was the subject on everyone's lips. Henry Fielding had reckoned
the whole aim of his *Inquiry* had been 'to rouse the civil power from
its present lethargic state.' This was its opportunity.

There was little sign of lethargy. Instead, Parliament tore into
domestic issues at a frenetic pace. It was in the early 1750s that the
old Julian calendar was finally scrapped and Britain entered the
same time-zone as the rest of Europe. Lord Chancellor Hardwicke
moved to outlaw the abuses of back-street weddings at the Fleet.

Henry Pelham introduced – although he later withdrew – a measure to increase the rights of Jews. The British Museum was established. There was a flood of proposals to mend and improve roads. And on 1 February 1751, just as *Gin Lane* went on sale at Hogarth's house in Leicester Fields, a parliamentary committee was appointed 'to revise and consider the laws in being, which relate to felonies, and other offences against the peace.'

The committee broke new ground. To start with, its membership was interesting. The committee included not only the Prime Minister, Henry Pelham, and most of the other leading parliamentary heavyweights, but also Henry Fielding's old school-friends George Lyttelton and William Pitt. James Oglethorpe was back in London and soon joined the meetings. Charles Gray, a Tory and the son of a glazier, was also an amateur archaeologist and a founding trustee of the British Museum. William Hay, the disabled MP for Seaford, had been campaigning on poor relief and disability for fifteen years.

Then there was the way the committee set about its business. Crime in the past had been dealt with *ad hoc*, but the new committee, which would meet for the next three years, would take a holistic approach, examining everything from legal aid to cleaning up trials, from the handling of stolen goods to protecting magistrates from malicious prosecution. It came up with ideas about improving the watch, and alternatives to the bloody parade of Tyburn. Later reformers would sometimes claim the 1751 committee as the moment when Parliament started to take reform seriously. It wasn't quite that. Most of its proposals got bogged down; only a few reached the statute book. A good number of its ideas belonged as much to the 'repressive' past as to any socially enlightened future. But it did create a background hum of social issues in Parliament. The spotlight was now firmly on crime. It was only a matter of time before MPs turned their attention to gin.

The immediate trigger for action, as usual, was a flood of petitions calling on Parliament to legislate. First to move was the City of London, nicely whipped up to a frenzy by Isaac Maddox's sermon. Others soon followed. The petitions attacked Madam Geneva from the usual angles and in the usual language. The difference this time was the range of directions they came from. In the past it had been the magistrates of Middlesex and Westminster who applied themselves to the gin problem. Now parish vestries started to lobby on their own account. On 1 March St Martin-in-the-Fields sent their own lobby to Parliament, and St Anne's Westminster followed a few days later. Within a week they were joined by seven others. The 'Lord High Steward and other officials of the City of Westminster' feared that gin-drinking, if not checked, 'may prove the destruction of religion and civil society.' Middlesex Quarter Sessions joined the chorus on 7 March.

Petitions came from outside London as well. There was a growing feeling that the gin problem was spreading to the country. 'The evil is increasing every day,' Josiah Tucker of Bristol thought, 'making its way from the Metropolis into the country towns, and even villages.' (That nicely matched the reformer's image of the big city's corruption poisoning the nation.) In 1751, petitions to Parliament would arrive from Bristol – both its Lord Mayor and its 'Society of Merchant Adventurers' – and from 'the Justices of the Peace, Clergy, Gentlemen, Merchants, Dealers, and Manufacturers, of the Town of Manchester.' A petition from Norwich reported 'a manifest change ... amongst the ... common people in their habitations, cloathing, and manner of living,' and laid it all at the door of Madam Geneva. A final, late entrant in the line-up of petitions was that den of debauchery and drug abuse, Henley-upon-Thames.

The buzz of voices calling for legislation was rising to a roar. At the bar of the House of Commons, a succession of experts testified to the trail of devastation Madam Geneva left behind her. Eminent doctors like Dawson, physician to St George's Hospital, confirmed that between 1734 and 1749 hospital admissions had risen from 12,710 a year to 38,147. Asked to account for the change, Dr Dawson 'answered, from the melancholy consequences of gin-drinking, principally.' City of London officials testified that one house in fifteen in the City was a gin-shop. Saunders Welch, High Constable of Holborn, capped that with evidence that the 7,066 gin-shops in his division amounted to almost one house in five. In St Giles's, things were even worse. 'There were about 2,000 houses and 506 gin-shops, being above one house in four; besides about 82 two-penny houses of the greatest infamy, where gin was the principal liquor drank.' Two bakers, John Wyburn and John Rogers, reported 'that the consumption of bread amongst the poor was greatly diminished since the excessive drinking of gin . . . The poor laid out their earnings in gin, which ought to purchase them bread for themselves and families; and that, in many of the out-parts, the bakers were obliged to cut their loaves into halfpenny-worths, a practice unknown to the trade till gin was so universally drank by the poor.'

In the hands of the newspapers, these statistics became even more terrifying. Daniel Carne, High Constable of Westminster, had testified that 2,200 of the 17,000 houses in Westminster sold gin. But someone was spinning the press again. The figure that took the headlines that week claimed a shocking 17,000 gin-shops in London. There was a good deal of exaggeration on all sides. The statistics which the City of London put before the House were swollen by the inclusion of ordinary alehouses. When the City constables returned records of unlicensed spirit-sellers, they could only come up with a total of 274 in the whole City.[29] The figure was not widely publicised.

Orchestrating the parade of evidence to the House in the second week of March was a rising parliamentary star. Thomas Potter, second son of the former Archbishop of Canterbury, would die young, never fulfilling his promise, but in 1751 he was 'a handsome clever youth,' closely linked with the Prince of Wales's faction. Horace Walpole remarked that session that 'the Prince has got some new and very able speakers, particularly a young Mr Potter ... who promises very greatly; the world is already matching him against Mr Pitt.' (Potter's private life was less promising. Leading a rakish existence from his father's apartments in Lambeth Palace, he had got a rector's daughter, a Miss Manningham, into trouble, and been forced to marry her. 'Oh, my dear Charles,' he wrote to his friend, Charles Lyttelton, 'I am no more what I was, no more the careless, the cheerful, the happy man thou knowest, but unhappy, miserable beyond remedy. In short I am – married, and married to a woman I despise and detest.')[30]

Thomas Potter was on the committee looking into crime, and he was close to the reformers. On 12 March, with the petitions flooding in, Corbyn Morris published his *Observations* on the London death rate and dedicated it to Potter. The day it came out, as Horace Walpole put it, 'Potter produced several physicians and masters of workhouses to prove the fatal consequences of spirituous liquors, which laid waste the meaner parts of the town, and were now spreading into the country.' As always, the reform campaign made no mistakes in its timing.

But it was on the same day, 12 March, that the bandwagon for a hardline new Gin Act received its first check. The spanner would be thrown into the works by Henry Pelham, Prime Minister and brother of the Duke of Newcastle.

It wasn't for nothing that Henry Pelham was seen as Robert Walpole's political heir. He was worried about his revenues. On 12 March he tried to have the physicians' evidence ruled out of court.

The reason, to Horace Walpole at least, was transparent. Pelham 'believed no remedy could be found for the evil, and yet imposing new duties would greatly diminish the Revenue.'[31] The government had only been cohabiting with Madam Geneva for eight years, but already they couldn't imagine life without her.

The reformers held a trump card. Back in 1743 there had been a war on. Ministers had been able to claim an urgent need for cash. In 1751, Isaac Maddox could ask what the country was coming to if it had to raise its revenue from vice 'even in a time of public peace and tranquillity.'[32] The zealots were in a better position to prise ministers' hands off spirit revenues than at any time since 1738.

The way to do it was through a massive increase in the 'still-head' duties paid by malt distillers. There would be no more messing around with compound distillers or Parliamentary Brandy. And the increase would be big enough to kill the trade outright. It would 'fall short of the ends intended by it,' in the view of one reformer, 'unless the duty is so high as to prevent the common sale of this commodity.'[33] And when Thomas Potter's draft Bill was published, it showed every sign of living up to expectations. The extra two shillings a gallon which he proposed for the spirits duty would represent more than half the cost of spirits. Giving evidence in 1745, the spirit dealer Stephen South told a select committee that malt distillers sold their spirits at around 1/10 a gallon, or £23 a ton, and profits ran at £3–4 a ton. Thomas Potter's new duty by itself would have come to more than £25 a ton. There would be no more getting drunk for a penny and dead drunk for tuppence.

Henry Pelham 'spoke greatly against it,' Horace Walpole remembered. Pelham could see a black hole opening up in government finances. But all he managed to win was an adjournment. The bandwagon for a return to prohibition seemed unstoppable. Given time, Henry Pelham might put the case for keeping the pragmatic policy of 1743, but he didn't have time. He had only won himself seven days. The debate would resume on 28 March.

But someone's lucky star — either Henry Pelham's or Madam Geneva's — was shining on them. On 20 March, even as Henry Pelham was on his feet in the House of Commons, Frederick, Prince of Wales, slumped onto a sofa complaining of pain in his stomach. Doctors would later diagnose the bursting of an abscess caused when the Prince had been struck by a tennis ball some weeks earlier. By next morning the heir to the throne was dead. It would be a month of mourning and funeral arrangements before debate on the Gin Bill could be resumed.

It wasn't only the fear of lost revenues that worried men like Henry Pelham. The measures which Thomas Potter put forward on behalf of the reformers would have meant a return to prohibition, but there were plenty of politicians and commentators who could remember the lesson of 1736, even if Isaac Maddox and Henry Fielding had forgotten it.

For some, it was no longer good enough simply to rail against the times, as reactionaries had been doing ever since the Glorious Revolution, to talk wistfully about a golden past and demand the eradication of vice. It was no longer enough to lambast gin-drinkers, prostitutes and the idle poor, to string up petty criminals, and drag blasphemers off to court.

In many areas of social concern, writers were starting to look for causes behind vice and immorality. When it examined prostitution in March 1751, *The Rambler* had no doubt 'that numbers [of women] follow this dreadful course of life with shame, horror and regret.' Prostitutes had always been the villains of London's streets; now they were being turned into victims. 'Where can they hope for refuge?' the paper went on. 'The bully and the bawd . . . fatten on their misery, and threaten them with want or a gaol, if they shew the least design of escaping.'[34] Back in 1736 the *Daily Post* had attacked brutal conditions in the army, declaring that 'if [soldiers] were treated in other respects with civility and humanity, the opportunities of being vicious would not only be taken from them, but they would insensibly grow ashamed of their vices, and endeavour to behave themselves.'[35] The 'spirit of humanity' would be celebrated by the reformer John Brown in the mid-1750s. Even the traditional dependence on the noose to enforce law and order was starting to be questioned. 'It is surely a vain attempt to put a stop to such crimes by the halter,' the *London Evening Post* argued in June 1751. 'If we would really prevent such intolerable disorders, we should, like skilful physicians, remove the cause of them, and not vainly fight against the effects.'[36]

There was plenty of this new humanity in Henry Fielding's novels, but in his *Inquiry* he seemed to have gone back to an older, harsher vision of the age. Dr Johnson, for one, attacked the *Inquiry*'s prescriptions for law and order, complaining that 'all seem to think that . . . we can only be rescued from the talons of robbery by inflexible rigour, and sanguinary justice.'[37] A writer who hadn't forgotten prohibition criticised Fielding's divisive focus on vice among the poor in the March *London Magazine*, querying whether 'there is any pleasure, or any vice, in which the great are allowed to indulge themselves, that can effectually by law be denied to the little.' When it came to gin, some writers, at least, were starting to go beyond shock and horror and wonder why people abused alcohol in the first place. 'Poverty may not only be the effect, but the cause of dram-drinking,' one suggested, 'wherefore it is to be wished, that any attempt to prevent the latter, will be accompanied with a relief to the former.'[38]

To commentators like that, the absolutist position adopted by Henry Fielding and the zealots looked more like a throwback to the Societies for Reformation of Manners than a practical solution to the problem. Prohibition, after all, had been tried once and it had failed disastrously. The pragmatic policy started in 1743, by contrast, had had visible results.

There had been changes in Parliament's attitude to prescriptive legislation as well. It had been a scarring experience to watch the Gin Act being ignored. To many, 1738 was a lesson that parliaments could not simply dictate popular behaviour and expect to be obeyed. 'The good of the people,' the *Gloucester Journal* had argued as prohibition fizzled out in 1738, 'is the great end for which all government is established ... When [government] discovers a riotous spirit in the people, it must not trust in ... stifling the discontents of the subjects by a military force ... The wisdom and goodness of a government ought to shew themselves, by looking ... into the real causes of a riot, and using all possible means to redress all true grievances of the people.'[39]

That kind of thinking, well mixed with cynicism and greed for revenue, had underpinned the Gin Act of 1743. The Act had been realistic about Parliament's powers; it had accepted that the poor would go on drinking gin for as long as gin offered them any comfort. It had been a compromise. Henry Pelham's aim, in the month after the Prince of Wales's death, was to return to that compromise.

There was plenty of lobbying going on as well. This time it wasn't coming from the Company of Distillers. The clique who ran the Company were beyond effective action. A Quarterly Assembly in 1748 had been cancelled because members 'thro' age, infirmity or otherwise do seldom attend.' When they tried to put together a lobbying committee in 1751, those 'who were [nominated] to be of the ... Committee declaring their unwillingness to attend ... the Court did not think fit to ... proceed any further thereon.'[40] Among the malt distillers, though, there was no such defeatism. In mid-March they were reported to be hampering City magistrates' attempt at a clamp-down on gin-shops. They worked hard behind the scenes. The line they pushed throughout 1751 was that the renewed prohibition campaign was a political ambush dreamed up by the opposition 'calculated rather to serve the purposes of a party . . . determined to distress the administration, than that any material benefits were expected from it.'[41]

With the death of Frederick, Prince of Wales, the opposition had lost their figurehead and *raison d'être*. Whether that was the cause, or whether it was the malt distillers' string-pulling, Henry Pelham's need for revenue or Parliament's sobering memories of prohibition, the Gin Bill which the Prime Minister himself laid before the House on 23 April looked very different from the one Thomas Potter had first proposed. There was no sign of any two shilling-a-gallon duty. The spirit duty would now go up by a modest fourpence halfpenny, to one shilling a gallon. There would be limited increases in duties on low wines, but it was a long way from a ban on gin. The proposals, as even Horace Walpole commented, were 'slight ones indeed for so enormous an evil!'[42] They fell far short of what Henry Fielding and Isaac Maddox had called for. There would be no return to prohibition.

The 1751 Gin Act was a defeat for the zealots, and a victory for the pragmatic policy of 1743. Seven years before, as the *Westminster Journal* recalled in summer 1751, the 1743 Act 'was asserted . . . to be [a] first necessary tax, which, tho' it might produce no great effects in itself, would at least make way for a second, that would be more sensibly felt; till, at length, these fatal spirits should be raised to a price at which few would be able, and none willing, to purchase them.'[43] Events had borne the policy out. The black market had gone. Nearly 30,000 retail licences were now being taken out every year. With its modest increase in duties, following the course set out in 1743, the 1751 Gin Act represented the triumph of realism over principle, restriction over prohibition.

The 1751 Act was realistic in more than its modest duties. Maybe the work of the reform committee was spilling over into the way Parliament looked at all its legislation. The 1751 Gin Act showed a new concern with detail, a new professionalism. The committee charged with drafting the Act took a month over it, and their time was well spent. There was proper consultation, for a start. Within a week of starting work, they sent a draft to the Commissioners of Excise for their comment, and asked to see a draft of the Commissioners' own suggestions. One measure was obvious enough. The 1747 Act which had allowed distillers to sell spirits would be repealed. There would be a push to squeeze small traders out of the industry. The retail licence would be doubled to £2. Licences would be available only to inns, alehouses and taverns – and only to such of those as were prosperous and well-established. Grocers and chandlers' shops were specifically excluded. Penalties for unlicensed gin-sellers would go up.

For the first time, legislators were getting to grips with the whole supply-chain for gin. It had long been complained that gin-sellers sold spirits on credit, allowing workers to run up huge tabs by the end of each week. Under the new Act, spirit-sellers would no longer be able to go to court to recover small debts for spirit sales. Any dealer who sold gin up to the value of a pound did so at his own risk. From now on, unlicensed retailers would themselves be able to inform on the distillers who supplied them. They wouldn't only be able to claim their reward; they would be given immunity from prosecution as well. It would be a foolhardy distiller who sold gin to an unlicensed shop, when the gin-seller had only to hand in his name to avoid prosecution, make £5 and walk away scot-free. Spirits would be banned from gaols. Payments to informers would be speeded up. There were detailed provisions to reduce licensing fraud and fraud by distillers.

The new duties in the 1751 Gin Act were small enough. But

its effects, and its significance, would go much further than those modest duties implied. For the first time legislators had actually made an effort to understand how the gin industry worked.

By the time the new Gin Act received royal assent, on 25 June, a clamp-down on gin-shops was already under way. At the beginning of March, the *Whitehall Evening Post* reported that 'upwards of 50 licensed distillers were convicted before the Commissioners of Excise, for suffering tippling in their shops, and fined in the penalty of £10 each.'[44] Another forty would be convicted in April, and there would be even bigger sweeps in May and June. Middlesex magistrates joined the clamp-down as well, with a move against unlicensed dealers in Bagnell's Marsh and other slum areas.

And when the new régime came in on 1 July, it was strictly enforced. Middlesex magistrates got wind that dram-shops were trying to reclassify themselves as alehouses so as to make themselves eligible for spirits licences. In response, Quarter Sessions recommended JPs 'not to licence any house which hath not been heretofore a publick house, has not been so within the space of three years last past, or which hath been converted into a private house since the same was a publick one.' In some Westminster parishes, anyone who applied for a licence was required to 'bring four substantial housekeepers to vouch for his honesty and sobriety.' At a City of London licensing sessions, the *Gentleman's Magazine* reported that 'only 27 licences, viz. 25 for former victualling houses and two for new coffee-houses, were granted.'[45] Forty alehouses were suppressed in St James's, Westminster in late September, and another forty in Tower Hamlets a month later.

The clamp-down certainly gave the impression of a government getting to grips with gin. For some gin-drinkers, it was all too much. 'A few days since,' reported the *London Morning Penny Post* on 29 July, 'a poor man who lives in Long Ditch, Westminster, having got together near two bottles of gin to serve him when the Act took place, laid a wager with a neighbour that he and his wife could between them drink it off, fasting; which they accordingly did ... and both continued well for some hours, but the next morning were both found dead in their bed.' There was a certain amount of griping about Excise. One 1752 print showed Excise men staving in the casks of an unlicensed gin seller. 'If this be Angleterre,' commented a bystander, 'me go to France.'

No one, though, could carp at the Act's results. In 1751, just over seven million gallons of English spirits paid duty. The figure hadn't changed substantially since 1744. In 1752, the quantity of spirits produced dropped below four and a half million gallons for the first time in twenty years. There had been no change in corn prices, no new war, no other obvious influence coming into play. Spirit production would remain more or less steady for the next six years.

If the tide had turned in 1743, then the Gin Act of 1751 saw gin visibly ebbing out of London. Even reformers could see the achievement in that. Whatever they had called for at the time, they were quick to claim the 1751 Gin Act as their own. In his *Inquiry*, Henry Fielding had ruled out anything 'less than absolute deletion' of the spirits industry. But in the pages of the *Covent Garden Journal*, a year on, he would assign credit to Isaac Maddox for the success of a law, 'which, if it hath not abolished, hath very considerably lessened the pernicious practice of gin drinking.'[46] Six years later, the reformer George Burrington would report that 'the lower people in late years have not drunk spirituous liquors so freely, as they did before the good regulations ... settled by Parliament ... We do not see the hundredth part of poor wretches drunk in the streets.'[47] Credit was widely given to the new Gin Act. 'The custom,' Jonas Hanway would recall at the end of the decade, 'of the common people's drinking great quantities of a most inflammatory and poisonous liquor, certainly created an incredible devastation amongst the children of the poor, till the hand of providence interposed, by the instrumentality of His Majesty's ministers, to arrest the dreadful progress of it.'[48]

But if Madam Geneva had lost her power over Londoners, it wasn't all down to His Majesty's ministers. The times were changing as well. She had made her home in a chaotic city of gamblers and speculators, a city of danger and opportunity, a city of risk. By the mid-point of the century, London could seem a very different place. 'The people themselves,' as Jonas Hanway put it, 'seem at length to have discovered, that health and pleasure, food and raiment, are better than sickness and pain, want and wretchedness.'[49] The decades since the Glorious Revolution had been a gin-fuelled adventure, a rollercoaster ride. For many, by 1751, it was time to get off.

# CHAPTER SIXTEEN

## THE MIDDLE CLASSES

By the middle of the eighteenth century, spirits weren't the only kind of transformation on offer in London. Those who wanted it could try out a drug far more potent even than gin.

It all started in May 1738, just after the acquittal of Roger Allen, the Thrift Street rioter. On Wednesday 24 May, a young cleric was attending a religious meeting in Aldersgate Street. Listening to Luther's preface to the Epistle to the Romans, at 'about a quarter before nine' in the evening, he felt his heart 'strangely warmed.' That was all there was to it; in his diary he sounded a bit disappointed there were no angels or trumpets. But 24 May 1738 was the transfiguring day of John Wesley's life.

Everyone had to hear the good news. In London that autumn Wesley threw himself into his new ministry. He preached in prisons and workhouses. He rode the cart to Tyburn with the condemned. Even that wasn't enough. On 2 April 1739 'at four in the afternoon, I submitted to be more vile, and proclaimed in the highways the glad tidings of salvation, speaking . . . to about three thousand people.'

Wesley's fellow 'enthusiast', George Whitefield, followed his lead the same month. On 29 April Whitefield preached to 20,000 (by his own estimate) on Kennington Common. Thousands more flocked to hear Wesley at Blackheath and Kennington. On 6 May, at one of Whitefield's meetings, 'some supposed there were above 30 or 40,000 people, and near fourscore coaches . . . and there was . . . an awful silence among them.'

The evangelists didn't silence their congregations with dry commentaries on church matters. Theirs was faith distilled into its purest spirit, a heady draught which intoxicated the crowds. Garrick said he would give £1,000 to be able to utter 'Oh!' like Mr Wesley. Of William Romaine, another charismatic who began his ministry in 1738, it was said that visitors came to London 'to see Garrick act and Romaine preach.'[1] And the message was as intoxicating as the delivery. Religion was a transfiguring experience. There was more to it than dutiful church attendance. It could alter your whole life.

The establishment hated it, of course. Transformations were exactly what they wanted to avoid. 'It is monstrous to be told that you have a heart as sinful as the common wretches that crawl on the earth,' the Duchess of Buckingham exclaimed. 'This is highly offensive and insulting and at variance with high rank and good breeding.'[2]

The establishment was missing the point. Methodism and Madam Geneva may have seemed equally addictive, equally intoxicating, and equally dangerous in their effect on the people ('Piety as well as gin helps to fill up their leisure moments,' was one dismissive verdict).[3] But religious zealots had one big advantage over gin-drinkers. They may have been insufferable, but they didn't dodge work, abandon their families or pass out on the pavement. In turning from bottle to Bible, people were taking a step towards responsibility. For some, at least – the thousands who craned on tiptoe and shushed their neighbours to hear John Wesley preach — conspicuous consumption, drink, gambling and whores were out. A more sober future beckoned.

Religion was only part of it. Sometime in the 1740s, the middle classes came out of their shell. They had always existed, of course, although no one knew quite what to call the third of Londoners who earned something between £50 and £400 a year. There had always been attorneys and wealthy shopkeepers, curates and apothecaries. But the eighteenth-century town opened up a whole range of new opportunities for them. It offered new ways to use what wealth and leisure time they had, new ways to express themselves. By 1750, Londoners could find better places to spend their money than the dram-shop or gambling-table. 'Every clerk, apprentice, and ... waiter,' Smollett exaggerated, 'maintains a gelding by himself, or in partnership.'4 They could spend money on their homes. 'What is an article of necessity in England,' Grosley noticed on his visit, 'is mere extravagance in France. The houses in London are all wainscotted with deal; the stairs and the floors are composed of the same materials.'5 An English commentator reckoned that 'peasants and mechanics ... freeholders, tradesmen and manufacturers in middling life, wholesale dealers, [and] merchants ... have better conveniences in their houses and ... more in quantity of clean, neat furniture, and a greater variety [of] carpets, screens, window curtains, chamber bells, polished brass locks, fenders etc., (things hardly known abroad among persons of such rank) than are to be found in any country of Europe.'6

The middling tradesman saving up for new carpets and curtains was not going to spend his time crashed out at the local dram-shop. From his comfortably furnished home, perhaps in one of the new terraces springing up all over London, he set out to explore a more orderly way of life. One writer in 1752 took the measure of London on a hot June Sunday. He noticed the gin-drinkers, of course, but other Londoners now caught his eye as well. He saw 'citizens who have pieces of gardens in the adjacent villages, walking to them with their wives and children, in order to drink tea ... after which they load themselves with ... roots, salads and other vegetables to bring home to supper.' Old women fed the ducks in St James's Park; children thronged the railings in the middle of London Bridge. In the summer sunshine, anyone with a flat roof, 'especially such as have prospects of the river Thames,' could be seen 'taking the advantage of the fineness of the weather, and drinking tea, beer, punch, and smoking tobacco there, till the dusk of the evening.' On Westminster Bridge he saw 'hundreds of people, mostly women and children, walking backward and forward ... looking at the boats going up and down the river; and sitting on the resting benches to pick up new acquaintance.'[7]

Indoors, the middle classes hurried to dinner parties, boring each other with 'a great deal of insignificant discourse among people who are strangers to each other, and have met casually at some friend's house to dinner, about the fineness or dullness of the weather, beauty of their children, goodness of their husbands, and badness of their several trades and callings.'

The anonymity of the town had been one of its dangers. Now it was being softened by clubs. 'Bodies of men (known by the name of rural societies)' were seen on that June Sunday, 'straggling about the fields, cracking merry jokes, making ludicrous remarks on the places they go to, and settling where to dine, and what to spend at dinner.' There were picnics on the river, 'young people ... taking spells of the oar to relieve each other, while they refresh themselves with the tongue, ham, bread, butter, wine and punch which they took on board.' There was sport. The bloodthirsty spectacles of combat and animal-baiting at Clerkenwell were giving way to organised games. The 'healthful and manly exercise of rowing on the river Thames' was certainly a change from the brandy-shop. Saussure remarked, in 1728, that 'the English are very fond of a game they call cricket.' ('For this purpose,' he explained, 'they go into a large open field, and knock a small ball about with a piece of wood. I will not attempt to describe this game to you; it is too complicated ... Sometimes one county plays against another county.')[8]* By the mid-1730s cricket matches were being publicised and the press reported them enthusiastically. On 20 September 1736 the papers announced 'on Kennington Common, the greatest match at cricket, that has been known for many years, between the gentlemen of Kent and those of Surrey.' Surrey won by two wickets. Formal rules of cricket arrived in 1744. There were new rules for boxing as well; thuggery was being transformed into noble science. The champion of England, Jack Broughton, opened a boxing academy in the Haymarket in 1743, offering 'muffles ... that will effectively secure [participants] from the inconveniency of black eyes, broken jaws, and bloody noses.'

Suddenly, there was more for middle-class townsfolk to do in their leisure hours than strut along the Strand, aping the languid habits of their superiors. At work, meanwhile, even the hazards of business were starting to be tamed. A 1739 commentator remarked on the 'box and tradesmen's clubs which ... meet at taverns, inns, coffee and alehouses ... whereby ... a good correspondence [is] cultivated, for the mutual improvement of their respective business.'[9] Being middle class became something to be celebrated for its security, its freedom from ups and downs. 'The calamities of life,' Robinson Crusoe's father advised him, 'were always shared among the upper and lower part of mankind; but ... the middle station had the

* Misson had been equally perceptive about English football: 'This is kicked about from one to t'other ... by him that can get at it, and that is all the art of it.'

fewest disasters, and was not exposed to so many vicissitudes . . .
The middle station of life was calculated for all kinds of virtues and
all kinds of enjoyments . . . Peace and plenty were the handmaids
of a middle fortune . . . Temperance, moderation, quietness, health,
society, all agreeable diversions, and all desirable pleasures, were the
blessings attending the middle station of life; [and] this way men
went silently and smoothly thro' the world, and comfortably out
of it.'[10] In a life of temperance, moderation, quietness and health,
there was no room for Madam Geneva.

The middle classes were starting to become conscious of their
own virtues. There was a growing self-help literature to guide them
through their new world. Their dinner parties might be planned
from Hannah Glasse's *Art of Cookery made Plain and Easy*, published
in 1747, or *The Family Magazine, Containing Useful Directions in All
the Branches of House-keeping and Cookery*, which appeared from
1741. They no longer had to keep referring to those above or
below them to define who they were. A new kind of sentimental
patriotism emerged around the middle of the century as well. Its
appeal was no longer just to duty, but to something emotional, a
sense of belonging. Britain was a club which anyone could join,
and tub-thumping songs were composed to celebrate membership.
Thomas Arne's 'Rule Britannia' would be written in 1740; 'God
Save the King' would become a popular anthem at the time of the
1745 rebellion. In John Brown's *Estimate of the Manners of the Times*,
written in 1757, he would see Britain's strength as based not only
on 'the national capacity' and 'the national spirit of defence', but
on 'the national spirit of union.'

He saw other new developments as well. One was 'the spirit
of humanity.' There was a new mood in the air. In February
1751, Hogarth's *Four Stages of Cruelty* appeared alongside *Gin
Lane* and *Beer Street*. Concern for the humane treatment of animals
was already becoming more widespread. The Eton tradition of

'hunting the ram' (not just hunting it; clubbing it to death) was banned in 1747. Nor was it only animals that were being seen in a new sentimental light; attitudes to children were changing as well. Children's books started to appear. John Newbury's *Pretty Little Pocket Book* would be a runaway success in 1742, and many others would follow. Writers cast a sentimental eye on children. One, walking round London at dusk, noticed – as if they had never been there before – children sitting 'in back-alleys and narrow passages, very busy at their several doors, shelling peas and beans for supper, and making boats, as they call them, with bean shells and deal matches.'[11] Tom Jones' landlady described a little girl nursing her mother: 'Molly . . . is but thirteen years old, and yet, in my life, I never saw a better nurse . . . what is wonderful in a creature so young, she shows all the cheerfulness in the world to her mother; and yet I saw her – I saw the poor child . . . turn about, and privately wipe the tears from her eyes.'[12]

Sentiment had arrived. In literature, Swift and Pope had both died during the 1740s, and with them had passed away the harsh wit and vitriol of the Augustan coffee-house. Biting verse satire was replaced by sentimental prose. Middle-class readers of the 1740s sobbed for *Pamela* and wept buckets over *Clarissa*. Even sensible Sophia Western, in Henry Fielding's *Tom Jones*, couldn't resist a good novel. '"There appears to me a great deal of human nature in it,"' she protested when her aunt caught her reading *David Simple*, '"and in many parts, so much true tenderness and delicacy, that it hath cost me many a tear." "Ay, and do you love to cry then?" says the aunt. "I love a tender sensation," answered the niece, "and would pay the price of a tear for it any time."'[13]

The world of Moll Flanders – the world of Jonathan Wild and the South Sea Bubble, Madam Geneva's world – suddenly seemed very far away. The party, or nightmare, of the Age of Risk was coming to an end. If anyone still needed intoxication, they were as likely to turn to John Wesley's new religion as to fall into the arms of Madam Geneva. The Gin Craze had been born from an age of highs and lows, opportunities and risks. It reflected the euphoria of boom, the despair of bust. By the middle of the century, though, the middle classes were promoting new virtues of stability and responsibility.

It was only a matter of time before such habits, such fashions in behaviour, should spread further across society. Reformers soon spotted that the key to changing manners wasn't dragging the cursing poor off to prison; it was persuading them to be more middle class. 'Household economy,' one complained, 'has not the least appearance among these wretched people. Mutual affection and tenderness between husband and wife, the chief comfort and happiness of a family, is turned into brawls, strife, perpetual wranglings and everlasting jars. Parental love for their natural offspring is converted into a cruel neglect and careless disregard.'[14] Good housekeeping, marriage and the family, love for children: these were all middle-class virtues, and that was where the future lay. The same writer thought that the poor were not so far gone in vice, 'but that they may be reclaim'd . . . if the better sort of people . . . will but every man begin the work . . . The generality, the vulgar . . . will soon follow their example.'[15]

Signs of change were noted approvingly. The tireless chronicler who wandered round London on a June weekend in 1752 noticed 'careful old mothers of families, whose pangs and infirmities prevent their taking natural rest, lying in bed, considering how their circumstances are, and what method is best to take for the future . . . Wives and servant girls . . . who live in courts and alleys, where one cock supplies the whole neighbourhood with water, taking the advantage before other people are up, to fill their tubs and pans, with a sufficiency to serve them the ensuing seven days . . . Poor people that lodge in low-rented houses, going to each other, and after paying their awkward compliments, borrowing saucepans and stewpans, for the dressing peas, beans, bacon and mackerel for dinner.' One of Walpole's agents told him, in 1736, that 'most of the common people of what rank or denomination soever . . . are linked together in clubs for the mutual subsistence and support of one another.'[16] Though 'the rabble, or those who compose the mob,' were 'still very insolent and abusive', thought *A Brief Description of London* in 1776, they were 'much mended in this respect within the last fifty years.'[17] Its author even credited them with 'good nature and humour.' Baretti, writing in August 1760, found that 'in the space of ten years, I have observed that the English populace have considerably mended their manners [in their attitude to strangers] and am persuaded that in about twenty years more they will become quite as civil . . . as the French and Italians.'[18]

There were sticks as well as carrots to the change in London manners. Most important was the economy. Living standards had been high all through the decades of good harvests and cheap food – all through the gin-drinking years. By the mid-century that boom had come to an end. Real wages had climbed all through the 1740s, but they went into steep decline when food prices rose and the population began growing. The peak probably came sometime around 1743, the year the Gin Craze reached its zenith. During the 1750s, the real wages of London bricklayers, to take one example, fell by almost ten per cent, and there were worse times ahead. One modern index of real wages has spending power in 1760 slumping back past the level of the early 1720s – the years when the Gin Craze, and the panic about gin, both took off in earnest.[19] For decades it had been a standard lament about the poor that they would work only until they had enough to live; then they would head off to the dram-shop. If life was getting dearer all through the 1750s, it was hardly surprising that they would abandon Saint Monday and seek thriftier gods to worship.

It wasn't just a large sector of the population who were yearning for security and stability. London was changing as well. The city where Madam Geneva had made her home sixty years before had been a chaotic place, the battleground of entrepreneurs and con-men, pick-pockets and whores (or so, at least, it chose to represent itself). By the middle of the century, that image was changing. When Canaletto arrived in 1746, he and his imitators painted London as a city of politeness and civility rather than squalor and danger. Londoners suddenly seemed to look about themselves with new eyes. Public-spirited types were shocked to notice that 'a city famous for its wealth, commerce, and plenty, and for every other kind of civility and politeness,' should have streets 'which abound with such heaps of filth, as a savage would look on with amazement.'[20]

Back in the 1720s they either hadn't noticed the filth, or hadn't known what to do about it. Now they took action. It started with street lighting. A Lighting Act was passed for the City of London in 1736. Spitalfields followed suit two years later, Shoreditch in 1749. Foreign visitors would be amazed by London's brilliance. 'In Oxford Street alone,' Archenholz would exclaim, 'there are more lights than in all Paris.'[21] Lighting wasn't the only improvement. The Fleet River, symbol of a sordid past, would be covered over in 1747. The Thames was bridged at Westminster, embanked above London Bridge. Public building projects transformed the centre of town. Parliament Street, a new ceremonial approach from St James's to the Palace of Westminster, was begun in 1738. William Kent's new Treasury had been completed in 1736; his Horse Guards would follow in 1753.

By the 1750s tracts were appearing thick and fast to condemn the city's defects – from open cellars and projecting steps to broken pavements and dilapidated houses – and to suggest improvements.

'A greater degree of true public spirit,' wrote the MP Charles Gray, one of the members of the 1751 parliamentary committee on crime, 'seems to be very happily rising among us, and more attention to be paid than formerly to matters upon which the real welfare of the nation depends.'[22] There was a growing belief that things could be improved. Corbyn Morris's *Observations* on London mortality ended with 'proposals for a better regulation of the police* of this metropolis.' His models were the aqueducts and viaducts of ancient Rome. Rome's monuments, he pointed out, were 'all built at the public expense for public convenience.' A generation before, no one had believed either in public expense or public convenience. But a generation before, change itself had been regarded with suspicion. Change belonged to the gamblers, to the speculators and social climbers, to Madam Geneva. Reformers didn't look forwards; they looked back – back to an old England of social certainties and unchanging order. By the 1750s, that attitude was wearing thin. 'To rail at the times at large,' wrote the reformer John Brown in 1757, 'can serve no good purpose. There never was an age or nation that had not virtues and vices peculiar to itself: And in some respects, perhaps, there is no time nor country delivered down to us in [hi]story, in which a wise man would so much wish to have lived, as in our own.'[23] No wise reformer of the 1720s would have chosen to live in his own vicious age; he would have chosen Vergil's Rome, or the reign of Alfred. But some had started looking for ways to improve the present, rather than dreaming about the past. They had begun to embrace change. They had invented progress.

Captain Thomas Coram had dreamed ever since 1722 of opening a hospital to care for London's foundling children. Walking to and from the City at night had 'afforded him frequent occasions of seeing young children exposed, sometimes alive, sometimes dead,

* Meaning civil regulation.

and sometimes dying.'[24] Back in 1722, no one had listened. It wasn't until 1741 that the Foundling Hospital finally opened its doors in Hatton Garden. It would be the high-profile charity success of the 1740s. It became fashionable to visit the hospital and give your name to a Foundling Hospital child. Handel conducted his first benefit concert in the unconsecrated chapel in May 1749. Many reformers would be involved with it (including many from the campaign against gin). Hogarth donated his own portrait of Coram at the opening of the chapel; Commons Speaker Arthur Onslow gave a prayer book. The chapel would be consecrated with an inaugural sermon by Isaac Maddox, Bishop of Worcester. (Thomas Coram, sadly, would miss out on all this triumph. He fell out with the General Committee in 1742; his wife died; he ran into financial difficulties. He would be remembered at the end of his life sitting in the hospital arcade in a shabby red coat, handing out gingerbread to the children.)

The Foundling Hospital wasn't just a new institution for London. It was a whole new way of looking at charity. Back in 1709, Atterbury had written that 'the value of our gift depends not on the success of it.'[25] Charity, in his view, was there to benefit giver as much as recipient ('Our part is to chuse out the most deserving objects . . . and when that is done, all is done, that lies in our power: the rest must be left to Providence'). But the Foundling Hospital had a specific social purpose, and it would be judged by its results. To achieve them it would bring to the business of charity a new efficiency of organisation and fund-raising. Instead of railing against the institutions of the new age — marketing, subscription, the joint-stock company — it would use them to achieve its ends. There was no coincidence in that. Aristocratic support had been needed to get the project off the ground, but the huge majority of the hospital's active supporters were untitled, and the biggest group were merchants. By the 1750s a new kind of reformer was emerging. Jonas Hanway embodied the type. Tire- less and professional, grounded in business, he brought to reform an unquenchable thirst for improvement, promoting church, trade and empire through projects from foundlings to fallen women, poor boys to sailors.*

The Foundling Hospital broke ground in another way. Its end was to help that very embodiment of the Age of Risk, the foundling. Foundlings had always been vilified. They overturned the traditional idea that you were defined by your birth and must bear the consequences of it. Without known parents, foundlings had no place in traditional society and were punished for it. They carried their mothers' sin on their shoulders. Now reformers set out to help them. Many foundations followed the Foundling Hospital's lead. The Lock Hospital for women with sexually transmitted diseases opened in 1746, and two smallpox hospitals in the same year. The Lying-in Hospital for Poor Married Women would open in Covent Garden in 1749, and Queen Charlotte's Hospital for Unmarried Mothers in 1752. Many of them broke taboos, as the Foundling Hospital did. The Magdalen Hospital, opened in 1758, aimed to reclaim prostitutes. It wasn't long since the fallen woman had been held up as the cause of the age's vices, not as its victim.

Through such institutions, the risks of the age were being tamed. Its villains – whores, foundlings and bankrupts – started to attract society's pity as well as its fear and loathing; they were offered help rather than curses. It didn't happen overnight, of course. But a new mood emerged in the middle of the century, one which promoted stability above risk, public spirit over private gain. Out of doors, reformers worked busily to improve the city; indoors, families were discovering the docile pleasures of middle-class life. There were

---

* He also pioneered the umbrella and fell out bitterly with Dr Johnson over the merits of tea-drinking.

no gin-drinkers in the paintings of Canaletto. The frenetic world which had created Madam Geneva was passing. 'Were the same persons who made a full tour of England thirty years ago,' the *Gentleman's Magazine* wrote in 1754, 'to make a fresh one now they would find themselves in a land of enchantment. England is no more like to what England was than it resembles Borneo or Madagascar.'[26]

The reactionaries of the Societies for Reformation of Manners had turned into the reformers of the 1750s, men like Jonas Hanway, busily sending poor boys off to a life at sea, or Henry Fielding's half-brother John, blind magistrate of Bow Street, who campaigned tirelessly to improve London's law and order. It was in the gin years that the nineteenth-century reform movement had its roots. Vigorous Christians started campaigns; writers and artists joined the chorus (in the 1750s it would be Hogarth and Henry Fielding; eighty years later, Dickens and Cruikshank); the end result was rational legislation which extinguished the problem and improved the lot of the poor.

Even at the time, the tight-knit reform lobby claimed the 1751 Gin Act as its own. In later years they would claim the whole victory over gin. For Dorothy George, writing in the liberal reform tradition in the 1930s, it was 'a turning point in the social history of London.'[27] Before the 1751 Act, vice and misery had roved unchecked among the poor; afterwards, an orderly succession of campaigns and reforms had steadily improved their lot. The 1751 Gin Act was the first step on a road which led onwards and upwards towards clean drinking-water, pensions and the Welfare State. (Liberal historians would routinely exaggerate the figures for early eighteenth-century spirits production, usually by adding the quantities of low wines produced to the spirits that were made from them.) For subsequent reformers, the battle against gin seemed to provide a blueprint for how society could be improved.

It wasn't quite like that at the time. Reformers in the mid-eighteenth century had wanted Madam Geneva dead, not tamed; they had done their best to drive her out of town. Henry Fielding could show benevolent compassion on every page of his novels (*Tom Jones*, after all, was *The History of ... a Foundling*), but when it came to gin he was a zealot. Isaac Maddox could extend sympathy to foundlings but not to gin-drinkers. John Fielding could be pragmatic about most fallen women, but not about Madam Geneva.

There was something about her that still stuck in their throats. Back in 1743, all rational argument supported a policy of pragmatism and demonstrated that prohibition had failed, but for the bishops compromise was still too hard to swallow. The stench of the alchemist's workshop still clung to Madam Geneva. Reformers couldn't rid themselves of the idea that the distiller's alembic performed an evil magic, that it was unnatural, an insult to God. Somewhere at the back of their minds they still saw witches burning at the stake.

So reformers were the first to cheer when, in 1757, the government suddenly did exactly what they had wanted all along. They banned all distilling from grain and malt. For the first time in seventy years, the fires went out on the London distilling industry. The magic potion stopped dripping from the still-heads.

# CHAPTER SEVENTEEN

———•———

# THE DEVIL'S PACT

It wasn't anything to do with Thomas Wilson, or Henry Fielding, or any of the reformers. In 1757, Britain faced a crisis more serious even than the Seven Years War. In 1757, after forty years of generally cheap corn, after ten years in the 1740s which were 'as good . . . as ever were known in succession,'[1] the harvest failed.

In London, Parliament wasted no time in banning exports of corn and malt. On 11 March, they followed with an Act 'To prohibit . . . the making of low wines and spirits, from wheat, barley, malt, or any other sort of grain.' It was a temporary measure, passed 'for a limited time.' But in May the ban was extended until the end of the year, and when the next harvest proved no better, it was extended again. The distillers lobbied for all they were worth, but this time their pleas fell on deaf ears. Parliament was scared of the distillers, but it was more scared of a hungry mob who couldn't afford bread. In the end, the ban on distilling corn would stay in place for four years. The sun started to shine again only in 1760. That year the corn grew, and the arguments started in earnest.

Parliament faced a quandary. The trouble was that three years of prohibition had whetted the appetites of reformers for more. They had seen the effects of a ban for themselves. 'Certain it is,' wrote one campaigner, 'that the prohibition of Gin put an end to drunkenness.'[2] Spirits could still be made from imported molasses and sugar, but it was a trickle compared with what the distillers had made before. In 1760, they would produce barely a quarter of the amount they had made in 1751. And, most important of all for the reformers, higher prices put spirits beyond reach of the poor. 'On stopping the use of this intoxicating poison,' the same writer went on, 'it was almost incredible to see what a change there soon appeared among the same order of people, how they again at once became sober, industrious, vigorous, hardy, brave and governable.' It was a good time to make the case. Sober soldiers and gin-less sailors had just won Britain her *annus mirabilis*, with stunning victories over the French in North America and Europe. Freed from the tyranny of Madam Geneva, the poor seemed eagerly to have embraced middle-class virtues. 'The very poor themselves,' the writer went on ecstatically, 'talk'd with gladness and thankfulness of their deliverance from rottenness and rags.' It seemed impossible – unthinkable – that any government could contemplate letting the distillers charge their stills again. 'Is it already to be forgot,' he finished, 'how the infection of gin-drinking spread even among our women and children, and how, by the universality of it, our streets were pestered with scenes of horror and distress? . . . In the reign of Gin . . . was there a manufacturer, or indeed a housekeeper, that could manage or depend on their servants or workmen?'

But the ban had only ever been a temporary measure. Now the price of corn was falling again, and the distillers wanted their trade back. In 1760, Sir Joseph Mawbey, one of the biggest malt distillers in London, put pen to paper and published a detailed list of *Queries in Defence of the Malt-Distillery*. He didn't deny the 'reformation amongst the manners of the people, since the stoppage of the malt distillery.' But Sir Joseph could find reasons for it besides the ban on distilling. In 1748, peace and the return of the troops had caused a crime wave. Remobilisation in 1756 had had the opposite effect. Yesterday's drunkards were now toiling across a plain somewhere in India. And any change in behaviour at home could be ascribed to the Act of 1751. '[Was not] the quantity of malt spirits, made before the [ban],' he asked, 'inconsiderable, in comparison of what were formerly made; and ... did not [that Act] reduce the consumption more than a third and consequently remove great part of the evils of dram-drinking?'

Among reformers, Sir Joseph's arguments provoked instant outrage. Two sets of *Answers* were published, one ('intended to save millions') 'shewing it to be both a religious and political sin to distil spirits from corn.' One paper in particular, the *Monitor*, took up the reform case. In a series of articles, widely reprinted, it tore headlong into the distilling industry. Desperate to revive memories of the bad old days, it even exhumed Judith Defour ('How shocking is it to remember that wretched mother, who murdered her own child, threw it into a ditch, and stripped it of cloaths, just put on by a charitable person, to pawn them for nine pennyworth of gin'[3]). The more frightening statistics from the physicians' evidence from 1751 were repeated, as was the memory of a time when '7,000 out of 12,000 quarters of wheat, sold in the London markets per week, were converted into spirituous liquors.' It was zealotry at its most zealous. The *Monitor* would return to the subject no fewer than eleven times in the course of spring 1760. It would dig up all the old chestnuts about distillers adulterating spirits. It would threaten the end of British liberties. The extreme case was pushed to its limits. 'Reason and sound policy,' the paper thundered, 'religion and self-interest, our duty to God, our neighbour, and to ourselves, enforce the expediency, and necessity of continuing the prohibition.'

Pragmatists were caught in the middle. While the reformers ranted on one side, distillers were clamouring for the return of their 'property' on the other. In the background, meanwhile, landowners were wondering what to do with all their surplus barley.

To some eyes, though, that offered an opportunity. Three years of prohibition had softened the distillers up to accept duties which they would normally have fought tooth and nail. Desperate to be seen as responsible, they were even making the case for higher duties themselves. One supporter of Sir Joseph Mawbey went into print arguing for 'the laying such a farther duty on all spirits, as, though it may prevent excess in the use of them, may still not be so great, as to debar the poor, on necessary occasions, the proper use of them.'[4] They would accept anything if it would only get the stills working again. But the opportunity wouldn't be there forever. If, as one pragmatist argued, 'the prohibition were to be continued till greater plenty shall come, the clamor would be so great to have it opened, that the distillery would not readily submit to the high duties exacted at present; therefore this seems to be the critical juncture, at which we can make the best terms in favour of the regulations necessary to be enforced, for the safety of the people.'[5]

In print, the distillers may have produced honeyed words ('Gin being dear has produced sobriety,' was one demure line, 'gin being kept as dear will secure sobriety'[6]). Behind the scenes their lobbying was as ruthless as ever. A Bill was introduced to restore corn distilling – with increased duties – in March 1760. Egged on by the reform camp, the City had voted for a petition against it 'by a great majority.' But letters soon appeared in the papers urging them to change sides. By the time the Bill reached the Lords, a second petition was voted down by the City by 43–42.[7]

Other cracks started to appear in the prohibitionist position.

There were, after all, those who profited from the ban on distilling corn. West Indian sugar planters were rumoured to have increased rum imports from 650,000 gallons to well over a million gallons. Their aim, according to Sir Joseph Mawbey and his followers, was obviously 'to procure the temporary prohibition to become a permanent law. The true motive of [the reformers] is undoubtedly their interest.'[8] When the *Monitor*'s righteous indignation began to look less than impartial, support for prohibition fell away. The *Gentleman's Magazine* had started out advocating prohibition, but the scales soon fell from its eyes. '[People] now find how much they have been abused,' it wrote sorrowfully, 'by the interested relations of sugar-planters, West India factors, brandy-merchants, sugar-bakers, brokers, and brewers; all of whom have very good reasons for espousing the sugar distillery in opposition to the malt distillery.'[9]

And so, once again, the pragmatists triumphed. 'The price of British-made spirits,' one commentator wrote after the new Act went through, 'which after the prohibition could only be made from molasses, rose considerably, and it was found that the consumption diminished in proportion. This hint could not escape the eye of government. The determination was, by some means or other to keep the price of spirituous liquors at that height to which they had risen upon the prohibition. This was about £21 17s. 6d per ton above what they had been before.'[10]

Either by good luck or good judgement, the compromise which Carteret had introduced back in 1743 had turned into a consistent policy. The 1746 and 1751 Gin Acts had ratcheted up spirit duties. Since then there had been an extra pound added to spirit licence fees by way of stamp duty (the war was on its way; there was a £2m loan to finance, and by now governments knew exactly where to turn for cash). When it came to enforcement, Acts in 1753 and 1754 had closed loopholes in the 1751 Act, clamped down on unlicensed retailers and limited spirit imports. Now an extra fivepence a gallon went on low wines made from corn, and a full one and threepence extra on corn-based spirits, more than doubling the spirit duty.

It all meant a big change for London drinkers. Back in 1745, spirits had sold at £23 a ton. After the Act of 1760, the spirit duty alone would come to more than that. The whole point of gin was that it had been cheap, but it was cheap no longer. Slowly, by dribs and drabs, drinkers started to wander across the page from Gin Lane back into Beer Street.

Porter had been around for almost forty years, but at threepence a pot it had never been able to compete with Mother Gin. 'For a halfpenny a man may get a dram of Geneva,' the *Daily Post* had commented in the bad old days of 1736, 'tho' he has not always three halfpence to purchase a pint of porter.'[11] With three halfpence in his pocket, a gin-drinker could be nearing dead drunk and on his way to the free straw. All that changed with the distillery ban. 'Gin is now so dear, or else so very bad,' wrote Henry Fielding's half-brother John in 1758, 'that good porter gains the pre-eminence, and I doubt not, but at year's end, there will be found a considerable increase in the consumption of that commodity.'[12] Confirmation came from *An Essay on Bread* published in the same year. 'Porter is almost become the universal cordial of the populace,' the author claimed, 'especially since the necessary period of prohibiting the corn-distillery; the suppression presently advanc'd the price of that common poison Gin, to near three times its former price, and the consumption of beer has kept pace with such advance.'[13]

The price of a pot of porter went up to threepence halfpenny in 1760, but it still looked attractive alongside expensive gin. Maybe porter suited the new mood of the times as well. It was an aspirational drink, a middle-class drink. Porter, as one commentator put it, was designed 'for the suppers of such people who are too poor to drink wine, and too rich to drink table-beer.'[14] Whatever the reason, spirit production didn't recover from the distillery ban between 1757 and 1760. Between the 1751 Act and the onset of the ban, it averaged four and a half million gallons a year; the two decades after 1760 saw it level out below two and a half million gallons.

The Gin Craze was over; the panic which accompanied it could subside. But Madam Geneva hadn't been outlawed. 1743, the turning-point, had been a pact with the devil, and so were the Acts which followed it – 1760 most of all. The authorities got tax revenues, control of the industry and, in the end, a declining drink problem. In return, Madam Geneva got to move out of the back-streets into smart new accommodation.

In 1790, Thomas Pennant made a tour of London, publishing a book to describe what he saw. One day he took a boat across the river to Lambeth, and there he halted in amazement. He found himself looking at 'the vast distilleries, till of late the property of Sir Joseph Mawbey.'

Two hundred years later, that site would be the Beefeater Gin Distillery. In 1790, there weren't just stills and vats on the site. For years, distillers had been profiting from sidelines as well. Pennant commented that 'there are seldom less than two thousand hogs grunting at this place; which are kept entirely on the grains.'[15] Distillers' hogs victualled the navy which was spreading British empire overseas. Reformers threw up their hands in horror at the idea of 'a still, that can daily work one hundred and forty quarters of corn . . . or more corn in a week than grows in a whole county.'[16] But that was the other side of the devil's pact. With 1760, the industrialisation of gin arrived in earnest.

It was happening to beer as well. The previous two decades had seen the emergence of the great names who would dominate

London brewing for the next two centuries: Samuel Whitbread, Felix and Sir William Calvert, Benjamin Truman, Parsons, Hope. By 1748, a dozen breweries were producing more than a third of the strong beer in London. Samuel Whitbread's huge Chiswell Street brewery went up in 1750. (Thomas Pennant thought 'the sight of a great London brewhouse exhibits a magnificence unspeakable.')

Among distillers, the ban of the late 1750s did much to weed out the smaller players. It was tough even for well-financed companies. William Currie's house saw profits of £2,000–£3,000 a year slump until they were barely breaking even.[17] Without corn mash in the vats, the number of hogs they could raise was virtually halved. According to one later author, only twelve of London's 'capital' houses weathered the storm of the late 1750s.[18]

But for those who did survive it – and another long ban when the harvests failed again between 1766 and 1773 – there were profits to be made from a smaller market with fewer players in it. Thomas Cooke's distillery was producing 300,000 gallons of corn spirits a year by the mid-1760s, as well as keeping 3,000 hogs on spent wash.[19]* William Currie's company took on a new partner when the ban ended, and enlarged its stock value to £36,000. The company's profits soared. They could barely make spirits fast enough. A letter to one customer complained that 'casks are extremely scarce with us at present, [we] therefore desire the favour of you to return them as soon as possible.' Frantic messages were despatched to London in search of fresh stocks of yeast.[20]

Malt distilling had always been a game for the rich. As stills

* Unfortunately, Cooke was one of his own best customers. In September 1743 he recorded in his diary, 'Whereas for about 6 years past I have been grievously tormented by drinking strong liquors, therefore for the future I intend by God's assistance to drink nothing but to lead a temperate life.' Five broken deadlines followed.

grew ever larger, it became even harder to force a way into the industry. Back in 1747, Robert Campbell had reckoned a distiller needed up to £5,000 to start in business.[21] But when William Currie started his company with two partners in 1749, they set out with a joint stock of £17,000 and outgoings of over £18,000.[22] The days of the back-street distiller were over. Gin was no longer a social problem; it was big business. Lobbying against the corn ban in 1757, a supporter listed the trades that depended on the London distillery: 'coopers, backmakers, coppersmiths, wormmakers, smiths, bricklayers, plumbers . . . all concerned in the coal trade . . . all employed in ploughing, sowing, reaping, and thrashing five or six thousand quarters of corn per week, for six or seven months in the year; the labourers, farmers . . . landlords . . . those that carry it to the sea or waterside, the captains or masters . . . sailors or bargemen, who bring it to London . . . lightermen, cornfactors, cornporters, carmen, millers, and many others that are concerned in bringing spices, seeds, sugars &c. from abroad, besides those that are employed in making spirits.'[23] From the government's point of view, there were clear advantages in having the industry controlled by a small number of powerful players. Carteret had set out the vision in 1743, arguing as his Bill's 'principal advantage' that it would 'bring the trade under some regulation, by confining it to those, who have some credit, and live comfortably by their businesses.'

Sir Joseph Mawbey, elected MP for Southwark the year after the distillery ban was lifted, had no interest in drunken gin-wives lying in the gutter outside his distillery. So the Gin Act of 1760 did everything it could to push the industry into the right hands. First, subsidies were offered on all spirits exports. There was nothing wrong with gin tipped down foreign throats. William Currie's firm went into the export market with a will. 'The exportation of spirits is a branch we intend to cultivate,' the partners agreed; 'the intent of the legislature & of the ministry is to encourage it as much as possible.'[24] They kept at it, despite burning their fingers with unreliable shippers and bad debts from Portuguese merchants. In the following year, 1761, there were even more obvious measures to encourage industrial concerns. A minimum limit was set on the size of distilleries, ostensibly to help the Excise Office keep track of production. From now on, distillers had to have a capacity of 100 gallons. If they wanted to qualify for export subsidies, they needed even more – a low-wine still with a minimum capacity of 800 gallons.

There had been a growing tendency for malt distillers to buy up compounders. That was outlawed in the 1760 Act, but the measure was repealed after only a year. From the 1760s on, the industry would be concentrated in fewer and fewer hands. When Parliament surveyed the malt distillers in 1803, it would find that just nine names owned ninety per cent of still capacity. And those names, by the 1760s, were starting to sound familiar. The Booth family had begun as brewers and vintners in the 1740s. By 1751 John Booth was selling gin; his Turnmill Street distillery opened soon afterwards. Robert Burnett was already in business by then, with a huge distillery on the waterfront in Vauxhall. At the end of his career, he would be knighted, and would become a Sheriff of the City of London. Alexander Gordon founded his distilling business in 1769. By the end of the century, Gordon's and Booth's would be sending out more than half a million gallons of gin a year.

Distilling had come a long way from the days of Dudley Bradstreet. There was no longer a still in every chandler's shop. The 'running, shabby fellows' had been swept away. But for those who remained, there were ever-increasing profits to be made. By 1783, William Currie's company would be valued at £80,000. Still thriving in 1845, the firm invested £30,000 in a Vine

Street compounding firm called Tanqueray's. Soon afterwards they merged with Gordon's.

But by then the wheel had come full circle. 1760 brought in an uneasy truce between drinkers and reformers. Gin didn't go away. The papers in 1764 reported two gin-soaked builders at Gray's Inn drunkenly lobbing bricks at each other; one was hit on the head and died.[25] Pierce Egan described his Regency swells looking for low-life kicks in 'All Max', a gin-shop in Whitechapel: 'Lascars, blacks, jack tars, coal-heavers, dustmen, women of colour, old and young, and a sprinkling of the remnants of once fine girls, &c., were all *jigging* together. *Heavy wet* was the cooling beverage, but frequently overtaken by *flashes of lightning*.'[26] Panic about gin didn't disappear either. In the 1790s, Hannah More would show all the old hatred of Madam Geneva in *The Gin-Shop; or, a peep into a prison*:

> The state compels no man to drink,
> Compels no man to game;
> 'Tis gin and gambling sink him down
> To rags, and want, and shame.

Gin-drinking had been a response to insecurity. The Gin Craze had been born from a culture of risk and opportunity in a town that offered both in abundance. And as the population of London started to boom at the end of the eighteenth century, as industrialisation gathered pace, conditions in the slums could only worsen, and with them the lot of immigrants working long hours in squalid conditions.

Francis Place campaigned against drink all his life, but even he could understand 'the sickening aversion which at times steals over the working man, and utterly disables him for a longer or a shorter period, from following his usual occupation, and compels him to indulge in idleness.' Maybe it would have been helpful if someone back in 1736 had stopped to wonder what made the poor turn to drink in the first place. 'It is not easy,' Place went on, 'for any one who has not himself been a working man, accurately to estimate the agreeable sensations produced by the stimulus of strong liquor . . . yet so constant are these effects, that he who has scarcely any other means of excitement producing enjoyment, will in almost all cases . . . endeavour to produce them as often as he has the power, and dares venture to use it.'[27]

Soon into the nineteenth century, London's population burst a million. Newly anonymous, newly insecure, slums sucked in migrants to a world of hard work and ill health; a new world of risk. Maybe that would have been enough by itself to ignite a second Gin Craze. But in 1825, as if they were determined to recreate the conditions of the early eighteenth century, the government decided to throw fuel on the flames. They declared free trade in spirits.

Free trade was the call on every side – beer was liberalised at the same time. Old restrictions were to be swept aside; the economy would boom. Eighty years of pragmatic control over gin were ended. The cost of a spirit licence was more than halved, and spirit duties slashed. The result was dramatic. In 1826, spirit production more than doubled, hitting a level that hadn't been seen since 1743. By the end of the decade more than 45,000 licences were being issued every year.

'Everybody is drunk,' Sydney Smith wrote to John Murray. 'Those who are not singing are sprawling. The sovereign people are in a beastly state.'[28] They soon had new places to be beastly in. In the gin debate back in 1743, Lord Talbot had given the House of Lords a dire vision of what London could expect if Madam Geneva was allowed to settle down in the city. 'We may expect to see a long catalogue of drams wrote in gold letters upon every sign-post,' he had warned, 'and those that enter will certainly find . . . casks or vessels piled up a-top of one another, with a luscious description of its contents in capital letters upon every one. Nay . . . these casks [will be] exposed to the view of every [passer-by], and the shop or public room always full of customers . . . These, and many more allurements than I can think of, will certainly be made use of by those that are to be licensed to sell spirituous liquors.' In 1834, giving evidence to the House of Commons select committee on Drunkenness, a Tothill Street grocer described the new Gin Palace which had just opened across the road from his shop: 'It was converted into the very opposite of what it had been, [from] a low dirty public house with only one doorway, into a splendid edifice, the front ornamental with pilasters, supporting a handsome cornice and entablature and balustrades, and the whole elevation remarkably striking and handsome . . . the doors and windows glazed with very large squares of plate glass, and the gas fittings of the most costly description . . . When this edifice was completed, notice was given by placards taken round the parish; a band of music was stationed in front . . . the street became almost impassable from the number of people collected; and when the doors were opened the rush was tremendous; it was instantly filled with customers and continued so till midnight.'

Gin Palaces arrived in the late 1820s, and soon they were everywhere. The Select Committee on Drunkenness (which could do nothing to stem the tide) heard that 'there is a company formed in London for the purpose of buying any old free public house that can be met with, and they are then fitted up in the palace-like style in which they are now seen.' In Lambeth's New Cut, one witness told them, 'I suppose there are £25,000 being spent in building gin-shops. I should think they must cost £7,000 or £8,000 each house.'

It was a new Gin Craze, and the new Gin Panic soon followed. The phrase was coined by Henry Fearon, pioneer of the Gin Palace, in a newspaper article in 1830. Anti-spirits societies appeared in Glasgow and Ulster in 1829, and spread to Blackburn in 1830. On 1 September 1832, in Preston, Lancashire, seven pioneers signed the pledge of total abstinence, and for the next forty years, through interminable feuds, mergers and divisions, children's rallies and temperance tracts, marches and fund-raising events, campaigns in Parliament and thunderous sermons from the pulpit, through rows between prohibitionists and moral suasionists, through Bands of Hope and anguished confessions from penitents, the panic about drink would run uncontrolled.

There were more sober voices as well. In the early 1830s a young journalist called Charles Dickens visited one of the new Gin Palaces. He found gilt-labelled barrels, plate glass, polished mahogany and despair. He was shocked by the drunkenness and the tawdry splendour, shocked by the 'throng of men, women and children,' who, as the evening ended, dwindled 'to two or three occasional stragglers – cold, wretched-looking creatures, in the last stage of emaciation and disease.' But he withheld judgement. 'Gin drinking is a great vice in England,' Dickens wrote in conclusion, 'but wretchedness and dirt are greater and until you improve the homes of the poor, or persuade a half-famished wretch not to seek relief in the temporary oblivion of his own misery, with the pittance, which, divided among his family would furnish a morsel of bread for each, ginshops will increase in number and splendour.'[29]

## EPILOGUE

*The bill now before us may indeed, Sir, very properly be called an experiment: It is, I believe, one of the boldest experiments in politics that was ever made in a free country.*
William Pulteney, House of Commons prohibition debate, 16 February 1736

*Our country has deliberately undertaken a great social and economic experiment, noble in motive and far-reaching in purpose.*
Herbert Hoover, Presidential Election Campaign, 1928

On 16 January 1919, the Eighteenth Amendment to the Constitution was ratified by the necessary three-quarters of the States, and America faced prohibition.

It was the culmination of a long campaign by reformers to save America from itself. Prohibition came in at a time of dizzying economic growth and frightening social change; a time of risk. The great cities were swelled by hordes of immigrants. They were fuelled by speculation, given over to wild hedonism. Prohibition was the attempt of small-town America to hold back the tide. Change had got out of hand. America no longer seemed a land of certainties, of farmers tilling their own ground and praying in church on Sunday. Suddenly it was a country of strange languages and overnight millionaires, of saloons and nightclubs, dancing girls and jazz music. Prohibition dragged America back to safe ground.

America had always been suspicious of the town. 'Those who labour in the earth,' wrote Thomas Jefferson, 'are the chosen people of God.'[1] The Constitution had avoided a metropolitan capital. State assemblies would meet not in the big towns, but in rural centres like Albany. America was to be a land of godly farmers governed by wise and independent country gentlemen.

By the end of the nineteenth century it had all gone wrong. The Civil War had been followed by rapid industrialisation and economic growth. Immigrants had flooded in. By the turn of the century, America was no longer a land of villages. It was no longer a land of whites, or Protestants, or even of Anglo-Saxons. In the cities, migrants huddled in anonymous slum dwellings. And the cities themselves were changed beyond recognition. New grids of streets cut across farmland; unimaginable new buildings rose up into the sky. New York and Chicago became places of transformation. Vast fortunes were made by men who had never held a plough. The Jazz Age celebrated modernity and high spending. It was a time of neurotic hedonism. Nightclubs and cinemas gave New Yorkers the same risky pleasures that Londoners had once found in the theatre and masquerade. Silent movies lingered endlessly on the lives of the decadent rich: their silks, their cocktails, their extravagance.

'It was borrowed time anyhow,' wrote F Scott Fitzgerald of the age he characterised, 'the whole upper tenth of a nation living with the insouciance of grand ducs and the casualness of chorus girls.'[2] Walter Lippmann, surveying Prohibition in 1927, saw exactly what it all meant to conservatives. 'The evil which the old-fashioned preachers ascribe to the Pope, to Babylon, to atheists, and to the devil,' he wrote, 'is simply the new urban civilisation, with its irresistible scientific and economic and mass power. The Pope, the devil, jazz, the bootleggers, are a mythology which expresses symbolically the impact of a vast and dreaded social change.'[3]

Alcohol was the conservatives' scapegoat. Just as gin had in the 1720s, it became a focus for all the evils of the age. Drink threatened America's security and damaged its economy. 'King Alcohol,' fumed the *National Temperance Almanac* in 1876, 'has . . . filled our prisons, our alms-houses and lunatic asylums, and erected the gibbet before our eyes. He has destroyed the lives of tens of thousands of our citizens annually . . . He has turned . . . hundreds of thousands . . . to idleness and vice, infused into them the spirit of demons, and degraded them below the level of brutes. He has made thousand of widows and orphans . . . He has introduced among us hereditary diseases, both physical and mental, thereby tending to deteriorate the human race.'[4]

If booze was responsible for all the evils of the age, then Prohibition, as in 1736, became the panacea. That was the reformers' message; its eventual triumph was achieved through Christian fervour allied to impressive powers of organisation. In 1736 it was Thomas Wilson who navigated the bandwagon towards prohibition. Two centuries later it was Wayne B Wheeler, working behind the scenes, who organised the propaganda and made the connections.* The drinks companies in America were powerful, just as the London malt distillers were powerful, but the reformers outmanoeuvred them at every turn. On 16 January 1920, the Volstead Act came into force, and America turned dry.

---

* By the time of his death, Wayne B Wheeler was one of the most influential power-brokers in Washington. 'Wayne B Wheeler had taken snuff,' commented Senator Bruce of Maryland, 'and the Senate, as usual, sneezed. Wayne B. Wheeler had cracked his whip, and the Senate, as usual, crouched.'

The authorities had been expecting trouble on the night Prohibition came in, but in the end it was a damp squib. There were mock funerals for John Barleycorn at Maxim's and the Golden Glades. The Hotel Vanderbilt gave away free whisky. At Reisenweber's, ladies were handed compacts in the shape of coffins. The protests, though, were only symbolic. 'The big farewell,' as the *New York Evening Post* put it, 'failed to materialise.' Maybe the authorities assumed $1,000 fines and six month jail sentences would be enough to deter anybody. The truth was rather different. There were no riots because there would be no Prohibition. In the great towns and cities, the Volstead Act was a dead letter from the start.

Reformers had feared crime and a subversive population. Prohibition gave them both. By criminalising one of America's biggest industries, they handed it over to bootleggers like George Remus and Lucky Luciano. In Chicago, news reports were soon full of the feud between Big Jim Colosimo and Johnny Torrio. Al Capone was waiting in the wings.

Worst of all, Prohibition – just as it had in 1736 – turned ordinary citizens into criminals themselves. Men and women who paid taxes and went to church found themselves law breakers just by pouring a glass of beer. Prohibition drove a wedge into society. For many, it was a straightforward split between rich and poor. The Yale Club had bought up fourteen years' supply of booze before the Volstead Act came into force. As a result, 'the workers,' as one Union leader put it, 'who have no cellars . . . learn to hate their more fortunate fellow citizens more bitterly and uncompromisingly.'[5] 'Very few [working men],' the Wickersham Commission reported towards the end of Prohibition, 'have any respect for the Prohibition laws and do not hesitate to say so. They consider these laws discriminatory . . . and therefore have no compunction in violating them.'

Alienation fuelled a cult of subversion. Some had seen it coming. 'This law will be almost impossible of enforcement,' Fiorello La Guardia, future mayor of New York, wrote to Andrew Volstead even while his Act was passing through Congress. 'And if this law fails to be enforced ... it will create contempt and disregard for the law all over the country.'[6] Criminals became elevated, as Jack Sheppard or Dick Turpin had been, into popular heroes. The speakeasy and nightclub started to develop their own counter-culture. Eighteenth-century Londoners had drunk Blue Ruin, Bob Makeshift and South Sea Mountain. In their turn, Americans in the Roaring Twenties rolled under the table in the clutches of Old Horsey, Happy Sally, Soda Pop Moon, or Jersey Lightning.

Some of them didn't get up again. Eighteenth-century gin had been a deadly concoction of poisons, flavourings and malt spirit. The 'bathtub gin' produced under Prohibition was no better. Industrial alcohol was poisoned by law to make it unpalatable. Bootleggers added glycerine and oil of juniper to make gin, caramel and creosote to make whisky. When New York authorities tested seizures in 1928, they found that nearly all the booze they tried still contained poisons. Some reckoned 50,000 Americans were killed, blinded or paralysed during Prohibition.

Even so, Prohibition never stopped people drinking. But to the American authorities, just as to Robert Walpole and Thomas De Veil, that was soon no longer the point. 'The issue is fast coming to be recognised,' President Harding would proclaim, 'not as a contention between those who want to drink and those who do not ... but as one involving the great question whether the laws of this country can and will be enforced.'[7] By the mid-Twenties, Prohibition was no longer about drink; it was about government authority. Faced with widespread disregard of the law, the authorities determined to force it through. Brigadier General Lincoln Andrews was appointed Prohibition 'Czar' on April Fool's Day 1925. Draconian punishments were made still harsher.

The only effect of the clamp-down, as in 1738, was to fill up the prisons. By 1929, federal convictions for liquor offences had doubled, and the government had started work on six new jails. Out at sea, meanwhile, as in the early eighteenth century, Prohibition had created an uncontrollable problem of smuggling, as schooners and speedboats queued up along the coast to deliver their illicit cargo. And the manner of the clamp-down only alienated even more of the population. 'As a class,' wrote Stanley Walker, city editor of the *New York Times*, '[prohibition agents] made themselves offensive beyond words, and their multifarious doings made them the pariahs of New York.'[8] Ninety-two would be killed in the course of Prohibition.[9] Agents' $40-a-week pay made them as susceptible to corruption as Edward Parker had been two centuries earlier. The bootlegger George Remus claimed he only ever found two people who turned down a bribe. Magistrates of the 1730s had complained of constables who were gin-sellers themselves. In 1926, Mayor William E. Dever of Chicago told Congress that sixty per cent of his police force were in the liquor business.[10]

Prohibition had failed. The reformers' attempt to outlaw it had succeeded only in worsening the problem; along the way they had managed to undermine the contract between the American government and the society they governed. And for politicians, there were still worse problems to wrestle with. For as long as booze was being sold under the counter, they made no money from it. And by 1932, politicians needed all the revenue they could get. The Wall Street Crash had brought a frenzy of speculative growth to a close. The costs of the New Deal lay ahead.

The cold winds of Depression had their effect in other ways

as well. In the 1750s, falling standards of living had played their part in reducing gin-drinking. For out-of-work Americans in 1930, there was no longer money to spend at the bar. An Age of Risk – of transformation and change, opportunity and calamity – had come to an end. A time of vanishing social hierarchies and increasing individualism was replaced by one which offered new visions of social responsibility (a vision which would be reinforced a decade later, when the Second World War created a role for America as global superpower).

And so America made its pact with the devil. The politicians had their drink revenues; reformers comforted themselves with the end of the crime wave; and for companies like Seagram's (founded by Samuel Bronfman, who had once been Canada's biggest bootlegger), the profits began to pile up. John Barleycorn was allowed to stay in America.

On 21 December 1970, President Richard Nixon met Elvis Presley in the Oval Office. They didn't talk about rock'n'roll; they talked about drugs. Both President and King were worried about what was happening to young people in America. Elvis wanted to help. He wondered if he could be become an honorary agent at large to help fight drugs. Nixon wanted all the support he could get. The corruptions and cover-ups of the Watergate affair were still two years away. In 1970, narcotics, and what was wrong with American young people, were foremost on the President's mind. The war on drugs was about to be declared.

During the 1960s, a whole pharmacopia of drugs had suddenly appeared on the streets of western cities. Heroin and cannabis had a long history in some parts of the world, but had never been used in the west on any large scale; alongside them emerged new synthetic chemicals like LSD. The novelty of drugs was a large part of their threat. Alcohol was hallowed by time and custom. Every western culture had embedded drink in a web of traditions and habits, in traditional drinking places like the English pub or German wine cellar. Narcotics were different. They were taken in new ways, by new people. Their effects seemed different and terrible.

They weren't the only thing about the 1960s that was new. Drugs burst on the world in a decade of unsettling social and economic change. Old manners and customs were swept away. The Old World's foundations were rocked by a sexual revolution, a revolution in classes and generations, a revolution of manners. Suddenly, cities like New York, London and San Francisco seemed to offer unprecedented possibilities. People no longer needed to follow a single path from factory to grave. They could transform their clothes, their accent, their music. They could transform themselves. And waves of speculation over the next four decades provided new ways for people to become rich – from media moguls to Wall Street traders, Loadsamoney to dotcom millionaires – and poor again.

There were endless new ways to spend money as well. Social change whipped up a fashion firestorm. The consumer society was (re-)born. A 1950s salary might have gone into a nest-egg for a rainy day. Now it would disappear in new clothes, household goods, music, and the exploding business of leisure. With the arrival of television, there was a huge and brash new medium to broadcast the changes of the new age. Not even the retired colonel living down a leafy lane in Kent could escape what was happening on Carnaby Street. Advertising reached everyone, everywhere.

But it didn't mean that everyone had to like it. The changes of the 1960s brought unprecedented opportunities, but also frightening uncertainties. It was a new Age of Risk, febrile and exhilarating, narcissistic and neurotic. Beyond the bright lights, the sports cars to covet and the celebrities to emulate, beyond the freedoms of air travel or contraceptive pill, the new age seethed with old spectres. Crime soared, and so did the fear of crime. Families broke down; old communities were eroded; violence filled cinema screens. Squalid urban slums mushroomed behind the advertising hoardings.

Drugs were soon singled out as a focus for society's fears about its own transformation. As in the early eighteenth century, Drug Craze and Drug Panic were joined at the neck. The problems were familiar, and so were the fears. Drugs produced crime. It wasn't just heroin addicts committing robbery to pay for their addiction; the drug-user was uncontrolled, more likely to attack strangers, a menace. Drugs broke down families. A whole generation was growing up unable to fulfil their useful role in the economy. Soon there would be fears that NATO security was at risk because American servicemen were debilitated by drugs. Prisons were said to be overrun with heroin. New spectres began to stalk the nightmares of city-dwellers. The crack addict wove along the pavement contemplating attacks on strangers; in the basement crack den, addicts lay stupefied in half-darkness; 'crack babies' were born to addict mothers who abused social security to fund their habit. Judith Defour was back on the streets.

Before 1970, there had been little government attention paid to drugs. The change, when it came, was dramatic. In Britain, the 1971 Misuse of Drugs Act classified and outlawed harmful substances. In America, Richard Nixon declared war on the scourge of the age. Drugs prohibition had arrived.

There was optimism to start with. 'We have turned the corner on drug addiction,' the President announced in 1973. A Drug Enforcement Agency report in 1978 declared that 'heroin availability continues to shrink.' The truth was simpler. A whole sector of society had simply opted out of the law. In 1970, only fifteen per cent of Britons had tried an illegal drug. Twenty-five years later, that figure had risen to forty-five per cent. In 1991, twenty-six million Americans experimented with drugs.[11]

Society feared crime, and it feared a subversive counter-culture.

Prohibition fuelled both. The entire drugs industry, one of the world's fastest-growing, was handed over to criminals, and the costs of illegal heroin addiction soon created a crime wave. A 1994 West Yorkshire survey reported that nearly all young offenders in their sample were regular drug-users. About half of the murders in the United States every year were reckoned to be drugs-related.[12]

By opting for prohibition, governments had ruled out every other control they might have had over drugs. They couldn't draw revenues from them. They couldn't control where drugs were manufactured, sold or consumed. They had no influence over the industries which grew the raw materials for drugs, processed, transported, marketed and distributed them – nor over the profits they made. They had created a global criminal industry, and along-side it, a smuggling problem to dwarf the brandy-runners of the eighteenth century and Rum-Rows of Prohibition-era America.

The law was ignored, and with disregard came disrespect. Drug-use created a subversive counter-culture with its own language and its own customs. Prohibition also had a terrible effect on the health of drug-users. In the back-streets of St Giles's, gin-drinkers had been sold dilute spirits contaminated with alum and sulphuric acid. Impure heroin, cut with bleach or cleaning fluid, would have an even more devastating effect on modern drug-users. It would kill 15,000 a year, according to one American estimate, while contaminated needles spread the modern plague of AIDS.

But there would be no change in the law. By the 1980s, drugs policy was no longer about the social causes of drug abuse, nor about the safety of users. It was about enforcement. In 1982, Vice-President George Bush launched the South Florida Task Force, the most ambitious attempt so far to stamp out drugs. In office as President, he would spend $40bn on the war on drugs. His initiatives had only one measurable effect: they filled up the jails. By 1990, over half of federal inmates were drug offenders.

At more than 25,000, they outnumbered the entire federal prison population a decade earlier.

And all along, there was never any sign that the war on drugs could be won. On 24 March 1743, after six and half years of prohibition, William Pulteney told the House of Lords, 'It is well known, that punch and drams of all sorts, even common gin not excepted, are now sold openly and avowedly at all public houses, and many private shops and bye-corners; and it is likewise known, that they are now sold as cheap as they were before the present law was enacted.'[13] In December 1999, Barry Shaw, chief constable of Cleveland police, reported that 'there is overwhelming evidence to show that the prohibition-based policy in this country since 1971 has not been effective in controlling the availability or use of proscribed drugs. If there is indeed a war against drugs, it is not being won . . . Illegal drugs are freely available, their price is dropping and their use is growing. It seems fair to say that violation of the law is endemic, and the problem seems to be getting worse despite our best efforts.'[14]

In 1743, a British ministry, undemocratic, amateurish, un-supported by statistics, Civil Service or analytical tools, still managed to grasp the reality that the battle against Madam Geneva was lost, and that its costs in social disunity and crime were far worse than gin. Western governments of the late twentieth century held out against such a moment of truth. For modern politicians, as for 1730s reformers, drugs were too closely linked with all the evils of the new Age of Risk: with the loss of traditional values, with family breakdown and crime. No one could compromise on drugs without seeming to condone those changes.

What few of them noticed was that Drug Craze and Drug Panic might be Siamese twins; that it might be the very same forces of fear and uncertainty which drove young people to drugs and conservatives to family values. Just as in early eighteenth-century

London, or America in the Roaring Twenties, a new age has offered intoxicating transformations, a heady cocktail of opportunities and risks. In every metropolis, dealers reckon up their odds on the trading floors, and corner shops are littered with discarded scratch-cards. Televisions flash out their images of cars and holidays to those who will never be able to afford afford them; while in the shopping streets, plate-glass windows display clothes and cosmetics which promise to transform secretaries into supermodels.

The consequences should surprise no one. Somewhere a new Henry Fielding is shaking his head over the frivolity of the age, a Thomas Wilson is carving his career out of family values, and a Dr Stephen Hales is throwing up his hands in honest dismay. And somewhere, out of sight in the back-streets, Madam Geneva is still loitering along the gutter, barefoot in a ripped party dress, dispensing her gifts of comfort and misery, ecstasy and death.

# NOTES

## INTRODUCTION: The Alchemists

1  William Phillip, *A Book of Secrets, translated out of the Dutch*, 1596
2  de Mayerne, *The Distiller of London*, p96
3  Morwyng, *The Treasure of Euonymus*, p161
4  Morwyng, *The Treasure of Euonymus*, p127
5  Morwyng, *The Treasure of Euonymus*, p83
6  Forbes, *Short History of the Art of Distillation*, p106
7  Forbes, *Short History of the Art of Distillation*, p97; Tlusty, 'Water of Life,

Water of Death: The Controversy over Brandy and Gin in Early Modern Augsburg', p20

8  Brennan, *Public Drinking and Popular Culture in Eighteenth Century Paris*, p214

9  Hales, *A Friendly Admonition to the Drinkers of Brandy, and other Distilled Spirituous Liquors*, p1

10  *A Dissertation upon Drunkenness*, 1727, p14

## CHAPTER ONE: The Glorious Revolution

1  Blunt, *Geneva: a poem. Address'd to the Right Honourable Sir R— W—*, 1729

2  van der Zee, *William and Mary*, p283

3  Defoe, *Brief Case of the Distillers*, 1726, p17

4  P Clark, *The English Alehouse*, p211

5  Defoe, *Brief Case of the Distillers*, 1726, p18ff

6  Filby, *A History of Food Adulteration and Analysis*, p157

7  Davenant, *An Account of the Trade between Great-Britain, France, Holland etc*, first report, 1711, p42

8  Ward, *London Spy*, XI, p205

9  Ch(H), P28/6

10  Filby, *A History of Food Adulteration and Analysis*, p158

11  Malcolm, *Anecdotes of the Manners and Customs of London during the Eighteenth Century*, p131

12  Ward, *London Spy*, II, p32

13  Ward, *London Spy*, IX, p165

14  Davenant, *Essay upon Ways and Means of Supplying the War*, p133

15  de Saussure, *A Foreign View of England*, 16 Decemeber 1725

16  Defoe, *Review*, 9 & 19 May 1713

17  Chamberlayne quoted in Lecky, *History of England in the Eighteenth Century*, p476

18  Defoe, *Brief Case of the Distillers*, 1726, p18ff

19  de Saussure, *A Foreign View of England*, October 1726

20  de Saussure, *A Foreign View of England*, 7 February 1727

21  Lecky, *History of England in the Eighteenth Century*, p477

22  French, *Nineteen Centuries of Drink in England*, p294

23  Porter, 'The Drinking Man's Disease'

24  Lindsay, *The Monster City*, p37ff

25  P Clark, *The English Alehouse*, p209

26  *A Dissertation upon Drunkenness*, 1727

27  Defoe, *Brief Case of the Distillers*, 1726

28 Quoted on title-page of Blunt, *Blunt to Walpole: a familiar epistle in behalf of the British Distillery*, 1730
29 Place, *Drunkenness*, notes, BM Add. MSS 27825
30 PH, 22 March 1743
31 *A Dissertation upon Drunkenness*, 1727, p14
32 *The Tavern Scuffle*, 1726

# CHAPTER TWO: London

1 Smollett, *Humphrey Clinker*, p117
2 Inwood, *History of London*, p260ff
3 Defoe, *A Tour thro' the whole Island of Great Britain*, 1724–5
4 Earle, *A City Full of People*, p50
5 Defoe, *Everybody's Business is Nobody's Business*, 1725
6 McKendrick, Brewer & Plumb, *The Birth of a Consumer Society*, p52
7 *Low-life, or One Half of the World Knows not how the Other Half Live*, p10
8 Phillips, *Mid-Georgian London*, p45
9 Ward, *London Spy*, VIII, p138
10 Fielding, *Tom Jones*, p171
11 Fielding, *An Inquiry into the Causes of the Late Increase of Robbers*, p26
12 Inwood, *History of London*, p314
13 *Angliae Tutamen ... Being an account of the banks, lotteries, mines, diving, draining, lifting, and other engines, and many pernicious projects now on foot, tending to the destruction of trade*, 1696
14 Chancellor, *Devil Take the Hindmost*, p81
15 Davenant, *The True Picture of a Modern Whig*, 1701
16 Earle, *The Making of the English Middle Class*, p151
17 Andrew, *Philanthropy and Police*, p15
18 Rudé, *Hanoverian London*, p71
19 Fielding, *Tom Jones*, p416
20 Fielding, *An Inquiry into the Causes of the Late Increase of Robbers*, p38
21 Smollett, *The Adventures of Roderick Random*, pp315 & 320
22 Tom Brown, *Amusements Serious and Comical, Calculated for the Meridian of London*, 1700
23 Sherlock, *A Letter from the Lord Bishop of London to the clergy and people of London and Westminster on occasion of the late earthquakes*, 1750, p9
24 *A Trip through the Town*, 1735
25 de Saussure, *A Foreign View of England*, 16 December 1725
26 Defoe, *Complete English Tradesman*, i, pp312–5
27 Grosley, *A Tour to London*, i, p55

28  Earle, *A City Full of People*, p82

29  Burke, *The Streets of London*, p59

30  de Saussure, *A Foreign View of England*, 29 May 1727

31  Egmont Diary, iii, p279

32  Burrington, *An Answer to Dr William Brackenridge's Letter concerning the Number of Inhabitants within the London Bills of Mortality*, 1757

33  Wrigley and Schofield, *The Population History of England, 1541–1871*, 1981

34  Fielding, *An Inquiry into the Causes of the Late Increase of Robbers*, p83

35  OBPP, 7–10 September 1720

36  Earle, *A City Full of People*, p206

## CHAPTER THREE: South Sea Mountain

1  20 February 1720, quoted in Chancellor, *Devil Take the Hindmost*, p64

2  21 April & 24 June 1720, quoted in Cohen, *The Edge of Chaos*, pp201 & 214

3  *A Letter to the Patriots of Change Alley*, 1720

4  *Mist's Journal*, 26 March 1720

5  *Mercure Historique et Politique*, July 1720

6  *Applebee's Original Weekly Journal*, 5 August 1720

7  Cohen, *The Edge of Chaos*, p207

8  Cohen, *The Edge of Chaos*, p244

9  Speck, *Stability and Strife*, p197ff

10  *Weekly Journal*, 1 October 1720

11  *Applebee's Original Weekly Journal*, 1 October 1720

12  *London Gazette*, 25–29 April 1721

13  *Weekly Journal*, 18 November & 28 October 1721

14  LMA, Middlesex Order Book, MJ/OC/1/fol.s 126–8

15  Shoemaker, 'Reforming the City: The Reformation of Manners Campaign in London' in Davison, Hitchcock, Kiern and Shoemaker, *Stilling the Grumbling Hive*, p100

16  Curtis and Speck, *The Societies for the Reformation of Manners*, p46

17  Woodward, *An Account of the Rise of the Societies for Reformation of Manners*, 1698

18  Shoemaker, 'Reforming the City: The Reformation of Manners Campaign in London' in Davison, Hitchcock, Kiern and Shoemaker, *Stilling the Grumbling Hive*, p101

19  Joseph Butler, Bishop of Durham, 1736, quoted in Porter, 'English Society in the Eighteenth Century Revisited', p279

20  Pope, *A Farewell to London. In the Year 1715*

21  Johnson, *London*
22  Short, *New Observations ... on City, Town, and Country Bills of Mortality*, 1750
23  Fielding, *An Inquiry into the Causes of the Late Increase of Robbers*, p17
24  *Craftsman*, 13 December 1735
25  Gordon and Trenchard, *Cato's Letters*, 1720–22
26  Beattie, *Crime and the Courts in England*, pp516–7
27  de Saussure, *A Foreign View of England*, February 1726
28  *Daily Journal*, 5 February 1726
29  Pope, *Epilogue to the Satires*, Dialogue I, 159ff
30  *The Occasional Monitor* 1731, p8
31  *London Magazine*, January 1737
32  Andrew, *Philanthropy and Police*, p22ff
33  Porter, *English Society in the Eighteenth Century*, p90
34  Andrew, *Philanthropy and Police*, p24
35  Bulstrode, *A Charge delivered at the General Quarter Sessions*
36  LMA, Middlesex Sessions Papers, 1721/May/2

## CHAPTER FOUR: The Magistrates

1  LMA, Middlesex Sessions Papers, 1721/May/2
2  Landau, *Justices of the Peace*, p202
3  Fielding, *Voyage to Lisbon*, footnote to introduction
4  Babington, *A House in Bow Street*, p36
5  LMA, Westminster Order Book, January 1726
6  LMA, Westminster Order Book, WJ/OC/1
7  LMA, Middlesex Sessions Papers, 1721/Oct/8–9
8  LMA, Middlesex Order Book, MJ/OC/1/fols 126–8
9  LMA, Middlesex Sessions Papers, 1721/May/2
10  LMA, Middlesex Sessions Papers, 1721/Oct/8–9; also in Middlesex Order Book, MJ/OC/1/fol.181
11  *London Journal*, 20 January 1721
12  Curtis and Speck, *The Societies for the Reformation of Manners*, p55
13  *The Poor Man's Plea to all the Proclamations, Declarations, Acts of Parliament, etc....  for a Reformation of Manners*, 1703, quoted in Burtt, *Virtue Transformed*, p60
14  Mandeville, *The Fable of the Bees*, vol. 1, Remark G, p82ff
15  LMA, Westminster Order Book, WJ/OC/1, 15 February 1725, p75
16  Dolins, *Two Charges of Sir Daniel Dolins* 1725
17  LMA, Middlesex Sessions Papers, 1725/Dec/48–51
18  LMA, MR/LV/34/3

19  *The Tavern Scuffle*, 1726

20  *Of the Use of Tobacco, Coffee, Tea, Chocolate, and Drams*, 1722, Section VII

21  Petition of Royal College of Physicians, 19 January 1726

22  GL, MS6207/1, General Quarterly Court, 5 January 1725

23  GL, MS6207/1, General Quarterly Court, 12 July 1726

24  Defoe, *Brief Case of the Distillers*, 1726, p2

25  *Daily Journal*, 5 February 1726

## CHAPTER FIVE: The First Gin Act

1  Gonson, *Five Charges to Several Grand Juries*, 1728, Charge to the Grand Jury of Tower Hamlets, 16 July 1728

2  LMA, Middlesex Order Book, MJ/OC/3 fol.151

3  PH, vol VIII, 25 February 1729, p710

4  Croker, *Lord Hervey's Memoirs*, p124

5  Ch(H), P28/6 & P28/25

6  PH, House of Lords debate, 24 March 1743, p1257

7  Brown, *The Interest of the Compound Distiller Consider'd*, 1733, p13ff

8  *The Case of the Master, Wardens and Company of Distillers of London*, 1729

9  *A Proposal most humbly offered to the honourable House of Commons to prevent the excessive drinking of spirituous liquors*, 1729

## CHAPTER SIX: Corn

1  GL, MS6207/1, 6 May & 30 May 1729

2  GL, MS6207/1, General Quarterly Court, 8 July 1729

3  GL, MS6207/1, General Court, 30 September 1729

4  *The Distillers Petitions to His Majesty*, 1729

5  Blunt, *Blunt to Walpole: A familiar epistle in behalf of the British Distillery*, 1730

6  Thompson, 'The Moral Economy of the English Crowd', p85

7  Defoe, *Review*, 9 May 1713

8  Ch(H), P28/6

9  PH, House of Lords debate, 23 February 1743

10  *Diaries of Thomas Wilson*, 17 November 1735

11  Allen, *Ways and Means to Raise the Value of Land*, 1736

12  PH, House of Lords debate, 22 March 1743

13  Defoe, *Brief Case of the Distillers*, 1726, p5

14  Defoe, *Complete English Tradesman*, ii, part 2

15  *The Farmer Restored, or the Landed Interest Preserved*, 1739, p12

16  Ormrod, *English Grain Exports*, p68

17  PRO, T 64/274/58–9

18  *True State of the British Malt-distillery*, 1760, p33

19  *Gentleman's Magazine*, October–November 1752

20  Mathias, *The Brewing Industry*, p435

21  *A Collection of Letters Published in the Daily Papers*, 1736, letter ii

22  *An Inquiry into the Causes of the Present High Prices*, 1767, quoted in Mingay, 'The Agricultural Depression', p326

23  Speck, *Stability and Strife*, p126

24  Allen, *Ways and Means to Raise the Value of Land*, 1736

25  Mingay, 'The Agricultural Depression', p324

26  *The Occasional Monitor*, 1731

27  2 Geo2 c17

28  PH, House of Lords debate, 22 March 1743, p1217

29  Brown, *The Interest of the Compound Distiller Consider'd*, 1733, p8

30  PRO, T 27/25, Treasury Out Letter Book, 10 March 1731, & PRO T 29/27, Treasury Minute Book, 23 March 1731 & 25 March 1731; GL, MS6207/1A, General Court, 25 March 1731

31  GL, MS6207/1A, General Quarterly Court, 11 July 1732

32  GL, MS6207/1A, General Quarterly Court, 11 January 1732

33  CJ, 19 February 1733

34  2 Geo2 c17

35  Eboranos, *Reasons for Promoting the British Distillery*, 1733

## CHAPTER SEVEN: The Christians

1  OBPP, 27 February–1 March 1734, pp82–4

2  Burtt, *Virtue Transformed*, p58

3  *Diaries of Thomas Wilson*, p47, footnote

4  Allan and Scholfield, *Stephen Hales*, pp109–12

5  Allan and Scholfield, *Stephen Hales*, p81

6  Hales, *A Friendly Admonition to the Drinkers of Brandy*, 1734

7  *Diaries of Thomas Wilson*, 19 December 1731

8  CUL, SPCK Minutes, vol. xvi, 1734–6 (SPCK.MS.A1/16), 29 April 1735

9  *Diaries of Thomas Wilson*, 13 December 1735

10  CWAC, St James's Parish Vestry Minutes, June 1735, fol 99

11  Sedgwick, *The House of Commons 1715–54*, p174

12  *Diaries of Thomas Wilson*, 19 August 1735

13  Presentment of the Grand Jury of Tower Hamlets, 6 October 1735

14  Presentment of the Grand Jury of Middlesex, 25 September 1735

15 CUL, SPCK minutes; *Diaries of Thomas Wilson*, 28 October 1735; LMA, Middlesex Order Book, MJ/OC/4/fol.s 47–8

## CHAPTER EIGHT: Prohibition

1 LMA, Middlesex Order Book, MJ/OC/4/fol.s 54–7
2 *Diaries of Thomas Wilson*, 19 January 1736
3 *Diaries of Thomas Wilson*, 14 March 1736
4 Egmont Diary, ii, 5 February 1736, p229
5 *A Collection of Letters Published in the Daily Papers*, 1736, letter ii
6 *Daily Post*, 30 March 1736
7 *Daily Journal*, 1 April 1736
8 *Daily Gazetteer*, 19 February 1736
9 *Gentleman's Magazine*, March 1736, p166
10 *London Daily Post and General Advertiser*, 29 March 1736
11 *London Daily Post and General Advertiser*, 29 March 1736
12 *Diaries of Thomas Wilson*, 19 August 1735
13 *The Case of the Distillers Company and Proposals for Better Regulating the Trade*, 1736
14 Philanthropos, *The Trial of the Spirits*, p19
15 *Diaries of Thomas Wilson*, 15 February 1736
16 *Diaries of Thomas Wilson*, 26 August 1735
17 PH, 8 March 1736, p1037ff
18 Egmont Diary, ii, 8 March 1736, p240
19 *London Daily Post and General Advertiser*, 16 March 1736
20 *Diaries of Thomas Wilson*, 16 March 1736
21 *Diaries of Thomas Wilson*, 23 February 1736
22 *A letter from a Member of Parliament to his friend in the country*, 1736, p8ff
23 *A letter from a Member of Parliament to his friend in the country*, 1736
24 *Occasional Remarks upon the Act for laying a duty upon the retalers of spirituous liquors*, 1736, p9ff
25 PH, 16 February 1736
26 PH, 22 & 24 March 1743, p1241

## CHAPTER NINE: Summer Riots

1 Quarrell and Mare, *London in 1710. From the Travels of ZC von Uffenbach*, p73
2 PH, 1737, p1282
3 Sedgwick, *Lord Hervey's Memoirs*, p136
4 *London Daily Post and General Advertiser*, 15 July 1736

5 PRO, TS 11/1027

6 PH, 1737, p1282ff

7 PRO, TS 11/1027

8 Rogers, *Crowds, Culture and Politics in Georgian Britain*, p25

9 PRO, SP 36/39 fol 48 (formerly 91)

10 Ch(H) P70/2/2 & P70/2/14

11 OBPP, October 1736, pp199–204

12 Ch(H) P70/2/14

13 Ch(H) P70/2/14

14 PH, 1737, p1285

15 Ch(H) P70/1

16 PRO, SP 44/130, pp109–14

17 Ch(H) P70/2/2

18 Ch(H) P70/2/14

19 *Diaries of Thomas Wilson*, 14 September 1736

20 *An Account of the Melancholy Circumstances of Great Britain*, 1743

21 *Craftsman*, 5 June & 14 August 1736

22 Battestin, *Henry Fielding*, p209

23 De Veil, *Memoirs of the Life and Times of Sir Thomas Deveil, Knight*, p43

24 *Daily Gazetteer*, 17 August 1736

25 Ch(H) P70/2/1

26 Ch(H) P70/2/7

27 CUL, SPCK Minutes, 28 September 1736

## CHAPTER TEN: The Death of Madam Geneva

1 *Daily Journal*, 30 September 1736

2 *London Magazine*, October 1736

3 *London Daily Post and General Advertiser*, 29 September 1736

4 Sedgwick, *The House of Commons 1715–54*, p174

5 PH, 1737, p1287

6 *London Daily Post and General Advertiser*, 4 October 1736

7 *Grub Street Journal*, 30 September 1736

8 Ch(H) P70/2/4

9 *London Daily Post and General Advertiser*, 28 September 1736

10 *Daily Post*, 24 September & 1 October 1736

11 *London Evening Post*, 30 September 1736

12 PH, 1737, p1287

13 *Craftsman*, 11 September 1736

14 GL, MS6207/1A, General Quarterly Court, 12 July 1737

15  *Grub Street Journal*, 23 September 1736

16  *Craftsman*, 2 October 1736

17  *London Daily Post and General Advertiser*, 28 September & 4 October 1736

18  *Read's Weekly Journal*, 23 October 1736

19  *Daily Post*, 15 November 1736

20  *Daily Post*, 4 December 1736 & *London Daily Post and General Advertiser*, 27 November 1736

21  *Daily Journal*, 14 October 1736

22  *London Daily Post and General Advertiser*, 2 November 1736

23  *London Daily Post and General Advertiser*, 22 October 1736

24  *Read's Weekly Journal*, 23 October 1736

25  *London Daily Post and General Advertiser*, 29 October 1736

26  De Veil, *Memoirs of the Life and Times of Sir Thomas Deveil, Knight*, p2

27  Quarrell and Mare, *London in 1710. From the Travels of ZC von Uffenbach*, p53

28  Ward, *London Spy*, VI, p110

29  *London Daily Post and General Advertiser*, 22 October 1736

30  *London Daily Post and General Advertiser*, 15 November 1736

31  Coxe, *Memoirs of the Life and Administration of Sir Robert Walpole*, iii, p357, Robert Walpole to Horace Walpole, 20–31 August 1736

32  *Diaries of Thomas Wilson*, 25 & 30 October 1736

33  *Diaries of Thomas Wilson*, 1 November 1736

34  *Daily Journal*, 22 September 1736

35  *Daily Post*, 2 December 1736

## CHAPTER ELEVEN: Bootleg

1  Bradstreet, *The Life and Uncommon Adventures of Captain Dudley Bradstreet*, p78ff

2  *Read's Weekly Journal*, 18 February 1738

3  PH, House of Lords debate, 24 March 1743, p1243

4  Porter, 'English Society in the Eighteenth Century Revisited', p254

5  Quarrell and Mare, *London in 1710. From the Travels of ZC von Uffenbach*, p146ff

6  Sedgwick, *Lord Hervey's Memoirs*, p201

7  *A Brief Description of London*, pxxiii

8  Phillips, *Mid-Georgian London*, p166

9  Linebaugh, *The London Hanged*, p187

10  Linebaugh, *The London Hanged*, p67

11  Porter, 'English Society in the Eighteenth Century Revisited', p253

12  Gilmour, *Riots, Risings and Revolutions*, p9

13  Fielding, *Covent Garden Journal*, 20 June 1752

14  Wilson, *Distilled Spirituous Liquors the Bane of the Nation*, 1736

15  Cooper, *The Complete Distiller*, chapter LV

16  Boyle, *The Publican's Daily Companion*

17  Bystander, *The Consequences of Laying an Additional Duty on Spirituous Liquors, candidly considered*, 1751, p16

18  *Craftsman*, 29 April 1738

19  Thomas Cooke, Distiller's Notes, BS Add MSS 39,683

20  Tucker, *An Impartial Enquiry into the Benefits and Damages ... from the present very great use of low-priced Spirituous Liquors*, 1751, p7

21  Filby, *A History of Food Adulteration and Analysis*, p222

22  *Grub Street Journal*, 27 January 1737

23  PH, 10 February 1737, p1281ff

24  PH, 10 February 1737, p1294

25  Davison, Hitchcock, Kiern and Shoemaker, *Stilling the Grumbling Hive*, p41

26  *Daily Post*, 27 April 1737

27  *London Magazine*, January 1737

28  PRO, Board of Excise Minutes, CUST 47/165, 14 January 1737, p129

29  PRO, CUST 48/13, 19 August 1737, p179

30  *Daily Journal*, 1 October 1736

31  *London Evening Post*, 16 August 1737

32  *Daily Post*, 27 November 1736

33  *Daily Post*, 30 October 1736

34  *Old Whig*, 24 June 1737

35  PRO, T 29/28, 30 August 1737; CUST 48/13, 31 August 1737, p179

36  *London Evening Post*, 29 October 1737

37  *London Evening Post*, 3 November 1737

38  *Daily Post*, 4 November 1737

39  *London Evening Post*, 5 November 1737

40  *London Evening Post*, 10 November 1737

41  *London Evening Post*, 19 November 1737

42  *Diaries of Thomas Wilson*, 23 December 1737

43  *London Evening Post*, 7 March 1738

44  *Craftsman*, 3 December 1737

45  *London Evening Post*, 5 January 1738

## CHAPTER TWELVE: Clamp-down

1  *London Evening Post*, 24 January 1738

2  *London Evening Post*, 24 January 1738

3 *London Evening Post*, 30 March 1738

4 PRO, PC/1/5/15, Westminster

5 *London Evening Post*, 16 August 1737

6 *London Evening Post*, 6 May 1738

7 *Daily Post*, 13 May 1738

8 Blackerby, *The Speech of Nathanial Blackerby Esq*, 1738

9 PRO, PC/1/5/15, Westminster, April 1738

10 De Veil, *Memoirs of the Life and Times of Sir Thomas Deveil, Knight*, p38ff

11 *London Evening Post*, 11 May 1738

12 De Veil, *Memoirs of the Life and Times of Sir Thomas Deveil, Knight*, p38ff

13 PRO, PC/1/5/15, Westminster, May 1738

14 *London Evening Post*, 19 August 1738

15 *Read's Weekly Journal*, 8 April 1738

16 *Gentleman's Magazine*, 1738, p698

17 *London Evening Post*, 13 May 1738

18 *London Evening Post*, 8 July 1738

19 Beattie, *Crime and the Courts in England*, p302

20 *London Daily Post and General Advertiser* & *London Evening Post*, 27 July 1738

21 *Read's Weekly Journal*, 22 July 1738

22 PRO, PC/1/5/15, Westminster, July 1738

23 PRO, PC/1/5/15, Westminster, October 1738

24 *Daily Post*, 8 May 1738

25 PH, House of Lords debate, 22 March 1743

26 *A Short History of the Gin Act*, 1738

27 *London Evening Post*, 9 May, 1 July & 29 August 1738

28 *London Evening Post*, 29 April 1738

29 *Read's Weekly Journal*, 12 August 1738

30 Sabourn, *A Perfect View of the Gin Act*, 1738

31 OBPP, October 1738, p155ff

32 *London Evening Post*, 17 August & 19 September 1738

33 PRO, Board of Excise minutes, CUST 47/166, 26 February 1737

34 *London Evening Post*, 31 December 1737, 5 January, 16 & 21 February 1738

35 PRO, CUST 47/165, 31 August 1736; CUST 47/167, 10 August 1737; & CUST 47/170, 16 November 1738

36 *Read's Weekly Journal*, 20 August 1737

37 Hardwicke Papers, BL Add MSS 35600, fol 94ff

38 PRO, PC/1/5/15

39 *Read's Weekly Journal*, 6 January 1739

40 *London Evening Post*, 25 December 1738

41 *London Evening Post*, 16 & 21 December 1738

42  PRO, T 1/309, 4 December 1742; *Gentleman's Magazine*, 21 December 1738

43  *London Evening Post*, 5 August 1738

44  *Read's Weekly Journal*, 29 July 1738

45  Stevenson, *London in the Age of Reform*, p9

46  *Read's Weekly Journal*, 22 July 1738

47  De Veil, *Memoirs of the Life and Times of Sir Thomas Deveil, Knight*, p38; LMA, MJ/OC/4, fol.107, 13 April 1738

48  *London Magazine*, January 1737

49  *Gentleman's Magazine*, 1738, p698

50  *Diaries of Thomas Wilson*, 10 May 1737

## CHAPTER THIRTEEN: Women

1  *A Dissertation on Mr Hogarth's Six Prints Lately Publish'd*, 1751, p10ff

2  *A Dissertation on Mr Hogarth's Six Prints Lately Publish'd*, p9

3  P Clark, *The English Alehouse*, p167

4  Defoe, *Life of Colonel Jack*, 2nd ed., 1723

5  *Grub Street Journal*, 27 January 1737

6  *Universal Spectator*, 17 December 1737

7  *Low-life, or One Half of the World Knows not how the Other Half Live*, p55

8  *A Dissertation on Mr Hogarth's Six Prints Lately Publish'd*, p12

9  *The Occasional Monitor*, 1731, p6

10  Trotter, *An Essay Medical, Philosophical, and Chemical on Drunkenness*, p65ff

## CHAPTER FOURTEEN: Repeal

1  All quotes for debate are from PH, 1743, p1199ff

2  *London Evening Post*, 24 February 1743

3  Hanbury Williams, *S—s and J—l, a New Ballad*, 1743

4  *Champion*, 1 March 1743

5  GL, MS6207/1, Court, 10 April 1744

6  LMA, MR/LV/6/65

7  *London Evening Post*, 31 March 1743

8  *London Evening Post*, 12 & 17 February 1743

9  Smollett, *History of England*, 1757

10  PRO, CUST 48/13, 31 January 1744

11  GL, MS6207/1, General Quarterly Court, 4 January 1746

12  *Considerations, humbly offered to the honourable the House of Commons, in behalf of the distillers of London, Westminster, and parts adjacent*, 1746

13  PRO, CUST 48/13, 31 January 1744

14 Beattie, *Crime and the Courts in England*, p233

15 Davison, Hitchcock, Kiern and Shoemaker, *Stilling the Grumbling Hive*, p83

16 *Whitehall Evening Post*, 17 January 1749

17 *Letters of Horace Walpole*, Horace Walpole to Horace Mann, November 1749, January 1750, March 1752

18 *Low-life, or One Half of the World Knows not how the Other Half Live*

19 Smollett, *History of England*

20 *Letters of Horace Walpole*, Horace Walpole to Horace Mann, 2 April 1750

21 Sherlock, *A Letter from the Lord Bishop of London to the clergy and people of London and Westminster on occasion of the late earthquakes*, 1750

## CHAPTER FIFTEEN: Gin Lane

1 *Low-life, or One Half of the World Knows not how the Other Half Live*

2 Smith, *State of the Gaols in London, Westminster, and the Borough of Southwark*, 1776, p49

3 Lackington, *Memoirs of the First Forty-Five Years of the Life of James Lackington*, p59

4 Rule, *Albion's People*, p110

5 Fielding, *An Inquiry into the Causes of the Late Increase of Robbers*, p96

6 Phillips, *Mid-Georgian London*, p279

7 Battestin, *Henry Fielding*, p148; Babington, *A House in Bow Street*, p96

8 Battestin, *Henry Fielding*, p435

9 Babington, *A House in Bow Street*, p72

10 Boswell, *London Journal*, 6 July 1763

11 *Whitehall Evening Post*, 8 January 1751

12 Babington, *A House in Bow Street*, p73

13 Fielding, *Voyage to Lisbon*, introduction

14 Maddox, *The Expediency of Preventative Wisdom*, 1751, p14

15 *Diaries of Thomas Wilson*, 17 April 1750

16 *London Magazine*, 8 February 1751

17 Hogarth, *Autobiographical Notes*

18 Lindsay, *Hogarth, His Art and His World*, p94

19 Hogarth, *Autobiographical Notes*

20 Morris, *Observations on the Past Growth and Present State of the City of London*, 1751

21 Tucker, *An Impartial Enquiry into the Benefits and Damages ... from the present very great use of low-priced Spirituous Liquors*, 1751

22 *Gentleman's Magazine*, 30 April 1751

23 *London Magazine*, March 1751, pp125–6

24 *Whitehall Evening Post*, 4 April & 21 February 1751

25 *London Magazine*, March 1751, pp125–6

26 *Read's Weekly Journal*, 2 February 1751

27 Lecky, *History of England in the Eighteenth Century*, p481

28 *Gentleman's Magazine*, April 1751, p165

29 CLRO Misc. MSS.82/17

30 Sedgwick, *The House of Commons*, p362

31 Horace Walpole, *Memoirs of the Reign of George II*, p66

32 Maddox, *The Expediency of Preventative Wisdom*, 1751

33 Fitzsimmonds, *Free and Candid Disquisitions, on the nature and execution of the laws of England, with a postscript relating to spirituous liquors*, 1751, postscript

34 *The Rambler*, March 1751

35 *Daily Post*, 3 April 1736

36 *London Evening Post*, 29 June 1751

37 *The Rambler*, 20 April 1751

38 Bystander, *The Consequences of Laying an Additional Duty on Spirituous Liquors, candidly considered*, 1751, p5

39 *Gloucester Journal*, quoted in *London Evening Post*, 23 December 1738

40 GL, MS6207/1, 24 May 1748 & 29 May 1751

41 Bystander, *The Consequences of Laying an Additional Duty on Spirituous Liquors, candidly considered*, p18

42 Horace Walpole, *Memoirs of the Reign of George II*, p106

43 *Westminster Journal*, quoted in *Gentleman's Magazine*, July 1751, p321

44 *Whitehall Evening Post*, 2 March 1751

45 LMA, Middlesex Order Book MJ/OC/5fol.235; *Gentleman's Magazine*, 31 October & 26 July 1751

46 Fielding, *Covent Garden Journal*, 10 March 1752

47 Burrington, *An Answer to Dr William Brackenridge's Letter concerning the number of inhabitants within the London Bills of Mortality*, 1757, p35

48 Hanway, *A Candid Historical Account of the Hospital for exposed and deserted young children*, p11

49 Hanway, *A Candid Historical Account of the Hospital for exposed and deserted young children*, p11

## CHAPTER SIXTEEN: The Middle Classes

1 Holmes and Szechi, *The Age of Oligarchy*, pp119 & 121

2 Porter, *English Society in the Eighteenth Century*, p48

3 Rule, *Albion's People*, p155

4 Smollett, *Humphrey Clinker*

5 Grosley, *A Tour to London*, i, p73
6 Josiah Tucker quoted in McKendrick, Brewer and Plumb, *Birth of a Consumer Society*
7 *Low-life, or One Half of the World Knows not how the Other Half Live*
8 de Saussure, *A Foreign View of England*, letter xii, p295
9 McKendrick, Brewer and Plumb, *Birth of a Consumer Society*, p203
10 Defoe, *Robinson Crusoe*, 1719, p12
11 *Low-life, or One Half of the World Knows not how the Other Half Live*
12 Fielding, *Tom Jones*, p636
13 Fielding, *Tom Jones*, p265
14 *A Dissertation on Mr Hogarth's Six Prints Lately Publish'd*, 1751, p25
15 *The Vices of the Cities of London and Westminster Traced from their Original*, 1751, p7
16 Ch(H) P70/2/14
17 *A Brief Description of London*, pxxiii
18 Baretti, *A Journey from London to Genoa*, i, p43
19 Landers, *Death and the Metropolis*, p65
20 Rudé, *Hanoverian London*, p135
21 Porter, *The Enlightenment*, p44
22 Gray, *Considerations on Several Proposals Lately Made for the Better Maintenance of the Poor*, 1751
23 Brown, *An Estimate of the Manners and Principles of the Times*, 1757, p15
24 McClure, *Coram's Children*, p19
25 Andrew, *Philanthropy and Police*, p19
26 *Gentleman's Magazine*, 1754, quoted in Porter, 'English Society in the Eighteenth Century Revisited', p270
27 George, *London Life in the Eighteenth Century*, 1925, rev. 1965, p49

## CHAPTER SEVENTEEN: The Devil's Pact

1 Sir Charles Smith, quoted in Ormrod, *English Grain Exports*, p125
2 *Short animadversions on the difference now set up between gin and rum, and our mother country and colonies*, 1760, p4
3 *The Monitor*, 12 January 1760
4 *True State of the British Malt-distillery, being a Defence of Mr M-wb-y's Queries*, 1760, p24
5 *Considerations Occasion'd by an Act of this Present Parliament, To prevent the excessive use of spirituous liquors*, 1760, p20
6 *London Chronicle*, 9 April 1760, p339
7 *Read's Weekly Journal*, 15 March & 5 April; *London Chronicle*, April 1760

8  *True State of the British Malt-distillery, being a Defence of Mr M-wb-y's Queries*, 1760, p2

9  *Gentleman's Magazine*, January 1760

10  *Considerations Occasion'd by an Act of this Present Parliament*, 1760, p2

11  *Daily Post*, 1 April 1736

12  John Fielding, *An Account of the Origins and Effects of a Police*, 1758, pxii

13  Jackson, *An Essay on Bread*, 1758

14  *Low-life, or One Half of the World Knows not how the Other Half Live*, p93

15  Pennant, *A Tour of London*, p33

16  *The Monitor*, 1 March 1760

17  UDV, TG-737, William Currie's Stock Book

18  *The Corn Distillery Stated to the Consideration of the Landed Interest*, 1783

19  Thomas Cooke, *Distiller's Notes*, BL Add MSS 39,683

20  UDV, TG-738, William Currie's Export Letter Book, letter to Pike and Spicer, 20 September 1760

21  Campbell, *The London Tradesman*, p33

22  UDV, TG-737, William Currie's Stock Book

23  Red Hot, *An Appeal to the Public concerning the Distilling Trade; with a rational scheme to extirpate it from the nation*, 1757

24  UDV, TG-738, William Currie's Export Letter Book, letter to Thomas Foxcroft, 1 November 1760, and letter to John Welch, 12 August 1760

25  Porter, *English Society in the Eighteenth Century*, p17

26  Egan, *Life in London*

27  Place, *Improvement of the Working People. Drunkenness—Education*, 1829, p14ff

28  Webb and Webb, *The History of Liquor Licensing in England*, p116

29  Dickens, *Sketches by Boz*, 1836, 'Gin-Shops', pp182–7

# EPILOGUE

1  Sinclair, *Prohibition: The Era of Excess*, p31

2  F Scott Fitzgerald, *The Crack-Up*, 1945, p15

3  Lippmann, *Men of Destiny*, 1927, pp28–31, quoted in Sinclair, *Prohibition: The Era of Excess*, p23

4  Sinclair, *Prohibition: The Era of Excess*, p70

5  Sinclair, *Prohibition: The Era of Excess*, p185

6  Behr, *Prohibition, the thirteen years that changed America*, p173

7  Sinclair, *Prohibition: The Era of Excess*, p278

8  Sinclair, *Prohibition: The Era of Excess*, p206

9  Coffey, *The Long Thirst*, p316

10  N Clark, *Deliver Us from Evil*, p165

11  Gordon, *The Return of the Dangerous Classes*, p144
12  Clutterbuck, *Drugs, Crime and Corruption*, pp123 & 156
13  PH, House of Lords debate, 24 March 1743, p1257
14  Quoted in the *Guardian*, 14 June 2001

# BIBLIOGRAPHY

———•———

Archive materials and literary works are not listed; nor are contemporary newspapers and other source materials whose titles in text and footnotes are self-explanatory. Long titles are generally not given. Where no author is given, publications are anonymous.

## Contemporary Publications

*Memoirs of the Times in a Letter to a Friend in the Country* (1737)

*Low-life, or One Half of the World Knows not how the Other Half Live* (1752)

*A Collection of all Statutes now in Force relating to Duties of Excise* (1764)

*A Brief Description of London* (1776)

Allen, William *Ways and Means to Raise the Value of Land* (1736)

Atlay, Jos *The Distiller's Vade Mecum* (1792)

Baretti, GMA *A Journey from London to Genoa* (1770)

Boswell, James *Boswell's London Journal* (1762)

Boyle, P *The Publican's Daily Companion* (1794)

Bradstreet, Dudley *The Life and Uncommon Adventures of Captain Dudley Bradstreet* (1755)

Campbell, Robert *The London Tradesman* (1747)

Child, Samuel *Every Man his Own Brewer* (1790)

Combrune, Michael *An Enquiry into the Prices of Wheat, Malt, and Occasionally of Other Provisions* (1768)

Cooper, Ambrose *The Complete Distiller* (1757)

Coxe, Archdeacon William *Memoirs of the Life and Administration of Sir Robert Walpole* (1798)

Croker, John Wilson (ed) *Lord Hervey's Memoirs* (1848)

Davenant, Charles *Essay upon Ways and Means of Supplying the War* (1701)

Davenant, Charles *An Account of the Trade between Great-Britain, France, Holland etc* (1715)

de Mayerne, Theodore *The Distiller of London* (1652)

de Saussure, César *A Foreign View of England in 1725–30* (1994)

De Veil, Thomas *Observations of the Practice of a Justice of the Peace* (1747)

De Veil, Thomas *Memoirs of the Life and Times of Sir Thomas Deveil, Knight* (1748)

Defoe, Daniel *A Tour thro' the whole Island of Great Britain* (1724–5)

Defoe, Daniel *Complete English Tradesman* (1726–7)

Egmont *Egmont Diary* (Historic Manuscripts Commission)

Grosley, M *A Tour to London* (1772)

Hanway, Jonas *A Candid Historical Account of the Hospital for exposed and deserted young children* (1759)

Hardy, John *The Retail Compounder or Publican's Friend* (1794)

Kalm, Pehr *Visit to England* (1748)

Lackington, James *Memoirs of the First Forty-Five Years of the Life of James Lackington* (1791)

Leadbetter, Charles *Leadbetter's Royal Gauger* (1755)

Lewis, WS (ed) *Three Tours through London in the Years 1748, 1776, 1797* (1941)

Linnell, CLS (ed) *The Diaries of Thomas Wilson* (1964)

Macky, John *Journey through England* (1722–3)

Mandeville, Bernard *The Fable of the Bees, or Public Vices and Private Benefits* (1714, 1724)

Misson, F M *Misson's Memoirs and Observations in his Travels over England* (1719)

Morwyng, Peter *The Treasure of Euonymus* (1559)

Paley, Ruth (ed) *Justice in Eighteenth Century Hackney: the Justicing Notebook of Henry Norris and the Hackney Petty Sessions Book* (1991)

Pennant, Thomas *A Tour of London* (1790)

Quarrell, WHG and Mare, Margaret (eds) *London in 1710. From the Travels of ZC von Uffenbach* (1934)

Shaw, Peter *Chemical Lectures for the Improvement of Arts, Trades and Natural Philosophy* (1731–2)

Smith, George *The Nature of Fermentation Explain'd; with the Method of Opening the Body of any Grain of Vegetable Subject, so as to obtain from it a Spirituous Liquor* (1729)

Strauss, Ralph (ed) *Tricks of the Town, or Ways and Means of Getting Money* (1747)

Walpole, Horace *Memoirs of the Reign of George II* (1847)

Welch, Saunders *Observations on the Office of a Constable* (1754)

Woodward, Josiah *Account of the Rise and Progress of the Religious Societies in the City of London etc* (1712)


## Tracts, Sermons and Satires (in chronological order)

*Further reasons humbly offered for the passing the bill for prohibiting the distilling of spirits and low-wines from corn* (1698)

*A Satyr upon Brandy* (1700)

*The Tavern Hunter; or a Drunken Ramble from the Crown to the Devil* (1702)

*Murder within Doors, or a war among ourselves, proving there are more kill'd by the Vintners, &c. than are sav'd by the Physicians* (1708)

Woodward, Josiah *A Dissuasive from the Sin of Drunkenness* (1711)

Awdle-Brains, Dorothy *The whole tryal indictment, arraignment and examination of Madam Geneva* (1713)

*The Case of the Distillers of London* (1714)

Bulstrode, Whitelocke *A Charge delivered ... at the General Quarter Sessions, Middlesex* (1718)

*Of the use of tobacco, coffee, tea, chocolate, and drams* (1722)

Chandler, Edward *A Sermon preached to the Societies for Reformation of Manners on January 4th 1724* (1724)

Defoe, Daniel *Everybody's Business is Nobody's Business* (1725)

Defoe, Daniel *A Brief Case of the Distillers and the Distilling Trade* (1726)

Dolins, Sir Daniel *Two Charges of Sir Daniel Dolins to the Grand Jury and other Juries of the County of Middlesex* (1726)

Slyboots, Saynought *The Tavern Scuffle* (1726)

*A Dissertation upon Drunkenness* (1727)

*Vinum Britannicum, or an Essay on the Properties and Effects of Malts Liquors, by a Physician in the Country* (1727)

Blunt, Alexander *Punchinello's Sermon preached at the Quaker Meeting in Gracechurch Street on Sunday May 14 1727* (1727)

Cowper, William *A Charge delivered ... at the General Quarter Sessions, held for the City and Liberty of Westminster* (1727)

Defoe, Daniel *Augusta Triumphans: or, the way to make London the most flourishing City in the Universe* (1728)

Gonson, Sir John *The Charge of Sir John Gonson to the Grand Jury of the City and Liberty of Westminster* (1728)

*Reasons humbly offered by the Maltsters of Surrey and Middlesex* ... (1729)

*The Case of the Master, Wardens and Company of Distillers of London* (1729)

*The Distillers Petitions to His Majesty* (1729)

*A Proposal most humbly offered to the honourable House of Commons to prevent the excessive drinking of spirituous liquors* ... (1729)

*The Case of the Company of Distillers of the City of London: with proposals for reforming the abuses practised in the distilling trade* (1729)

Blunt, Alexander *Geneva: a poem. Address'd to the Right Honourable Sir R— W—* (1729)

Blunt, Alexander *Blunt to Walpole: A familiar epistle in behalf of the British Distillery* (1730)

Gonson, Sir John *Five Charges to Several Grand Juries* (1730)

*The Occasional Monitor: or, short reasons offer'd to the farmers of England, that they may not be so readily deceived by the distillers subtle insinuations at this time* (1731)

*Reasons humbly offered by the Master, Warden, and Assistant of the Company of Distillers of London, for repealing the Act for laying a Duty on Compound Waters* (1731)

*The Character of the Times Delineated* (1732)

*Reasons humbly offered to the consideration of the honourable House of Commons, for encouraging the distilling of British spirits* (1733)

*The Case of the Master, Wardens, Assistants and Commonalty of the Company of Distillers* (1733)

Brown, J *The Interest of the Compound Distiller Consider'd* (1733)

Eboranos *A Collection of Political Tracts* (1733)

Buck, Stephen *Geneva. A poem in blank verse* (1734)

Drew, Robert *A Sermon preached to the Societies for Reformation of Manners* (1734)

Hales, Stephen *A Friendly Admonition to the Drinkers of Brandy, and other Distilled Spirituous Liquors* (1734)

Sherlock, Thomas *Sermon to Westminster Infirmary* (1735)

*The Case of the Sugar-trade, with regard to the duties intended to be laid on all spirituous liquors sold by retail* (1736)

*The Case of the Distillers Company and Proposals for Better Regulating the Trade* (1736)

*The Case of such of the Distillers as are the younger branch of the trade* (1736)

*A Proper Reply to the Trial of the Spirits* (1736)

*A Collection of Letters Published in the Daily Papers* ... (1736)

*The Life of Mother Gin* (1736)

*The Case of the Merchants, and others, of the City of Bristol, trading to the British Colonies in America* (1736)

*Occasional Remarks upon the Act for laying a duty upon the retalers of spirituous liquors* (1736)

*Reasons Humbly Offered to the Honourable House of Commons, for the effectual suppressing the excessive drinking of the liquor commonly called GIN* (1736)

*The case of the Working-coopers to the Distillers in and about the City of London* (1736)

*The Case of the Malt Distillers etc* (1736)

*An Impartial Enquiry into the Present State of the British Distillery* (1736)

*A letter from a Member of Parliament to his friend in the country, containing, his reasons for being against the late Act for preventing the retail of Spirituous Liquors* (1736)

*An Elegy on the Much Lamented Death of ... Madam Gineva* (1736)

*Reasons for an Additional Bounty and Drawback on the Exportation of Spirits made in Great Britain* (1736)

Eboranos *A Proposal to prevent the common tippling of spirituous liquors, in such manner as shall not any ways prejudice the Publick Revenue* (1736)

Holden, Adam *A Vindication of a Pamphlet Lately Published intituled The Tryal of the Spirits* (1736)

Juniper, Jack *The Deposing and Death of Queen Gin* (1736)

Philanthropos *The Trial of the Spirits* (1736)

Rudd, Dr Sayer *To the honourable the Commissioners of his Majesty's Excise. The Case of Dr Sayer Rudd, in answer to an information lodged against him, in the Excise Office, London, for retaling spirituous liquors* (1736)

Scrubb, Timothy *Desolation, or the fall of Gin* (1736)

Scrubb, Timothy *The Fall of Bob: Or, the Oracle of Gin* (1736)

Wilson, Thomas *Distilled Spirituous Liquors the Bane of the Nation* (1736)

*Mother Gin, a tragi-comical eclogue* (1737)

*The Worth of Liberty Considered* (1737)

Simpson, William *A Sermon preached to the Societies for Reformation of Manners* (1737)

*A Short History of the Gin Act* (1738)

Blackerby, Nathaniel *The Speech of Nathanial Blackerby Esq; at a general meeting of His Majesty's Justices of the Peace for ... Westminster* (1738)

Sabourn, Reay *A Perfect View of the Gin Act* (1738)

*The Farmer Restored, or the Landed Interest Preserved* (1739)

*A Letter to a Friend in the Country in Relation to the New Law Concerning Spirituous Liquors* (1743)

Gibson, Edmund *An Earnest Dissuasive from Intemperance in Meat and Drinks, with a more particular View to the Point of Spirituous Liquors* (1743)

Hanbury Williams, Sir Charles *S—s and J—l, a New Ballad* (1743)

Hanbury Williams, Sir Charles *Drink and be Damned* (1743)

*Considerations, humbly offered to the honourable the House of Commons, in behalf of the Distillers of London, Westminster, and parts adjacent* (1746)

Fielding, Henry *A Charge to the Grand Jury of . . . Westminster* (1749)

A Country Justice of the Peace *Serious Thoughts in Regard to the Publick Disorders* (1750)

Haywood, Eliza Fowler *A Present for Women Addicted to Drinking, adapted to all the different stations in life, from a Lady of Quality to a common servant* (1750)

Sherlock, Thomas *A Letter from the Lord Bishop of London to the clergy and people of London and Westminster on occasion of the late earthquakes* (1750)

Short, Thomas *Discourses on tea, sugar, milk, made-wines, spirits . . .* (1750)

Short, Thomas *New Observations . . . on City, Town, and Country Bills of Mortality* (1750)

*The Vices of the Cities of London and Westminster Traced from their Original* (1751)

*A Dissertation on Mr Hogarth's Six Prints Lately publish'd* (1751)

Bystander *The Consequences of Laying an Additional Duty on Spirituous Liquors, candidly considered* (1751)

Fielding, Henry *An Inquiry into the Causes of the Late Increase of Robbers, &c* (1751)

Fitzsimmonds, Joshua *Free and Candid Disquisitions, on the nature and execution of the laws of England* (1751)

Gray, Charles *Considerations on several proposals lately made for the better maintenance of the poor* (1751)

Hay, William *Remarks on the laws relating to the poor* (1751)

Maddox, Isaac *The Expediency of Preventative Wisdom* (1751)

Morris, Corbyn *Observations on the Past Growth and Present State of the City of London* (1751)

Philo-Patria *A Letter to Henry Fielding Esq; Occasioned by his Enquiry into the Cause of the late Increase of Robbers, &c.* (1751)

Tucker, Josiah *An Impartial Enquiry into the Benefits and Damages . . . from the present very great use of low-priced Spirituous Liquors* (1751)

Fielding, Henry *A Proposal for Making an Effectual Provision for the Poor* (1753)

Henry, William *An Earnest Address to the People of Ireland against the drinking of spirituous liquors* (1753)

Henry, William *A letter to Arthur Gore Esq, relating to the present abuse of spirituous liquors* (1755)

Brown, John *An Estimate of the Manners and Principles of the Times* (1757)

Burrington, George *An Answer to Dr William Brackenridge's Letter concerning the number of inhabitants within the London Bills of Mortality* (1757)

Red Hot *An Appeal to the Public concerning the Distilling Trade; with a rational scheme to extirpate it from the nation* (1757)

Mawbey, Sir Joseph *Queries in Defence of the malt-distillery* (1759)

*Short Animadversions on the Difference now set up between Gin and Rum, and our mother country and colonies* (1760)

*Full Answers to Mr M\*\*\*\*y's Queries in defence of the malt-distillery; shewing it to be both a religious and political sin to distil spirits from corn. Intended to save millions* (1760)

*An Oration, delivered before an audience of distillers, by Baalzebub* (1760)

*Answers to the Queries in defence of the malt-distillery* (1760)

*True State of the British Malt-distillery, being a defence of Mr M-wb-y's queries* (1760)

*Considerations Occasion'd by an Act of this Present Parliament. To prevent the excessive use of spirituous liquors* (1760)

Henry, William *A letter to the Right Honourable John Ponsonby, Speaker of the Honourable House of Commons, concerning the abuse of spirituous liquors* (1760)

Henry, William and Hales, Stephen *A New Year's Gift to Dram-Drinkers* (1762)

Hanway, Jonas *An Earnest Appeal for Mercy to the Children of the Poor* (1766)

Dossie, Robert *An Essay on Spirituous Liquors* (1770)

Smith, William *State of the Gaols in London, Westminster, and the Borough of Southwark* (1776)

## Miscellaneous

*Report from the House of Commons Select Committee on Drunkenness* (1834)

Egan, Pierce *Life in London* (1821)

Feltham, John *Picture of London* (1802)

French, RV *Nineteen Centuries of Drink in England* (1890)

Heberden, William *Observations on the Increase and Decrease of Different Diseases* (1801)

Lecky, William *History of England in the Eighteenth Century* (1883)

Malcolm, JP *Anecdotes of the Manners and Customs of London during the Eighteenth Century* (1808)

More, Hannah (pseudonym 'Z') *Cheap Repository: Patient Joe. Wild Robert. Dan and Jane; and the Gin-Shop* (1795)

Place, Francis *Report of Select Committee on Artisans and Machinery* (1824)

Place, Francis *Drunkenness* (1828)

Place, Francis *The Autobiography of Francis Place* (1972)

Rush, Benjamin *An Enquiry into the Effects of Spirituous Liquors on the Human Body* (1790)

Scarisbrick, Joseph *The Spirit Manual, Historical and Technical* (1891)

Trotter, Thomas *An Essay Medical, Philosophical, and Chemical on Drunkenness* (1804)

Webb, Sidney and Beatrice *The History of Liquor Licensing in England, Principally from 1700 to 1830* (1903)

Willan, Dr Robert *Reports on the Diseases in London* (1801)

Willan, Dr Robert *The Dreadful Effects of Dram-Drinking* (1804)

## Modern Articles

Amory, Hugh *Henry Fielding and the Criminal Legislation of 1751–2* (Philological Quarterly, I, 1971)

Barry, Jonathan *Consumers' Passions: The Middle Class in Eighteenth Century England* (Historical Journal, vol 34, 1991)

Clark, Peter *The 'Mother Gin' Controversy* (Royal Historical Society Transactions, vol 38, 1988)

Coffey, TG *Beer Street: Gin Lane. Some Views of Eighteenth-century Drinking* (Quarterly Journal of Studies on Alcohol, vol 26, 1966)

Hoskins, WG *Harvest Fluctuations and English Economic History 1620–1759* (Agricultural History Review, xvi, 1968)

Innes, Joanna *Parliament and the Shaping of Eighteenth-century Social Policy* (Royal Historical Society Transactions, vol 40, 1990)

Medick, Hans *Plebeian Culture in the Transition to Capitalism* (Culture, Ideology and Politics, Samuel, R and Jones, GS (eds), 1982)

Mingay, GE *The Agricultural Depression 1730–1750* (Economic History Review, 8, 1956)

Porter, Roy *English Society in the Eighteenth Century Revisited* (British Politics and Society from Walpole to Pitt, Black, J (ed), 1990)

Porter, Roy *The Drinking Man's Disease: The 'Pre-history' of Drinking in Georgian Britain* (British Journal of Addiction, 1985)

Rogers, N *Popular Protest in Early Hanoverian London* (Past and Present, 1978)

Rudé, G *'Mother Gin' and the London Riots of 1736* (Guildhall Miscellany, 10, 1959)

Shoemaker, R *The London 'Mob' in the Early Eighteenth Century* (Journal of British Studies, 1987)

Thompson, EP *The Moral Economy of the English Crowd in the Eighteenth Century* (Past and Present, 1971)

Tlusty, BA *Water of Life, Water of Death: The Controversy over Brandy and Gin in Early Modern Augsburg* (Central European History, vol 31, 1998)

Warner, J and Ivis, F *Gin and Gender in Early Eighteenth Century London* (Eighteenth Century Life, vol 24, 2000)

Warner, J and Ivis, F *'Damn you, you informing bitch': Vox Populi and the Unmaking of the Gin Act of 1736* (Journal of Social History, vol 33, 1999)

Warner, Jessica *The Naturalization of Beer and Gin in Early Modern England* (Contemporary Drug Problems, vol 24, 1997)

Warner, Jessica *Shifting Categories of the Social Harms Associated with Alcohol: examples from late medieval and early modern England* (American Journal of Public Health, vol 87, 1997)

Warner, Jessica *In Another City, in Another Time: Rhetoric and the Creation of a Drug Scare* (Contemporary Drug Problems, vol 21, 1994)

Warner, Jessica *Old and in the Way: Widows, Witches and Spontaneous Combustion in the Age of Reason* (Contemporary Drug Problems, vol 23, 1996)

## Modern Publications

Allan, DGC and Scholfield, RE *Stephen Hales: Scientist and Philanthropist* (1980)

Andrew, Donna T *Philanthropy and Police* (1989)

Ashton, TS *An Economic History of England: The Eighteenth Century* (1955)

Ashton, TS *Ecomomic Fluctuations in England 1700–1800* (1959)

Babington, A *A House in Bow Street: Crime and the Magistracy* (1969)

Barrows, Susanna and Room, Robin (eds) *Drinking: Behaviour and Belief in Modern History* (1992)

Battestin, MC and RR *Henry Fielding: A Life* (1989)

Beattie, J *Crime and the Courts in England, 1660–1800* (1986)

Behr, Edward *Prohibition, the thirteen years that changed America* (1997)

Boaz, David (ed) *The Crisis in Drug Prohibition* (1990)

Borsay, Peter *The English Urban Renaissance, Culture and Society in the Provincial Town, 1660–1770* (1989)

Brennan, T *Public Drinking and Popular Culture in Eighteenth Century Paris* (1988)

Brewer, John and Styles, John *An Ungovernable People: The English and their Law in the Seventeenth and Eighteenth Centuries* (1980)

Burtt, Shelley *Virtue Transformed: Political Argument in England 1688–1740* (1992)

Chancellor, Edward *Devil Take the Hindmost: A History of Financial Speculation* (1999)

Church, LF *Oglethorpe: A Study of Philanthropy in England and Georgia* (1932)

Clark, Jonathan *English Society 1688–1832: Ideology, Social Structure and Political Practice During the Ancien Régime* (1985)

Clark, Norman H *Deliver Us from Evil, an Interpretation of American Prohibition* (1976)

Clark, Peter *The English Alehouse: A Social History 1200–1830* (1983)

Clutterbuck, Richard *Drugs, Crime and Corruption: Thinking the Unthinkable* (1995)

Coffey, Thomas *The Long Thirst, Prohibition in America, 1920–33* (1976)

Cohen, Bernice *The Edge of Chaos: financial booms, bubbles, crashes and chaos* (1997)

Curtis, TC and Speck, WA *The Societies for the Reformation of Manners* (1976)

Daunton, M *Progress and Poverty: An Economic and Social History of Britain, 1700–1850* (1995)

Davison, L, Hitchcock, T, Kiern, T and Shoemaker, RB (eds) *Stilling the*

*Grumbling Hive: The Response to Social and Economic Problems in England, 1688–1750* (1992)

Earle, Peter *The Making of the English Middle Class: Business, Society and Family Life in London 1660–1730* (1989)

Earle, Peter *A City Full of People: Men and Women of London, 1650–1750* (1994)

Filby, FA *A History of Food Adulteration and Analysis* (1934)

Fletcher, A and Stevenson, J (eds) *Order and Disorder in Early Modern England* (1985)

Forbes, RJ *Short History of the Art of Distillation* (1948)

George, M Dorothy *London Life in the Eighteenth Century* (1966)

Gilmour, Ian *Riot, Risings and Revolutions: Governance and Violence in Eighteenth-century England* (1992)

Goldgar, B *Walpole and the Wits: The Relation of Politics to Literature, 1722–42* (1976)

Gordon, Diana R *The Return of the Dangerous Classes: Drug Prohibition and Policy Politics* (1994)

Gregory, J and Stevenson, J *Britain in the Eighteenth Century, 1688–1820* (2000)

Harrison, Brian *Drink and the Victorians* (1971)

Holmes, G and Szechi, D *The Age of Oligarchy: Pre-Industrial Britain, 1722–1783* (1993)

Inglis, Brian *Forbidden Game: A Social History of Drugs* (1975)

Innes, Joanna *Prisons for the Poor: English Bridewells 1555–1800* (1987)

Inwood, Stephen *A History of London* (1998)

Kinross, Lord *The Kindred Spirit* (1959)

Landau, N *The Justices of the Peace, 1679–1760* (1984)

Landers, John *Death and the Metropolis: Studies in the Demographic History of London, 1670–1819* (1993)

Langford, Paul *A Polite and Commercial People: England, 1727–1783* (1989)

Leuw, Ed and Marshall, Haen (eds) *Between Prohibition and Legislation, the Dutch Experiment in Drug Policy* (1994)

Lindsay, Jack *Hogarth, His Art and His World* (1977)

Lindsay, Jack *The Monster City: Defoe's London 1688–1730* (1978)

Linebaugh, P *The London Hanged: Crime and Civil Society in the Eighteenth Century* (1991)

Mathias, Peter *The Brewing Industry in England 1700–1830* (1959)

Mathias, Peter *The Transformation of England* (1979)

McClure, Ruth K *Coram's Children* (1981)

McCrea, Brian *Henry Fielding and the Politics of Eighteenth-century England* (1981)

McKendrick, Neil, Brewer, John and Plumb, JH *The Birth of a Consumer Society* (1982)

O'Gorman, F *The Long Eighteenth Century: British Political and Social History 1688–1832* (1997)

Ormrod, David *English Grain Exports and the Structure of Agrarian Capitalism 1700–1760* (1985)

Overton, Mark *Agricultural Revolution in England, the transformation of the agrarian economy, 1500–1850* (1996)

Paulson, R *Hogarth's Graphic Works* (1965)

Paulson, R *Popular and Polite Art in the Age of Hogarth and Fielding* (1979)

Paulson, R *Hogarth* (1993)

Phillips, Hugh *Mid-Georgian London* (1964)

Porter, Roy *English Society in the Eighteenth Century* (1990)

Porter, Roy *London, A Social History* (1994)

Porter, Roy *The Enlightenment: Britain and the Creation of the Modern World* (2000)

Reith, Gerda *The Age of Chance: Gambling in Western Culture* (1999)

Robson, Philip *Forbidden Drugs* (1999)

Rogers, N *Whigs and Cities: Popular Politics in the Age of Walpole and Pitt* (1989)

Rogers, N *Crowds, Culture and Politics in Georgian Britain* (1992)

Rudé, G *Hanoverian London* (1971)

Rudé, G *Paris and London in the Eighteenth Century: Studies in Popular Protest* (1970)

Rule, J *Albion's People: English Society 1714–1815* (1992)

Schivelbusch, Wolfgang *Tastes of Paradise: A social history of spices, stimulants and intoxicants* (1992)

Sedgwick, R *The House of Commons 1715–54* (1970)

Sinclair, Andrew *Prohibition: The Era of Excess* (1962)

Speck, WA *Stability and Strife: England 1714–1760* (1977)

Stark, Cameron, Kidd, Brian and Sykes, Roger (eds) *Illegal Drug Use in the United Kingdom* (1999)

Stevenson, J (ed) *London in the Age of Reform* (1977)

Stevenson, J *Popular Disturbances in England, 1700–1870* (1992)

Taylor, James Stephen *Jonas Hanway* (1985)

Uglow, Jenny *Hogarth* (1997)

van der Zee, Henri and Barbara *William and Mary* (1973)

Zirker, Malvin L *Fielding's Social Pamphlets* (1966)

# INDEX